THE FRUGAL HOMEOWNER'S GUIDE TO BUYING, SELLING, & IMPROVING YOUR HOME

Julie Garton-Good

Dearborn Trade
A Kaplan Professional Company

Acquisitions Editor: Jean Iversen
Managing Editor: Jack Kiburz
Project Editor: Trey Thoelcke
Interior Design: Lucy Jenkins
Cover Design: Scott Rattray, Rattray Design
Typesetting: the dotted i

Published by Dearborn Trade,
a Kaplan Professional Company

Printed in the United States of America

99 00 01 10 9 8 7 6 5 4 3 2

Library of Congress Cataloging-in-Publication Data

Garton-Good, Julie.
The frugal homeowner's guide to buying, selling, & improving your home / Julie Garton-Good.
p. cm.
Includes index.
ISBN 0-7931-2764-5
1. House buying—United States. 2. Home ownership—United States. 3. House selling—United States. 4. Residential real estate—United States—Purchasing. 5. Real estate business—United States. 6. Consumer education—United States. I. Title.
HD255.G368 1999
643′.12—dc21 98-31840
CIP

DEDICATION

This book is dedicated to the memory of my maternal grandmother, Martha Theodosia Dresser (1873–1962)—a savvy, Ben Franklin–type entrepreneur who taught me how to maximize my assets (both financial and personal) and think fast on my feet, as well as inspired me to pursue a life of entrepreneurial ventures and adventures in the real estate business. She is the original "Frugal HomeOwner™"!

CONTENTS

THE ECONOMIZING OWNER'S CREED
To Refinance, Repair, or Prepay—
Financial Management's the Way!

THE CREED OF THE SAVVY SELLER
Well Begun Is Half Done

PREFACE

"The way to wealth . . . depends chiefly on two words, industry and frugality; that is waste neither time nor money."

—*Benjamin Franklin,* Poor Richard's Almanac, *1733*

Ben Franklin had the right idea. In order to maximize what you have, being frugal is important.

But it's tough today, especially where owning a home is concerned. It's always another expense—fix the furnace, pay the property taxes—and one false move could end up costing you a huge chunk of cash.

In fact, there are six primary home owning missteps that can quickly strip profit from your home and your wallet:

1. *Not having clear-cut objectives.* Why are you buying a certain home? Why are you buying a home at all?
2. *Poor negotiations with the seller.* Could you/should you have better terms/price?
3. *Stopping the search for financing as soon as you locate a low interest rate.* Is it the lowest? What other factors should you consider?
4. *Mismanaging equity.* Do you know how to refinance? Does it make sense to prepay?
5. *Overimproving your home.* Even if you want and can afford an improvement, should you do it?
6. *Focusing on price alone when selling.* Selling strategy means more than top dollar.

This book addresses 11 Frugal HomeOwner laws to help you stop these leaks and profit through frugality.

Frugal doesn't mean cheap. Cheap is focusing on the least cost, with no concern for the quality. Frugal, on the other hand, comes from the Latin *frugalis,* meaning virtuous (which was later expanded to include the French word *frux,* meaning to enjoy). If you're a frugal homeowner, you manage your home in the most prudent, economical way, paying close attention to financial details that maximize your assets, empower your financial life, and increase the joy of home ownership!

Compiled from consumers' questions to my syndicated real estate column—called (you guessed it) "The Frugal HomeOwner™"—as well as vignettes from 25 years' experience as a real estate broker, real estate educator, and national speaker, this book contains three major sections:

1. Tips for Bargain Buyers (How to get the best bargain when you purchase.)
2. Striving to Be Economizing Owners (How to manage the day-to-day expenses of home ownership and soundly manage your home investment for the long run.)
3. Suggestions for Savvy Sellers (How to maximize profits when you sell.)

Whether you're starting out, winding down, or midstream in the home owning cycle, this book will provide you with the answers you need to make your ventures cost-effective.

Much like the format of Ben Franklin's *Poor Richard's Almanac,* this book contains page after page of cost-trimming, cutting-edge tips—on everything from refinancing online (Ben would be amazed) to protesting your property taxes (Ben would be proud!). And what could be more appropriate in our frugal journey than to pepper the pages with some of the master of thrift's most thought-provoking quotes—colloquialisms that span the generations with pragmatic insight.

Each chapter ends with reminders of the most Dangerous Dollars issues that could cost you big bucks as a homeowner, as well as the Perilous Pennies issues that can mount up over time.

Let *The Frugal HomeOwner* be your life-long almanac to maintaining and protecting one of the most precious savings accounts you'll ever own—your home equity.

Frugally yours,
Julie Garton-Good, DREI

THE BARGAIN BUYER'S CREED

Begin with the End in Mind.

• • • • •

"The borrower is a slave to the lender, and the debtor to the creditor; disdain the chain, preserve your freedom; and maintain your independency: Be industrious and free; be frugal and free."

—*Benjamin Franklin*

It's doubtful that Ben literally meant that we should never go into debt (especially to put a roof over our heads). But it does require that before taking the plunge into home buying we carefully think through our options, have objectives, and formulate a game plan to follow. Bargain Buyers "begin with the end in mind," knowing what they want to achieve with home buying in general, and buying a specific home in particular.

In fact, not isolating and focusing on objectives in home buying is the first bend where a fool and his money can part.

Making cost-effective decisions often requires that Bargain Buyers take a slow, circuitous route to home buying, making sure their timing is on target, their credit report is spruced up, and that they've gathered every single financial record required by the lender—all before they tour the first house! That's a Bargain Buyer. Willing to do what it takes to financially maximize home buying right from the start!

As you gain knowledge in the chapters that follow, remember the Bargain Buyer Creed: Begin with the end in mind. After all, no one truly makes money when they sell a home. The money is made in making a sound financial purchase—right from the start!

CHAPTER 1

The Frugal HomeOwner Law of Proper Timing

Timing Is Everything—Almost!

In an effort to move swiftly toward the American Dream of home ownership, overzealous buyers often overlook the important ingredient of timing. Timing is a reflection of what's happening (and what could potentially happen) in your life in the near future. These events could include marriage/divorce, relocation, job promotion/downsizing, or an upcoming inheritance that you'll use as a down payment on your first home.

Timing also includes shifts and changes in the residential real estate market and its potential impact on the soundness of your investment. Just ask a Californian how challenging it was to sell a home after a market downturn devalued real estate by 50 percent!

Contrarily, timing doesn't mean that you should wait to purchase until all of your astrological planets are spinning in the proper orbit! To be a Bargain Buyer, you should spend adequate time evaluating what you want to accomplish by purchasing, what (if anything) you stand to lose, and then apply these answers in the best way possible to financially maximize your purchase.

Last, timing means remembering the value of your time as you hunt for valuable resources, like online services to streamline the home buying process or the right real estate professional to give you one-on-one service.

RENT VERSUS BUY

Q. *My husband and I just completed graduate school and will be staying in the area for about 18 months. We don't know if we should buy now or wait. How can we evaluate this?*

A. You are wise to consider how long you plan to stay in the home. Even though U.S. government statistics show that home appreciation was up to an average of 4.7 percent in 1997 (that's $4,700 on a $100,000 home) compared to 3.6 percent in 1996, holding a home for a short time may not be financially sound. You need to apply your own information to see for sure.

With the advent of the World Wide Web, there are "rent versus buy" calculators online that can provide answers to your particular situation in seconds. One of my favorites is at www.homefair.com.

For example, rent versus buy requires such information as:

1. How long will you keep the property? (It's good to give a conservative estimate.)
2. What approximate rate of interest will you be charged for a mortgage?
3. What is your tax bracket?
4. What is the tax rate for property in the area in which you'd purchase?
5. What is the expected appreciation (3 percent is a good, conservative norm)?
6. What is the monthly rent for a property similar to the house you'd buy?
7. What is the price of the house you're considering?

Let's see if renting or buying for this 18-month period is better. For a house with a purchase price of $100,000 with an expected 3 percent annual appreciation (a similar property would rent for $700 per month) for buyers in the 28 percent tax bracket with financing at 7 percent, buying a home would not pencil out. You would need not only to recoup your initial down payment and closing costs, but you'd need cash to pay the second set of closing costs when you sold (between $6,000 and $10,000). What if the real estate market softened and your

$100,000 home was now worth closer to $95,000? More money lost. Consider all the dice to roll for a big investment.

How could this scenario turn out a little rosier? Perhaps a larger down payment would give you a bit more latitude. A mortgage lender could review the options with you. Is appreciation in the area stronger than the meager 3 percent we used? That also will slant the figures in your favor.

If it still doesn't pencil out as an investment, you may want to go for it anyway. After all, there are aesthetic benefits that you just can't put a price on like "pride of ownership" and being able to nail holes in your own wall.

Q. *My husband and I are having a debate about whether we should buy now (I say yes) or wait until we're relocated in a year or so (his choice). Which one of us is correct? P.S.—the lender said our mortgage payment would be only $50 more than our current rent; but we would need to buy down the mortgage to qualify.*

A. Without exact numbers like the amount of your down payment, etc., it's tough to tell. But at first glance, I'd say your husband wins!

How can you analyze this? First, add up all the closing costs the lender itemized for you, including any buy down points you need to pay to qualify for the lower interest rate. Buy downs are actually prepaid interest to buy a higher interest rate down to a lower one. For example, the lender would lower the loan's rate down from 8 to 7 percent if you were to pay more points up front. Because a point is equal to 1 percent of the amount financed, paying two more points on a $90,000 loan would cost you $1,800 more in cash at closing—not a good move when you'll be keeping the house for only a short time.

Add the total closing costs to the down payment you would make. That amount is what it will cost you up front to purchase.

For example, let's say that your closing costs (including buy down points) totaled $3,000. That, plus a $10,000 down payment, would equal $13,000 due at closing.

Now comes the tough part. Based on what you know about how property values have appreciated in the area you're considering, how much could you sell the house for in one year? In fact, let's be conservative and say that you could get only the $100,000 you originally paid for it. $100,000 minus your outstanding loan of $90,000 leaves $10,000 equity. But after you factor in your costs of sale of $7,000, only $3,000 remains. Because you spent $13,000 out of your pocket to initially purchase the home, you would have lost $10,000!

This example shows that holding on to property to gain appreciation is in large part the reason people make money when they sell a home.

"You will delay, but time will not."
—*Ben Franklin*

Q. *My job situation is a little precarious so I feel I should wait until next year to purchase a home. Besides potentially higher interest rates, are there any other financial impacts to consider?*

A. It seems that many would-be buyers are fence-sitting right now, concerned that their job and/or their industry may suffer cutbacks.

But your question is a good one because much of the costs of waiting can be found tallied up in terms of lost appreciation and equity. Here's an example. Assume that you want to purchase a $100,000 house using a 90 percent loan. If you purchase today at 7.5 percent, your payment will be $629.30 per month principal and interest.

Suppose you decide to wait. Luck is with you as interest rates actually drop one-half percent to 7 percent (wouldn't you love to have a crystal ball to determine this?). But because of appreciation (we'll use a meager 3 percent rate of inflation), the home now costs $103,000, making your 90 percent loan $92,700 and your monthly payment $617.38 principal and interest. You've saved $11.92 per month on your monthly payments by waiting to purchase. Or have you?

What about the $3,000 additional cost of the home? Divided by the monthly savings of $11.92, it would take you nearly 21 years to recoup the difference!

That's not all. By waiting to purchase, you need $300 more down payment, and a larger loan could mean more closing costs and would be tougher to qualify for. In addition, the lender's loan underwriting guidelines might have tightened, disqualifying you completely for the loan you need. And then there's the potential that the home you desire might not be on the market should you decide to wait.

We often forget that money is made in real estate with equity buildup and appreciation. These are impacted by length of ownership and compounding. As you can see by our example, 3 percent inflation can make a $100,000 home worth $103,000 next year and $106,090 the following year, compounding on and on. And don't forget the tax advantages, too.

While it would be uncomfortable to have a hefty mortgage payment and be unemployed, consider one last thought. If unemployment does strike before you purchase, it will take awhile to rebuild your employment history in order to qualify for a loan, even if you're ready to buy.

All things considered, and if you stay in the home long enough to recoup your costs, waiting to buy may end up costing you money.

"Ne'er take a wife till thou has a house (& fire) to put her in."
—*Ben Franklin*

Q. *My husband and I are both 75 years old and have been renting since we moved to Florida. We now have the opportunity to purchase the condo we're in but wonder if perhaps we're not too old to be doing this again, especially taking on a mortgage!*

A. If purchasing the condo will help you meet your objectives like securing your living arrangements for the future, then go for it! And add to that pluses like tax benefits, pride of ownership, and potential appreciation.

As with any major purchase, you need to weigh the potential obstacles as well.

While it's likely your debts are low, you must be able to financially qualify with a lender based on your monthly income (which could include pensions, Social Security, and interest income). You'd be paying property taxes and condo fees (which typically increase), and making the down payment would reduce the amount of ready cash on hand as well as interest income you might receive from it.

Another concern is that once you own the property, making the repairs and replacements shift from the landlord to you. These could include large capital items like air-conditioning units, stoves, and furnaces. Make sure you have, or set up, ample cash reserves to cover these possible costs.

Even though you like living in that condominium project as a renter, how does it compare to others in purchase value? Particularly with condos and town homes, projects can differ widely in market value, causing you to lose money if you decide to sell.

Home ownership is not just about costs. In making your decision, be sure to factor in how owning the condo will impact your physical comfort and mental well-being for the future. That should help lead you to the best decision.

"Plough deep while sluggards sleep, and you shall have corn to sell and to keep."
—Ben Franklin

REAL ESTATE MARKET CHANGES

Q. *I think we should purchase quickly before the summer home buying rush. Rates often edge up during that time and we are only marginally qualified for the type of loan we'll need. But my girlfriend says we should wait until fall as rates usually come down. Which of us is correct?*

A. While my crystal ball isn't polished enough to be certain, your guess may be more accurate. Your girlfriend's point is valid in that rates do tend to cool when peak demand falls off (usually after September). But your particular situation may warrant an earlier purchase.

Here's why. First, no one can control the interest rates. Depending on what's happening in the U.S. economy as well as internationally, rates could jump overnight. That's not a risk you can stand to take if you're only marginally qualified for a loan. (Unless you're willing to find a larger down payment or purchase a less expensive home—usually not very attractive options.)

Second, if you wait to purchase until later in the year, inventory for the type of property you're seeking might be depleted after the summer rush. And if demand for the type of home you want was high, that could drive up the price (supply and demand in action). If rates lower, you would save on interest payments but might have to pay thousands more on the purchase price.

Getting a jump on the summer home buying rush makes sense. No matter what's happening to rates, supply and demand often does cause mortgage rates to uptick at that time of year. Purchasing early could help you beat the rush, find a good selection of inventory, and potentially save you some interest costs at the same time.

If rates do come down and your girlfriend says, "I told you so," at least you'll be living in the house you wanted and can afford to eat a little crow!

Q. *Please explain the difference between a buyer's market and a seller's market.*

A. Buyer's and seller's markets are examples of supply and demand in action!

A buyer's market is characterized by the availability of many properties compared to the number of buyers who want them. This creates increased leverage for buyers with sellers contributing more to points, closing costs, etc., and/or reducing their sales price to capture buyers.

Conversely, in a seller's market, there are fewer properties for sale compared to the number of buyers. Prices are high, seller's have the upper hand in negotiating, and buyers become more competitive by paying at (or above) market price for properties.

In general, it will cost a buyer more to purchase a home in a seller's market. Buyers should make sure they'll own the property long enough to recoup their down payment and closing costs, especially because there is no tax write-off available when you lose money on the sale of your residence!

ALTERING YOUR LIFESTYLE AND YOUR HOUSING NEEDS

Q. *I am in the middle of a divorce, but want to buy a home for my daughter and myself. Is it possible to purchase a home before the divorce from my husband is final?*

A. Your attorney is the first one to consult. It's not impossible to purchase before your divorce is final, just a bit more tricky.

If you can personally carry all of your joint debt based on your income alone, there's a strong possibility that you can qualify before the final divorce decree. Even though your former spouse would not be on the loan with you, the lender might ask that he sign some documents at closing. This ensures that your former spouse agrees not to have any financial interest in the property you're purchasing, and protects you and the lender against any potential title problems. Obviously, your former husband needs to agree to this.

The lender's major concern is that until the divorce is final, your financial picture is subject to change. This is particularly true if child support or other similar agreements are still pending. The danger is that your former spouse could decide to try to alter a previous agreement that would drastically change your monthly income picture. Not only would this increase the lender's risk, but it might make the monthly mortgage payment tougher to make.

There is nothing wrong with checking with a lender to prequalify. Give the lender all of the facts and get advice as to properly timing the purchase (again, with your attorney's advice).

One last critical point. Make sure you don't start house hunting until you check with a lender. Committing to a purchase contract you may not be able to follow through on is not in your best interest and can add extra stress that you don't need right now.

Q. *We own land several counties north of where we live and want to retire there in ten years. Should we build now and rent the house out, or just keep the bare ground even though it doesn't generate any income?*

A. The answer lies in what you're trying to accomplish. If you truly want it to be the home for your golden years, then you may not want to build a house that will be lived in by someone else for the next ten years. But if you'd forego that for the income that could be generated, build-to-rent could be a more cost-effective alternative. In addition, completing the construction now would give you improvements that would appreciate and help grow your equity.

Now for addressing the construction issues. Because you're at a distance, if you build now you'd probably need to hire a reliable general contractor to keep you informed about progress and be prepared to take periodic trips to the site to monitor the work.

Don't forget that you'd be an absentee landlord and might want to pay a property manager to monitor the rental. Tenants might not keep your retirement dream home in the best of shape. Also, you'd need to be prepared to fund and orchestrate repairs to the property from time to time.

Last, but not least, is the issue of financing. If you weren't paying cash for the construction, obtaining a loan to build a second home or investment property will be more costly and difficult to obtain. Because the lender would not consider the house owner-occupied, a loan might require a down payment of up to 20 percent, higher loan fees, and traditionally a higher interest rate. Being tied down with a higher-than-market-rate loan may not be in your financial favor or something you want to be saddled with when you retire.

Upon sale, you can take a capital gains tax exemption of up to $500,000 of the equity from the sale of your home. Based on the hassle of owning and managing an income property long distance plus being able to pay cash later to build that spanking new dream home may make you realize that your bare ground looks pretty darn good just the way it is!

GETTING THE HELP YOU NEED WHEN YOU PURCHASE

Q. *Can I save time using the Internet to gather home buying information?*

A. Absolutely. There's nothing easier, faster, or more informational. The Web is not only revolutionizing the real estate industry, it's one of the best things to happen to homebuyers since the invention of the garage door opener! Not only can you gather information about the home buying process, mortgage rates and options, and available homes, you can do so in privacy and at your leisure. (A wide array of Uniform Resource Locators, or URLs, can be found in the Resource Guide at the end of this book.)

Here's how to get started. If you're a first time homebuyer who needs to know about the process, initially visit information-gathering sites like www.owners.com, www.homefair.com, ourbroker.com (not a brokerage, but Peter Miller, author and columnist), and, of course, yours truly at frugalhomeowner.com. Don't get bogged down initially filling in time-consuming forms and micromanaging the experience. Your mission is to feel comfortable with the process, not obtain your masters degree in real estate. (If you've seen how much time can pass while you're online, you know what I'm talking about.)

Next, visit several of the interest rate and mortgage sites like www.hsh.com, www.homeshark.com, and www.countrywide.com. If you're feeling comfortable enough with the process, go ahead and try one of the "how much home can you afford" calculators, check out your credit report online with lenders or by accessing sites like www.equifax.com.

Once your search leads you to specific properties at sites such as www.owners.com, www.realtor.com, or www.homeadvisor.com, you can gather support information about everything from crime rates (www.crimewatch.com) to schools (www.schoolreport.com).

To keep you informed of properties that suit your needs and to alert you when new listings come online, you may want to register with property locator services like www.matchpoint.com and homescout.com. This is a time saving way to keep abreast of what's new without going back to the drawing board each time you log on.

But there's a caution. Don't make the time saved counterproductive by trying to see everything that's available online. There are so many sites that viewing even a majority of them could take you days!

Q. *If we're looking at real estate information online, are there any "red flags" we should be aware of?*

A. Yes, there are. It's amazing how some people feel that because the property facts and pictures of the house are on the Internet, that it's sanctioned information (like printed words in a book, correct?). There is no Web god of real estate that patrols the information, guarantees the source, or even checks to see if the information is current. In fact, I recently visited a for-sale-by-owner site. I was interested enough to call the phone number provided, only to find out that the owner who placed the property online had died six months ago! (I guess it would be pretty tough to remove your listing once you're no longer "wired!")

Seriously, for all listings you need to check: (1) the source of the information (is it from an agent, the owner, a Board of REALTORS®?); (2) the accuracy of the information (sometimes this can only be done upon in-person inspection of the property); and (3) the timeliness of the information (has the zoning changed since the listing was posted? Have the property taxes changed?). Just as many people are hesitant to release their credit card numbers online, you may want to make inquiries solely using your e-mail address until you want your identity known. Prospective buyers often will contact agents this way for additional information and/or to ask questions anonymously.

Q. *Is there anything wrong with buying a property solely through an online listing? What are the cautions?*

A. Does this mean you're not going to view the property before you purchase it? What a brave soul you are! While I've heard of this happening in some international and/or commercial real estate sales situations, most people who are geographically able want to "kick the tires" before they make an offer.

If it's impossible for you to visit the property, it's a good idea to have a representative do so for you. You might hire a real estate attorney near the property to inspect it, draft the purchase agreement, check the title work, and assist in closing the sale. It's impossible to determine true property condition, sump pumps in basements, and neighborhood eyesores by looking at pictures online! Additionally, until electronic signature technology can be refined, you need to make sure that the person agreeing to sell the property is the real owner. It's less expensive to pay an attorney now to properly settle the sale than to have to file a lawsuit later to clear matters.

Q. *I found a for-sale-by-owner property that I want to purchase, but think I need help in negotiating and writing up the offer. Could I hire a real estate agent just for those services?*

A. Yes, you could. The real estate industry is realizing that "one size no longer fits all" when it comes to both buyer's and seller's needs. This new unbundled services or á la carte approach in the real estate industry is an excellent way for consumers to obtain the services they need, when they need them, often exercising more control over the home buying process. It's much like using any other type of consultant, such as a CPA, to acquire professional services.

I would suggest that you contact an agent (using a referral from another satisfied buyer is good) or visit some Web sites that belong to real estate companies near you. Tell the agent that you'd like to hire only the services you need, either paying an hourly fee or a flat fee. A percentage fee would not be in your best financial interest in this case, unless it was possibly a percentage of the savings realized by obtaining a much lower purchase price in using the services. The several hundred dollars such services could cost would be more than offset by the advocacy and the piece of mind you'll receive.

Q. *My concern is that if I work with just one real estate agent, I won't see everything available. Is this justified?*

A. I doubt that your true desire is to see everything available—but to find several of the best prospects from which to choose. Working with a real estate agent can accomplish that for you.

A good agent will listen to your needs and search through properties available (from both that agency's listings and those of the Multiple Listing Service), weeding out the inappropriate ones. He or she will probably then show you several to get your feedback, and repeat the process again until you find the right home. Additionally, the agent informs you of new properties as they become available and also those that may be for sale shortly. What could end up taking you months on your own can be done in a timely and cost-effective manner with the help of an agent.

Be candid with your feedback to the agent. When you see something you don't like, explain why. Point out features you do like in the homes you see. Your agent can give you better service with more information.

In most cases, you will be best served by dealing with only one committed agent versus "shopping the field" with a variety of agents and brokerages. If you make the agent aware that you are committed to work with him or her, there is no reason why the agent won't work diligently for you.

Q. *What is the difference between a buyer's broker/buyer's agent and a regular real estate agent? Is a buyer's broker paid by the buyer?*

A. A buyer's broker or buyer's agent is a real estate agent hired by the buyer to represent his or her interests. Real estate agents have typically listed property for sale and formed a legal relationship with the seller. Now buyers who desire to have their interests advocated can hire agents to represent them. It's an excellent way to obtain the negotiating and advocacy power you need as a buyer. Even as someone with a real estate broker's license, I use them myself when I purchase.

A buyer's agent negotiates on your behalf, does market analyses on properties you're interested in purchasing, and serves as a great asset to first-time buyers who often need a lot of information about purchasing real estate.

The buyer's broker can be paid by anyone—the buyer, the seller, or a third party—or could receive the cobroker (selling broker) share of the commission without it inferring that the buyer's agent represents the seller. This last method of compensation is the most common way to compensate a buyer's agent, but must be approved by both the seller and the listing broker before the property is shown to the buyer.

You can find a wealth of information about buyer's brokers at the National Association of Exclusive Buyer's Agents Web site, www.naeba.com.

Q. *The buyer's agent with whom I signed an employment contract called to say that she could show me "a great house that fits my needs," but not until she showed it to two other buyers/clients first! What gives her the right to prioritize those buyers if she's representing me, too? I'm in a hurry to buy!*

A. Just as one agent might be employed by several sellers to market their property, one agent could have several buyers signed as clients.

Review your written agreement to see if the issue of "multiple buyers for the same property" is addressed. Ideally, the agreement will specify how this should be handled. For example, first priority for showing could be given to the buyer who first signed the agreement with the buyer's agent or other similar guideline because it's tough to show the same property to (and equally represent) two buyers/clients simultaneously, especially in negotiations.

If working with multiple buyers for the same property is not addressed in your agreement, ask the agent how she came to this decision. If it's not in the agreement, the agent will be hard pressed to restrict you from seeing the property as soon as you want to see it.

Q. *We came across a real estate licensee who called himself a* facilitator. *Is that a special kind of agent?*

A. While the terms *facilitator, transaction broker,* or *nonagent* are fairly new to the real estate industry, they have received a fair share of press (both good and bad). Licensees who work as facilitators offer real estate services, but have no legal agency relationship to either buyer or seller. In other words, the licensee cannot negotiate nor advocate on behalf of the consumer when working as a transaction broker. The licensee stands neutral between the parties and helps facilitate the sale.

Some brokers and attorneys feel that this nonagency status might help the agent lessen his liability when working with consumers. But some states have purposely neither recognized nor sanctioned facilitators, feeling that their intermediary services are not in the best interests of consumers.

Realistically, most consumers work with agents to receive top-level services like negotiation and advocacy. And while it's up to each state to decide how licensees will work with consumers, buyers are voting with their feet—most often to the door of the agent who can represent their interests as buyers/clients.

Q. ***Is there a difference between real estate attorneys and other attorneys and can using them save you money?***

A. There is no additional formal law school training required to be a real estate attorney; but practicing real estate law requires a combination of financial/mortgage expertise, knowledge of the title industry, and inordinate people skills.

For example, on any given day, a real estate attorney might review a survey to write a legal description, discuss foreclosure options with a seller in arrears, and write an in-depth land sales contract (from scratch) that totals more than 30 pages. No two days are alike—no two clients' problems similar.

Depending on what you needed the attorney to do, a real estate attorney could save a buyer money. In most cases, you'd pay the same amount of money for a regular attorney to draft real estate documents as you would a specialist in real estate law. Why then, would anyone choose the former?

Don't forget that if you decide to work alone without the aid of a real estate agent, a real estate attorney can be invaluable in helping you write up a purchase agreement as well as troubleshoot the sale to closing.

"God works wonders now and then;
behold! a lawyer an honest man!"
—*Ben Franklin*

DANGEROUS DOLLARS AND PERILOUS PENNIES ISSUES

To maximize The Frugal HomeOwner Law of Proper Timing, avoid these Dangerous Dollars errors that can quickly strip big bucks out of your pocket:

- Don't purchase a home before you know (with some certainty) that you'll be staying put for awhile.

- Conversely, don't drag your feet to purchase, waiting for things to be perfect before you buy. Pencil out what you're losing in appreciation and equity buildup—you'll be amazed!
- Be cognizant of whether it's a buyers' or sellers' market to map out the best strategy for your purchase. With a buyer's market you may have more control and latitude with sellers, but need to be keenly aware of other buyers. In a seller's market, your offers must be strong and your negotiating sharp, keeping in mind that "he who hesitates is lost!"

And be aware of these Perilous Pennies issues that gradually let loose change mount into dollars:

- Realize how much money you're throwing away monthly for rent. In fact, you're already "buying" a house—for your landlord!
- Access online services first before setting foot out your door. Don't waste your time by not being prepared for the process.
- Choose real estate professionals and services based on *your* needs, not what the person or the service wants to deliver!

CHAPTER 2

The Frugal HomeOwner Law of Credit Consciousness

What You Don't Know about Your Credit, Someone Else Already Does!

Untangling your credit can be a nightmare. Credit postings that aren't yours. Obligations outstanding that you can prove were paid eons ago. And then there are the credit card accounts you closed out and sent back the cards for, still looming big as life all over your credit report!

If you've ever had onc or more of these credit glitches, you know it's not fun. Now compound this scenario with the seller anxious for his closing to proceed, your family in a tailspin to move, and the lender taunting, "You'll have to get a letter from your former spouse verifying that she's made the car payments on time before we can make you this loan." Ah, there are few other tensions quite like it!

By adhering to The Frugal HomeOwner Law of Credit Consciousness, you'll not only be aware that your credit report's in good shape, but you'll use your positive financial posture to negotiate a competitive interest rate and other mortgage perks with the lender.

The following questions will not only take the stress out of troubleshooting your credit picture, but give you additional insight into the important role credit plays in overall financial management.

As I'm known for saying, "Get a copy of your credit report and study it. You'll learn just how much other people already know about you!"

TYPES OF CREDIT REPORTS AND WHAT THEY SHOW

Q. *Can I obtain my own credit report, and how does it differ from the report the mortgage lender might pull?*

A. You can obtain your report by contacting one of the three primary credit reporting agencies in the country, Experian (formerly TRW), TransUnion, and Equifax. (Note the addresses, phone numbers, and Web addresses found in Figure 1.1.) The best way to do it (especially if you've never seen your report before and might have questions) is to check the yellow pages of your phone directory under "credit reporting agencies" for the office nearest you and walk in during their "consumer counseling" hours. If you choose to obtain your report by mail, you can contact the bureaus by phone and listen to detailed instructions on how to order your report. Alternatively, you could choose to order your report on the World Wide Web. Based on the company you order from and the state you live in, there may be a charge for the report (typically $15 or less).

FIGURE 1.1 Credit Reporting Agency Contact Information

Equifax
P.O. Box 740241
Atlanta, GA 30374-0241
800-997-2493
Order online at www.equifax.com

Experian
P.O. Box 2104
Allen, TX 75013-2104
888-Experian (888-397-3742)
www.experian.com (but online orders are not currently available)

TransUnion
P.O. Box 390
Springfield, PA 19064-0390
800-888-4213
Order online at www.tuc.com

Your information is called a consumer credit report. It's a broad overview of what creditors have reported about your accounts. And because not all creditors report histories on a consistent basis and/or the report you obtain may not contain information from all of the agencies, the report may have gaps. In fact, important credit histories like auto loans or student loans you've paid off might not even appear on this report.

But when the lender requests your credit report, it's much more in-depth. It's called a mortgage credit or merged report, and it will research each of the credit items you brought to the lender's attention during the loan qualifying appointment plus merge information from the other reporting agencies. This allows the lender to cross-check the information and compare any conflicting information between sources. This often uncovers more errors than you're able to detect in the consumer credit report.

Q. *What can a consumer expect to see on his or her credit report?*

A. You will be amazed at the depth of the credit report. You'll see which accounts are reported, the last payment received on each, as well as the past 12 to 18 months of payments and their timeliness. You'll also be able to see the highest balance on the account, the minimum repayment required monthly, and when the account was opened.

Be sure to take a detailed look on the report for who has checked your credit (usually showing for the past 24 months.) Anyone who has a valid business reason to check your credit may do so—with or without your permission. But, if you find that someone has maliciously checked your credit (without having a business reason to do so) it's punishable under federal law by a fine (which you receive) and/or imprisonment (which they receive!).

CREDIT SCORING

Q. *I've heard that mortgage companies are using credit scoring to evaluate borrowers. How does this work and what does your credit need to look like to have a good score?*

A. Credit scoring gives a numerical weighting to various financial factors like your income, debts, and job history. Lenders feel it can help predict the likelihood of mortgage default. While there are several credit scoring models, many lenders use the FICO (Fair, Isaac & Co.)

score and look for a minimum score of no less than 620 as an indicator of creditworthiness.

Errors on your credit report can cost points on your score. The past 6 to 12 months of credit history is perhaps the most important, and is a strong reminder to keep accounts current when anticipating a need to borrow.

Credit scoring also weighs how much available credit you have used. For example, if your balances are 75 percent or more of your credit limit, it can signal high financial leverage and higher risk to the lender. Because the lender compares the amount of debt you have to the amount of income you make, it's important to keep your outstanding credit reasonable for your income level.

Keeping a large number of accounts with zero balances also can lower your score because it increases the potential for you to live beyond your means. Decide which accounts to keep and close out the rest. In general, the longer the positive credit history, the better the score.

Opening new accounts can lower your score, as can having too many credit inquiries. Your score even can be affected when you transfer your balance to a new lower rate card, because you might not have closed out the old account. (If you've done this, inform the credit reporting agency to note this fact on your credit report, and be sure to close out the old account.)

As with other loan qualifying guidelines, credit scoring is merely one way to measure the financial strength of a borrower. But it's fast gaining acceptance by lenders as one of the more dependable ways to rate risk, predict foreclosure, and eliminate biases in granting credit.

Q. *Do lenders use ranges of credit scores to determine the credit strength of a buyer? And have there been any industry tests to see how accurate credit scoring is?*

A. Yes, to both questions. Lenders do use ranges of credit scoring, and there have been numerous tests to prove their efficacy. The Federal National Mortgage Association (FNMA) surveyed one million loan records and found that one in eight borrowers with a FICO score below 600 was either severely delinquent or in default. Contrarily, only one in 1,300 borrowers with scores above 800 had similar mortgage delinquency problems. From these and other surveys, the benchmark of concern is usually with scores of less than 620.

Most lenders who sell their loans into the secondary market use the following parameters when evaluating scores:

- *Scores greater than 660*—Credit risk is generally acceptable. In fact, a high score here can help compensate for other risks in the credit file.
- *Scores between 620 and 659*—Comprehensive review should take a closer look at potential risks. Supplemental credit documentation and letters of explanation may be required.
- *Scores below 620*—Cautious review is required. Borrowers may find themselves locked out of the best loans and terms available. The lender still may be able to make a loan if compensating factors can shore up the borrower's picture. In general, though, factors such as lower ratios, extra cash reserves, and/or a lower loan-to-value ratio on the loan won't compensate for unacceptable credit.

Q. *Is it possible that someone with extremely damaged previous credit could get a mortgage given credit scoring today?*

A. Yes. Even after major credit glitches like bankruptcy and foreclosure, in today's lending world of customized credit a borrower can usually qualify for some type of mortgage (albeit one with higher interest and/or more points and fees.) Instead of the top A category loans purchased by the secondary market (which we usually refer to as standard mortgages), a borrower only may be able to fit into a lesser category A–, B, C, or D rated loans called subprime.

Subprime loans are made to borrowers who have had damaged credit on a regular or extensive basis. Problems can fall into three primary areas of credit blemishes: mortgage credit, consumer credit, and public record postings. For example, the latter category would be someone with a foreclosure or a judgment against him or her.

After scoring and grading the borrower's credit, the lender would place the borrower in the appropriate category. For example, an A– borrower might be one with a 30-day late mortgage payment in the past 12 months; whereas a C subprime buyer might have had a bankruptcy discharged 14 months ago.

In addition to the borrower's credit, the amount of down payment plays a role in the type of subprime loan the borrower can obtain. In general, the larger the down payment, the weaker the credit can be.

Rates and points vary widely between loan categories. Depending on the loan types and market factors, B subprime loans might spread two or more interest rate points above standard fixed-rate 30-year loans so borrowers are advised to shop diligently before committing to a certain loan program.

"Pay what you owe and you'll know what's your own."
—*Ben Franklin*

GOOD CREDIT

Q. *What do mortgage lenders consider to be good credit? Is that the same as having perfect credit?*

A. *Good credit* for the purpose of qualifying for a mortgage loan doesn't mean that you've never been tardy paying an obligation. Although there are various ways to interpret credit, the secondary market (where loans are purchased as investments) considers a borrower to have "good credit" if the report shows nothing more detrimental during the past 12 months than the following:

- Revolving credit (like credit cards) with no more than two payments 30 days past due, and no payments 60 days past due
- Installment credit (like a car loan) with no more than one payment 30 days past due and no payments 60 days or more past due
- Housing debt (first or second mortgages, rent) with no payments past due

Thorough explanations must be provided to the lender for any late payments.

BLEMISHED CREDIT

Q. *How long do negative postings stay on a credit report?*

A. It depends on the type of negative postings. Derogatory information (like late payments, delinquencies) stay on a report for seven years. Bankruptcy stays on a credit report for ten years, as do foreclosures. Other types of negative postings, like recorded liens, stay on indefinitely.

But don't assume that negative information automatically pops off the report after the designated time expires. It often takes the watchful eye of the consumer to remind the reporting agencies that the clock has run out and the derogatory information should come off.

Q. *If I've declared bankruptcy, can I get a mortgage?*

A. Possibly. Most conventional lenders (especially the ones who sell their loans to secondary-market investors) will approve a previously bankrupt borrower for a mortgage loan within four years after a bankruptcy has been discharged. (The Federal Housing Administration—FHA—has been known to require only two years, or in rare circumstances one year.)

As with all adverse situations, explaining to the lender why they happened and how you will prevent them in the future is important. Bankruptcies caused by illness or death in the family or personal business failure may not reflect as harshly on the borrower as ignoring or mismanaging debts.

Q. *If my credit was poor 18 months ago, but has shaped up in the past 10 months, what are my chances for getting a home loan?*

A. In general, the past 6 to 12 months of credit history is most important to the lender. However, lenders consider a borrower's situation on a case-by-case basis, wanting to know what caused the poor credit and may require that you document it with letters of explanation. For example, circumstances outside of your control (illness, death in the family, loss of job) may not negatively impact your ability to obtain a mortgage. But if you just didn't pay your bills or were otherwise inattentive to your financial life, that could be a red flag to the lender that you'd do the same with a new mortgage.

CREDIT CHECKS ONLINE

Q. *We visited several mortgage sites online and two offered a free credit report—so we took their offers.*

But two weeks later when we finally settled on a lender, she asked if we'd been turned down by those companies because their inquiries appeared on our reports. Her underwriter is requesting we write a letter of explanation before they'll make us the loan!

A. With the advent of online services, this is happening more and more. A credit inquiry appears on your credit report no matter if it's done in person with the lender or via the Internet. Lenders check credit online to see how creditworthy a buyer is prior to quoting a mortgage interest rate and points. The lender you made application with was concerned that you might have applied with other lenders for mortgages and be obligated to pay them and/or were turned down by those lenders. That's why the letter of explanation might be necessary.

Shopping for the best interest rates and fees is no crime. But you could have obtained a fair idea of rates and fees without authorizing that your credit be checked, especially when the lender you finally apply with will run an entirely fresh report—one that you'll more than likely have to pay for!

In the future, you can request a range of rates and fees but may want to inform lenders in person and in cyberspace that "this rate inquiry does not authorize you to check my credit." You can reserve that right to the lender who receives your formal loan application.

CREDIT GLITCHES IN THE QUALIFYING PROCESS

Q. *If I have a negative posting that's being disputed with a creditor, is there any special way I can note that on my credit report?*

A. Absolutely. You are allowed to post a 100-word explanation on your report, designed to alert creditors as to why a bill is showing unpaid. In most cases, the posting stays on your report for six months, but can be renewed for additional increments of six months if necessary.

Q. *I was recently shocked to learn that my attorney in the divorce did not separate out my debts from my former husband's, even though the divorce decree showed how the assets were to be divided. How can I document this to the lender?*

A. Making the lender aware of the divorce decree is a start. But joint accounts mean joint liability. It sounds as though your former husband did not financially qualify to assume those debts—that's why they're still on your report.

Take a copy of the divorce decree to the lender and ask what will be required. Some debts may not be a concern. Others may require that you obtain photocopies of cancelled checks (both front and back) from your former spouse, showing that he's paying those debts in a timely fashion (particularly in the last 12 months). The lender is concerned that if your former husband falls behind on payments, you'll be liable for that coborrowed debt.

TROUBLESHOOTING ERRORS ON YOUR CREDIT REPORT

Q. *We checked our credit before going to the lender and found two errors that we told the reporting bureau about and then completed a Credit Dispute form. The bureau wrote us for more information, which we sent. But when we applied for a loan with the lender, both mistakes were still there. What happened?*

A. Just be patient. While it's true that the credit reporting agency tries to prove or remove the error within 30 days, this time frame begins anew after the complete information is received. This allows them to work on the problem with the full range of facts.

Even with the information, corrections often take up to 60 days to show on the credit report, especially because many creditors report only every 30 days.

Inform the lender of what you did and ask that it be confirmed directly with the creditor. The lender may make a lending decision after confirming that there was an error and that an amendment to the report is pending.

Be sure that you recheck your report with the credit bureau in approximately 60 days to make sure the error is off your report. If the credit reporting agency did not provide you with a merged report showing information from all three primary reporting agencies in the United States, you may need to pull reports from the other two companies to make sure their information is correct.

Additionally, the credit reporting agency must send a corrected copy of your report to anyone who received a copy in the previous 60 days.

Q. *The lender called to tell me that it appears that my credit report is tangled up with someone who has a similar name. How can this happen?*

A. It's estimated that this problem occurs in nearly 30 percent of all credit files. It can be caused when creditors report using an improper Social Security number, a common name without a middle initial gets misposted, and/or juniors, seniors, or other relatives' names are confused.

Check your credit report to see if your Social Security number is properly listed. It's best if you use your full name (including your middle name) when applying for credit.

Once corrected, check your report periodically to make sure that it stays free from error. Creditors might tell you that checking your report too often could indicate that you are waiting for something negative to be posted. To avoid this perception, post a note on your report stating that because of erroneous information previously posted, you periodically check your credit.

"Creditors have better memories than debtors."
—*Ben Franklin*

REPAIRING DAMAGED CREDIT

Q. *We want to sell the house we have and purchase a larger one, but are afraid to do so because of our credit. We've seen our credit report, complete with a myriad of open accounts with balances, and it can't help but hinder our ability to buy. Should we talk to the credit reporting bureau?*

A. No, talk to a lender. If you provide an idea of how much equity you have in your current home (based on what it could sell for), your monthly income, and your current debts, the lender can structure several options for you. You even can begin the process with a phone call.

Having equity in your current home gives you additional flexibility to pay off debts and hopefully buy that new one.

Q. *Because our credit problems are severe, we wonder if a credit counseling service might help?*

A. It's one option. The Consumer Credit Counseling Service is a nonprofit organization with locations throughout the United States. It will evaluate your income and ability to pay, analyze your debt, and request that you surrender your monthly income to them, from which they pay your creditors. Its goal is to help you reduce debt and make it manageable. The only cost is any volunteer contribution you wish to make. You can contact the location closest to you by looking under Credit Counseling Services in the yellow pages of your phone directory.

I would suggest that you first contact a mortgage lender for feedback on whether this approach is prudent for you. Some lenders are not proponents of it, claiming it does little to prove that the consumer can handle his or her debt and it's often tougher to get a buyer qualified for a mortgage after taking this route.

Q. *Responding to an ad claiming "repair credit within 30 days" has been a big mistake. We sent a check to the company and never heard a thing! Could we have untangled our credit by ourselves to get the mortgage?*

A. Yes, you could have. It is your right as a consumer to repair your own credit. Most companies claiming to repair credit do nothing more than what you could do as a consumer—and they charge a fee for doing it (or not doing it, as you found out!).

Consumers can be misled by companies claiming to remove blemishes and reinstate accounts in good standing. The truth is that no company (or person) can rewrite history. By law, negative credit information will stay on a credit report for a determinate period of time. So unless the information is erroneous (and can be corrected), no one could remove the adverse information.

Besides correcting your credit report yourself, there's one more action that could help you work through this. Contact the better business bureau and report the company that made false promises to you. They may have had previous reports; and your information could help others stay clear of them in the future.

"It's hard for an empty bag to stand upright."
—*Ben Franklin*

ESTABLISHING CREDIT WHEN YOU HAVE NONE (OR VERY LITTLE)

Q. *We don't believe in keeping our money in banks and we pay all of our bills in cash. How can we prove to a mortgage lender that we're creditworthy even though we don't have any credit references?*

A. Just because you pay your bills in cash doesn't mean that you don't have credit references. If you pay rent or utilities, those are references. Virtually any person or company that can document your repayment history can be a credit reference. In advance of applying for a mortgage, ask the lender what type of receipts and documentation will be required to paper trail your payment patterns. Lenders realize that not all borrowers handle their finances the same. Alternative methods of documentation are becoming much more acceptable in determining a borrower's creditworthiness. Find an enterprising lender who's willing to work around this minor roadblock.

Q. *We are a young couple trying to buy our first home. We have a car loan, three credit card accounts, and a good rental history. Would this be enough credit history for a home loan or should we take on more credit?*

A. Don't take on more credit! When the lender reviews your credit, it will evaluate several areas including the amount of your outstanding debt compared to your income, and how well you manage that debt. Taking on more debt now could skew your qualifying ratios.

If all of your creditors report to the reporting agency, the lender may have ample information on which to make a decision.

But if the accounts are too new to rate, or are not reported by the creditor, the lender may need additional references; but they don't always have to be debt references. Wait until you have a qualifying appointment with the lender to determine what else, if anything, you need to document.

"The second vice is lying; the first is running in debt!"
—*Ben Franklin*

Q. *I've been paying on a car loan for two years, but it doesn't show on my credit report. It's a good reference; how do I get it to appear there?*

A. Don't panic if a credit reference doesn't appear on your credit report. The type of report you received (a consumer's report) does not always reflect every credit account. In fact, not all creditors report accounts to credit reporting agencies.

Your concern can be remedied. Give the lender a complete list of credit references based on what you owe, loans you've paid off, and other credit references you feel paint a positive picture (just like you'll provide when you formally apply for a mortgage). Your car loan would be one such loan, and the lender can then make a special inquiry to the creditor to receive your payment history.

DANGEROUS DOLLARS AND PERILOUS PENNIES ISSUES

Focused on The Frugal HomeOwner Law of Credit Consciousness, take action to avoid these Dangerous Dollars issues that can erode your borrowing power:

- Check your credit well in advance of meeting with the lender (you even can do it online). Credit problems often take weeks or months to repair—precious time that could cost you major dollars in earnest money deposits, fallen transactions, and lost opportunities.
- Remove credit errors (and double-check their removal) as soon as you find them on your credit report. Even if credit errors don't disqualify you for the mortgage, they're likely to at least cost you a higher interest rate or additional loan fees—potentially thousands of dollars over the life of the loan!

Perilous Pennies points may appear innocent where credit is involved, but can restrict your borrowing power. Make sure to:

- Close out any open, zero-balance credit accounts appearing on your report because the lender may count a minimum monthly repayment amount against your long-term debt ratios for loan qualifying. Too much debt could limit the loan size and/or require that you make a larger down payment.
- Give the lender the names of positive credit references that don't appear on your credit report, especially large-purchase references like car loans, student loans, or other paid-in-full loans. An unmentioned reference might be the final piece of information the lender needs to cement your loan approval!

CHAPTER 3

The Frugal HomeOwner Law of Buyer Preparation

Forewarned Is Forearmed—And Can Cut Light-Years Off Your Loan Processing Time!

Have you ever wondered why some buyers sail through the home buying process while others seem to be caught up in a cruel game of homebuying pinball, bouncing from problem to problem? The critical difference lies in being prepared to buy. Preparedness encompasses itemizing your income and debts as well as knowing the questions to ask in "qualifying" a lender. (Yes, it makes perfect sense to interview a lender first to see if that company is prepared to make you the most cost-effective loan—and I'll show you how!)

Having your financial information in hand when you first visit the lender is critical today because your information is likely to be input directly into the lender's laptop computer and then processed using artificial intelligence software to underwrite the loan. Called handling the loan at "desk level," many lenders now are able to cut weeks off the processing time. In fact, several national lenders will guarantee that if the borrower comes to the application armed with the required financial information, the loan can close in as little as three business days! Just think how powerful your negotiating position with the seller would become if you could promise him or her a proceeds check before week's end! With the impact of technology and the advent of online banking—not to mention the lender's ease in accessing information regarding your employment history and your bank balance—lightning-fast closings may well become the norm, requiring sellers to be loaded up in the moving van before the property is even listed!

AFFORDABILITY—HOMEOWNERS' GREATEST CONCERN

Q. *One lender said not having enough money for the down payment was the number one problem with first-time buyers. Is this true?*

A. According to a national housing survey done by the Federal National Mortgage Association (FNMA, or Fannie Mae, found at www.fanniemae.com), which is responsible for buying mortgages in the secondary market, the lender is correct. Of the first-time homebuyers polled, 44 percent said that not having enough money for a down payment and closing costs was the number one roadblock to buying a home.

In second place was not earning enough income to make mortgage payments; 41 percent of homebuyers reported this concern.

Of the potential homeowners polled, 40 percent claimed that it was tough to find a home that they liked and could afford. Some expressed concerns that their limited budgets prevented them from qualifying for the type of house they wanted, especially one in a safe neighborhood with good schools.

It's interesting to note that these top three homebuying roadblocks all reflect issues of home affordability. Previous *Miami Herald* surveys confirm that home affordability is one of the major concerns facing Americans today, even for those who currently own homes.

Q. *I've heard that some lenders offer better fees if you apply online. How much could you save?*

A. It depends on how motivated the lender is to have your business. Yes, it's possible to save on the interest rate and/or the points, closing fees, or origination fees charged if you make application online. Savings could be as much as $1,500 on a $100,000 loan—now that's frugal! The rationale is that the process is more streamlined with less need for personal contact which could, in turn, reduce the lender's cost of business. In addition, buyers applying online are often more savvy and potentially more qualified, so there may be a bit of risk reduction (and thus incentive) for the lender to take the loan.

But you'll need to make a decision. Do you want to make a formal loan application online or would you prefer that a person calls to discuss mortgage options? I personally vote for (and have used) the latter because most online applications contain screen after screen of information to complete, numbers to provide—asking for information that's not usually at your fingertips when you're sitting in front of a computer screen.

Many mortgage sites allow you to send them a streamlined application that includes your name, phone number, e-mail address, best time to call, and the state in which you wish to buy property. You also can gather information on programs, rates, and points online and then request that deeper disclosures (e.g., closing costs) be faxed to you—all before you make a formal loan application. This also allows you time to check out companies you're not familiar with by calling the better business bureau.

While most mortgage companies use encrypted transmission to send your personal information (turning it from text to a secure code), some people still are leery of online security. But think about it. Information about our credit, medical history, and far more personal buying habits is freely circulating around the planet. So Web security could perhaps be one of our least personal worries!

If you go with the streamlined loan application offline, ask the lender to honor any online discounts. If they want your business, they will!

Q. *Does it make sense to pay cash for a house instead of being strapped with a mortgage?*

A. If you have an overall financial game plan and have decided what role owning a home will play in that plan, it will be much easier to weigh the pros and cons of this question. What are you trying to achieve, and how does paying cash for a home fit into this picture?

One positive to paying cash (besides not having a monthly mortgage payment) is the peace of mind owning a home free and clear can bring. There's something magical and liberating about having a safe haven that no one (except the tax collector) has a piece of. As America grays, more homeowners realize the stress too much debt can cause in their lives, and are finding ways to prepay their mortgages (or pay cash initially) to enjoy this freedom.

Not needing a mortgage also saves you tens of thousands of dollars worth of mortgage interest, having to pay discount points and other loan costs, *and* the hassle of applying for and closing a loan.

On the downside, tying up cash in your home would mean the loss of partial liquidity and potentially some financial flexibility. Financial planners tell us that in order to be financially secure, we need a minimum of six months in liquid assets plus a little more for emergencies. If you don't have financial padding comparable to this (in addition to what you'd pay for the house), you may be playing your cards too close to the vest.

Paying cash for a home also would take that money out of circulation, no longer generating interest and limiting your ability to fund new investments. No mortgage also means no interest deductions and could change your tax picture come April 15.

If you need to obtain a mortgage after acquiring the property, it would be considered a refinance and might not be as liberal in cash out. Points and other loan fees could be higher, and you would need to qualify financially based on your monthly income and debt.

One last cardinal sin homebuyers make in paying all cash for a property is failure to first pay off nondeductible credit card and revolving loan interest. It makes no sense to sidestep getting a mortgage that has potential tax benefits in lieu of paying off nondeductible debt with typically much higher interest.

The bottom line is to consult your total financial plan as well as your accountant or other financial adviser before rushing out to pay cash for a home.

CHOOSING THE RIGHT LOAN AND LENDER

Q. *We're first-time buyers and are so green we don't even know where to start when talking with a lender to find a cost-effective mortgage. Where do we begin?*

A. The best way for first-time (and repeat) buyers to begin is to answer the following four questions:

1. When applying for a mortgage, what is the amount of loan you can financially qualify for and what size payment would you be comfortable making as well? Buyers often can afford a payment larger than what their psychological barometer allows them to go with. (Listen to what it's telling you, or after closing you're likely to wake up with night sweats worrying about it.)

2. What is the amount of cash you'll feel comfortable parting with for the down payment and closing costs? This should be in sync with any other cash needs anticipated in the near future such as college tuition, down payment on a new car, and furnishing your new home. While it's great to use your savings for a down payment on a home, don't sacrifice your financial padding to do so.
3. How long will you hold the property and the mortgage? This is a critical question; yet many homebuyers don't even consider it when making financing decisions. The answer will help you decide whether it makes more sense to pay additional discount points to get the interest rate lower (advisable when holding the loan for a long time), or paying only a small to moderate amount down, fewer points, and a higher interest rate if you anticipate owning the property only for a short time.
4. If loans have fancy "bells and whistles" (like adjustable-rate mortgages with options to convert to a fixed-interest rate), do they make sense financially for what you want to achieve? For example, if you pay extra for the option to convert an adjustable-rate mortgage into a fixed rate, are you likely to use it based on how long you'll keep the property or the loan before refinancing? Lenders will print out computer comparisons showing exactly what various loans will cost.

Q. *We are seeking financing for our new home, and have found two lenders with identical rates. What other items, besides the interest rate and points, should we be comparing?*

A. You're wise to go beyond the lowest interest rate! Many buyers don't even think to pencil out the cost of the points if the interest rate is lower.

First, ask prospective lenders you're considering if they'll allow you to pay your own taxes and insurance and sidestep the impound or reserve account. Depending on the type of loan and amount of down payment you're making, the lender may waive the requirement that you pay a monthly escrow amount for taxes and insurance. This means that you would provide the lender with a paid receipt and annual insurance binder, but not have to tie your money up monthly for this cost.

Second, compare (line by line) the origination fees, warehousing fees, and other closing costs. Ask questions about what each fee does, what the charge is based on, and if it's included in the annual percentage rate (APR), because some are not. It's amazing how these can mount up—and, many of them are negotiable with the lender (it's just that borrowers fail to ask!).

Third, evaluate your loan prepayment options. Can payments be made at random and in varying amounts, or must they be equal to a full mortgage payment before being applied to the loan? If the payments are restrictive, it will be difficult for you to save interest by prepaying.

Last, which lender might fit any future need you have? If you anticipate car financing or an additional personal credit line in the future, would one lender be more likely to meet those needs than the other?

Evaluate the entire loan picture before you commit to work with one lender and/or one loan. It's the last chance you'll have to save money before closing.

Q. *The first lender I talked to about a mortgage quoted me an acceptable rate, but with very high points and I told him so. A second lender beat the points, but wanted to charge me private mortgage insurance (PMI) that would add to my monthly payments. Then, miraculously, the first lender decided he too could lend with fewer points and would waive the PMI. Is this common practice?*

A. The mortgage industry, like other professions, is in the business to maximize profits. But once a lender is able to evaluate how strong the applicant is, it's not unusual to find a way to meet or beat a competitor's offer.

Situations like the one you're describing often occur during the initial contact with the lender when a range of interest rates, fees, and loan programs are discussed. But once a mortgage credit report is pulled, your assets and debts analyzed, and your income verified, the lender would be able to weigh your risk as a borrower and potentially court you with lower interest rates and/or fees.

Information is definitely power when negotiating for the most cost-effective mortgage. I commend you for holding out for the best overall loan package, even if it did take diligent shopping and time to do it!

Q. *At loan application, the lender quoted me an approximate rate of interest. But two days later, he notified me that late payments in* *my credit would mean I'd have to pay almost 4 percent more interest if I wanted the loan. Was this a bait and switch scheme?*

A. It's tough to tell. Because the lender looks at the amount of risk involved when making a loan, a blemished credit report could add a higher potential for loan default, thus the requirement of higher interest.

But it concerns me that the rate jumped nearly 4 percent. It could signal a type of loan (and lender) you should steer clear of.

If you haven't done so already, go to the credit reporting agency and pull a copy of your credit report. You may uncover information you weren't aware of and/or you may be able to correct errors that would lower the interest rate quoted. Give the lender a chance to requote the rate and be sure to ask what the closing costs would be as well. In addition, ask your friends for references of lenders they've used and contact them for quotes.

Until you uncover and address your credit picture and obtain feedback from other lenders, you won't know how realistic it is to pay higher interest.

"Ere you consult your fancy, consult your purse."
—*Ben Franklin*

PREAPPROVED VERSUS PREQUALIFIED

Q. *A lender asked if we'd been preapproved before. Is this different than prequalified?*

A. Yes. Preapproved is a more in-depth approach to qualifying and means that, barring any unforeseen change in your financial picture (like a change of income or credit status), the lender agrees to make you a mortgage loan of up to a predetermined amount. This is a much stronger guarantee on the part of the lender than being prequalified.

Here's how it works. The lender gathers information from and about you including a mortgage credit report, the last three bank statements, the last two pay stubs, and copies of income tax returns. (This information can vary based on the type of loan and the lender's requirements.)

Based on the information, the buyer is preapproved for a mortgage amount of X, with a maximum interest rate of Y. The only limiting parameters placed on the loan might be that the lender reserves the right to receive an acceptable appraisal on the property before making the loan. You will know what you can afford and can use the information to make an offer to the seller.

Although preapproval is not mandatory for making an offer on a property, it adds another dimension of buyer strength.

Q. *What advantages are there for a buyer to be preapproved before looking at houses?*

A. A majority of buyers today are preapproved (particularly in very active sellers' markets where there are fewer properties for sale). From the seller's perspective, a preapproved buyer is a cash buyer. And a buyer who is not preapproved could be in a weakened position when negotiating with the seller, and/or could end up losing a property to a buyer whom the seller knows has a loan waiting in the wings.

Additionally, buyers who are not preapproved stand a greater potential for disappointment when they fall in love with a house, only to learn that they can't swing the financing and must "fall out of love." Ouch!

If a buyer is truly motivated about buying a home, and wants to put the best foot forward, preapproval is the first step.

QUALIFYING RATIOS

Q. *It's been a while since I've gotten a mortgage. What are the income-to-debt ratios currently used?*

A. Qualifying ratios depend on several factors—the type of loan, the amount of your down payment (as well as the lender originating the loan), whether that loan will be sold to the secondary market, and/or what that investor's requirements are. In other words, it depends!

In general, lenders who make loans to sell to secondary market investors use the following guidelines for conventional loans: Up to 28 percent of your monthly gross income can go toward paying your PITI payment (principal, interest, taxes, and insurance) plus any private mortgage insurance charge and/or condo or town home fee. And up to 36 percent of your monthly gross income could be attributable to your PITI payment *plus* any long-term debt that can't be paid off in ten months (or is a recurring cost). You can use the Quick Qualifying Worksheet in Figure 3.1 and the Loan Payment Table in Figure 3.2 to determine your

FIGURE 3.1 Quick Qualifying Worksheet

		Column A	Column B
Annual gross income:		$ ________	
Divide by number of months:		÷12	
Monthly gross income (Record it in both columns. Perform operations only on figures in the same vertical column.):		= ________	= ________
Lenders allow 28% of monthly gross income for housing expenses.			×.28
Maximum monthly housing expense allowance (Column B):			= ________
Lenders allow 36% of monthly gross income for long-term debt:		×.36	
Monthly expense allowance for long-term debt:		= ________	
Calculate your monthly long-term obligations below:			
Child support	$ _____		
Auto loan	+ _____		
Credit cards	+ _____		
Other	+ _____		
Other	+ _____		
Total long-term obligations	= _____		
Subtract total from your monthly expense allowance:		– ________	
Total monthly housing expense allowance:		= ________	
Look at the last amounts in Columns A and B above. Record the smaller amount.		$ ________	
About 20% of the housing expense allowance is for taxes and insurance, leaving 80% for payment of mortgage (principal and interest):		×.80	
Allowance monthly principal and interest (PI) expense:		= ________	
Divide this amount by the appropriate monthly payment from Figure 3.2:		÷ ________	
		= ________	
Multiply by 1,000:		×1,000	
Affordable mortgage amount (what the lender will lend):		$ ________	

qualifying ratios. Use the Mortgage Application Information in Figure 3.3 to check off what you'll need to bring to the lender. Qualifying ratios for other types of loans can be found in Chapter 5. And don't forget to access online calculators for computing ratios, like the one at homeadvisor.com.

Q. *We thought the qualifying ratios for a mortgage were 28 percent and 36 percent. But when we recently applied for a 95 percent conventional mortgage, the lender said that our total debt couldn't exceed 33 percent of our gross monthly income for the second ratio. Why is this more restrictive?*

A. The qualifying ratios of 28 percent and 36 percent are merely guidelines, usually primarily for loans with down payments of 10 per-

FIGURE 3.2 Loan Payment Table

Monthly payment for each $1,000 borrowed

	Term of Loan		
Interest rate	15 years	20 years	30 years
6.00%	$ 8.44	$7.16	$6.00
6.50	8.71	7.46	6.32
7.00	8.99	7.75	6.65
7.50	9.27	8.06	6.99
8.00	9.56	8.36	7.34
8.50	9.85	8.68	7.69
9.00	10.14	9.00	8.05

Note: Chart represents principal and interest only.

This table helps you calculate your monthly housing costs (not including property taxes, insurance, and any mortgage insurance premium). Each amount represents the principal and interest cost for each $1,000 borrowed.

For example, if you're considering a $100,000, 30-year mortgage at 8 percent, you would multiply 100 × $7.34 = $734 per month principal and interest payment.

FIGURE 3.3 Mortgage Application Information

Personal Information

- ☐ Social Security number(s) including coborrower
- ☐ Former address(es) if less than two years at present address

Employment Information

- ☐ W-2s; personal tax returns with all schedules, most recent two years
- ☐ Name, address, and phone number of employer(s); also dates of employment and gross income
- ☐ Previous employer(s) and/or school attended if less than two years in current position

If self-employed:

- ☐ Personal federal income tax returns for past two years
- ☐ Business returns for the past two years plus most recent year-to-date profit and loss statement

Current Housing Expense Information

- ☐ Amount of rent/first mortgage payment (P&I)
- ☐ Name, address, and phone number of landlord (if applicable)
- ☐ Amount of any other finance payments
- ☐ Hazard insurance
- ☐ Real estate taxes
- ☐ Mortgage insurance
- ☐ Other (including condo fees, flood insurance, etc.)

Monthly Income

- ☐ Pay stubs (most recent 30-day period)
- ☐ Other regular income
- ☐ Rental income
- ☐ Retirement/Social Security
- ☐ Alimony/child support (if you want it/them considered for the purpose of loan application)
- ☐ Commission income
- ☐ Investment interest/dividends
- ☐ Other

Monthly Obligations

- ☐ Auto loans/lease payments
- ☐ Revolving charge accounts (include account number and balance)

(continued)

FIGURE 3.3 Mortgage Application Information *(continued)*

- ☐ Real estate loans (state the outstanding balance)
- ☐ Alimony/child support
- ☐ Other

Assets

- ☐ Checking, savings, and investment account statements (most recent three months)
- ☐ Other certificates of deposit, bonds, etc.
- ☐ Real estate owned
- ☐ Vested interest in retirement fund (most recent statement)
- ☐ Automobile(s) owned (make(s) and year(s))
- ☐ Life insurance cash value
- ☐ Other

For New Construction (if available)

- ☐ Contract to build, plans, and specifications
- ☐ Purchase agreement with full address, including zip code
- ☐ Real estate agent's name, address, and phone number (if applicable)
- ☐ Property information

Other Information (if applicable)

- ☐ Divorce, bankruptcy papers
- ☐ If relocating, copy of corporate relocation agreement

cent or more. With only a 5 percent down payment, the loan is tougher to qualify for because it carries a greater risk of default and higher liability for the lender. That's why the lender is capping your PITI payment plus any long-term debt payments at 33 percent of your gross monthly income.

Additionally, when you use a small down payment, the lender also will evaluate your credit picture more carefully. There can be no room for delinquent payments, and the amount of debt you carry must be nominal and under control.

Besides the lender's guidelines and those of the secondary market where the lender sells the loan, the private mortgage insurance company also will want strong evidence that you can handle the mortgage. Because it protects the lender against your default during the early stages of the loan, the PMI company will evaluate both you and the property with its own set of guidelines.

INCOME THAT COUNTS FOR LOAN QUALIFYING

Q. *I've been told it requires two years of job history in order to secure a mortgage. Is there any way they would include school in this time as I've just completed my residency in medicine?*

A. School and other types of job training can count toward the employment qualification. This is particularly true when the level of knowledge required for a profession is substantial and/or highly technical. The lender needs assurance that you can now make a living in your chosen profession. Reviewing your scholastic standing and work habits during your residency can prove that.

Q. *I've been working two jobs for nearly two years. Will the lender count the second job as income for loan qualifying?*

A. Lenders recognize that second jobs help families make ends meet. But the lender wants to be assured that the income is likely to continue (just like your mortgage payment will!). That's why most lenders want to see a track record of at least two years of second-job income before counting it toward qualifying. (With a two-year track record, chances of the second income continuing are stronger.)

While the two-year work history requirement will make it pointless to get a short-term, part-time, or second job merely to qualify for a loan, the borrower can use that income for a higher down payment.

If the lender won't count the part-time income as qualifying income, it might use such income as a compensating factor. A second income can be a strong plus in underwriting the loan you can financially qualify for, and can help offset any less-than-perfect factors.

Q. *I'm awaiting loan approval for a new home and just received a cash bonus from my job. We'll use it to pay off some credit cards. Does the lender need to know this?*

A. Absolutely. It's a good idea to let the lender know of any change (positive or negative) to your financial picture during loan processing.

Paying off credit cards makes a difference in your overall debt picture and improves your debt-to-income ratio for qualifying.

If you didn't tell the lender of the changes and later found you couldn't qualify, you would have lost valuable time. If your purchase agreement is contingent on finding financing and you couldn't qualify, you could risk losing the house you want as well.

Even if you do qualify, less debt in your financial picture may allow you to negotiate better interest rates, points, and closing costs. Because less debt means that your risk of default to the lender is less, your loan application may be viewed more favorably.

The loan application documents you signed require that you inform the lending institution about your entire financial picture, so let the lender know about the good news and perhaps use it as a negotiating tool.

Q. *I am getting a pay increase in my job in 60 days. Is there any way I could include this for loan qualifying?*

A. Yes, you're in luck! Lenders will typically count pay increases for the purpose of qualifying if they will begin within 60 days of loan closing. (Note, that's not within 60 days of application, but loan closing.) To qualify, the increase has to be already approved with no other performance evaluation required. In addition, the employer will have to verify the increase in writing to the lender.

Q. *I've worked in commissioned sales for the past three years, and I've heard that it's tougher for people on commission to qualify for a home loan. Is this true?*

A. People who work on commission find it a bit tougher to qualify, but not impossible. Some lenders average the past several years' commissions, on the theory that commission income is less predictable than straight salary. If your commissions have been steadily increasing, the lender could agree to put more weight on the current commission income. You must sell the lender on why this income is likely to continue, including documenting a stable client base, providing commission agreements and 1099s, and perhaps other income tax records.

Q. *The lender told us that because we're self-employed, we'd need to provide extensive paperwork including a copy of our tax returns. Why are self-employed people punished like this?*

A. As self-employed folks, we're not really being punished by the mortgage industry—but it often does seem that way! It's just that self-employed borrowers statistically have shown a higher level of loan default over the years, plus there is a greater risk of embellishing income records (being both the employer and the employee).

Purchasers of loans in the secondary market (Fannie Mae, Freddie Mac, and Ginnie Mae) require certain documentation for self-employed borrowers. These typically include two years of signed copies of complete income tax returns (with all schedules attached), a balance sheet for the previous two years, and a year-to-date profit and loss statement (if you're a sole proprietor).

During the underwriting process, red flags may arise to alert the lender that the applicant is not telling the whole story and needs to be double-checked, especially regarding tax returns. These include expenses shown only in $100 increments ($200, $300), a tax payer in a high bracket who prepares his return himself, and a self-employed borrower who pays no estimated tax.

The lender also is concerned that if self-employment taxes have not been paid an IRS lien could take priority over the mortgage and wipe out buyer equity in the property.

The lender's requests are not meant to discriminate against your employment, but to provide information to both the underwriter and the investor who purchase the loan.

Q. *I am self-employed with fairly sporadic income, but do have good credit and a 30 percent down payment. Would a limited documentation loan work?*

A. It just might. Low-doc/no-doc loans are still around and are not just for the self-employed. Depending on how foreclosures ebb and flow (increasing the risk on these types of loans), you can find a variety of programs that will not require you to verify your income—just prove that you have the 25 to 30 percent minimum down payment, good credit, and the property you're interested in can appraise for the loan you're seeking.

Finding a cost-effective no-doc loan may take some diligent shopping. I suggest you check with mortgage brokers because they can shop broader markets to place higher-risk loans with nontraditional investors. Before jumping at the first loan offered, shop for the most competitive rates and fees. Some lenders penalize buyers by charging more of both because it's more work to place the loans with more perceived risk involved for investors.

Q. *What's the rationale behind lenders wanting a borrower to have at least three years of child support remaining before it can count as income?*

A. The lender needs guarantees in two areas regarding child support. First, that there is a strong, on-time track record of payments being received (preferably documented through court records). Second, that those payments can continue through the third year of the loan.

While the requirement is a secondary market guideline by investors who purchase loans, the three-year time frame makes financial sense. The toughest time for a new mortgage holder is typically the early months of home ownership when budgeting is critical. If child support is helping increase the borrower's cash flow during the first three years, the likelihood of default may be lessened and good payment habits will be established.

The lender will evaluate not only the quantity but the quality of the child support received. If payments are spotty and haphazard, child support may not be reliable enough to count as income but could be used as a compensating factor (which we'll explore further in Chapter 5.)

Q. *I'm considering buying a larger house and renting out the one I have. Will I have to show that I have tenants in order to qualify using the rental income?*

A. Yes. Depending on the qualifying requirements for the new mortgage, the lender may want to see a signed lease showing that the property is rented. (Otherwise the monthly payment on that mortgage would be added to your long-term debt picture for qualifying purposes.)

It's a common misconception that the entire amount of monthly rental income you'll receive will count for qualifying purposes. Most lenders will count only 75 percent of the rents as credits, but 100 percent of the monthly expenses on the rental house as debt.

For example, if you receive $1,000 per month rental income and the mortgage on the rental house is $900, you have a $150 monthly loss ($1,000 × 75% = $750 – $900 mortgage = $150 loss). This formula can change what you thought was an asset into a liability for getting a loan.

Before you shop for a replacement home, do yourself a favor and talk to a mortgage lender who can pencil out how the rental income will affect your qualifying picture, preapprove you for a new loan, and tell you what rental documents you'll need to provide so you won't have to piece them together later.

DEBTS COUNTED IN LOAN QUALIFYING

Q. *We'll need to replace our car soon, but also want to buy a home. Would a car payment make that much difference in loan qualification?*

A. It's amazing the damage $300 extra per month (today's median monthly car payment) can do to loan qualifying.

Here's an example. Let's say you're going for an $80,000 loan at 8 percent interest with a monthly payment (including taxes and insurance) of $700. Because most lenders on conventional loans will allow up to 28 percent of your gross monthly income to go to your house payment, you would need $2,500 monthly income to qualify.

Now add your long-term debts (usually those that will last ten months or more) to your house payment. Most conventional loan lenders allow this figure to be around 36 percent or less of your monthly income. If you had a credit card payment of $50 and a car payment of $300, you need to make $2,916 in monthly gross income to qualify. In other words, you need $416 additional monthly income to qualify because of the debts. This is a 16 percent increase and would equal $4,992 additional income over the year. While this might not seem like really big money, few people get 16 percent annual wage increases!

And don't think the lender can't tell that you're car shopping! A majority of car dealers pull a credit report prior to allowing someone to test drive a car. The lender will see "credit inquiry" noted on your credit report!

If your first priority is a home, get it first and worry about driving that new car off the showroom floor a little later.

"He that won't be counseled can't be helped."
—*Ben Franklin*

DOWN PAYMENTS

Q. *One set of parents says we should use at least a 10 percent down payment in order to keep our payment low. The other set says we should use a limited down payment to keep some savings. Help!*

A. Ah, yes—well-meaning parents! But the most definitive sources to help you weigh the pros and cons of a large versus small down payment is the lender. Besides owning a home, do you want liquid assets in case of an emergency or do you want a smaller monthly payment?

If you can only qualify for a mortgage by using a large down payment, then that's what you must do. But if you can use only a small down payment for your purchase and have the luxury of keeping money in savings, that may be even better.

It comes down to what you want to achieve. Loan qualifying aside, if you don't mind a larger monthly payment, will keep the house for a while, and don't have at least six months of monthly income in savings, a small down payment may be best. If the opposite is true and you'll have insomnia over a large monthly payment, may be moving soon, and have ample savings to feel comfortable, then putting more down may be for you.

The lender can crunch numbers and show you options in writing. You then can take those to both sets of parents to show them with facts how you arrived at *your* decision!

Q. *My husband and I are interested in buying our first home and heard that we could withdraw money from an IRA for the down payment. Please explain how this works.*

A. What a boon this is to home buying! Yes, it's possible under the tax law to withdraw up to $10,000 penalty-free from an individual retirement account (IRA) for first-time homebuyers to use for qualified acquisition costs (down payment and/or closing costs) on a principal residence. The IRS defines a first-time homebuyer as an individual (and his or her spouse) who has had no ownership interest in a home during the previous two years.

The buyer must use the IRA distribution to fund the home sale before the close of the 120th day after it's been withdrawn. The withdrawal can come from your own account and/or from the account of a parent, child, or grandchild, but can't total more than $10,000.

If it will be awhile before you buy a home, you might benefit to an even greater degree by setting up and then withdrawing your down payment and closing costs from a new Roth IRA. In addition to the penalty-free withdrawal benefit from the account, the Roth IRA is both penalty-free and tax-free if the account is held for five years. This means that even though you could create a Roth IRA in 1999, you wouldn't have the tax-free feature available to you until 2004. Most first-time buyers would have more to lose in equity by waiting five years than the tax savings would offset.

Your best bet is to contact your financial consultant or tax preparer on which IRA best suits your needs and tax situation.

Q. *I heard that it's possible to use your credit card to make a down payment on a house. Is this true?*

A. Yes, and it isn't even one of those late-night TV nothing-down ploys! The secondary market where loans are purchased has designed a mortgage for creditworthy buyers who have saved little or no down payment. Called "Flexible 97" (as in 97 percent loan), it requires only a 3 percent down payment that can come from the borrower's savings, a gift from a family member, a personal loan, and/or from a grant from an employer or a government agency. As you've pointed out, most unique is the fact that the 3 percent down payment can even come from the borrower's credit card! (But the borrower would need sufficient income to pay this off as a long-term debt.)

As with other types of low down payment conventional loans, the borrower's creditworthiness is important because equity is low in the early stages of the loan, creating a greater risk to the lender. Buyers considering this loan should check their credit before going to a lender to make sure their report is error-free.

Before pulling out that plastic, make sure that you borrow against a credit card with a low interest rate and prioritize a quick payoff plan in your budget so you're not paying hefty nondeductible interest.

For more information, you can contact either a local lender or Fannie Mae direct for information at 800-7FANNIE (Monday through Friday from 9 AM to 5 PM ET) or its Web site at www.fanniemae.com.

Q. *Our daughter needs a bit more down payment for the home she's buying. Would it be a good idea to borrow against some certificates of deposit (CDs) we have instead of cashing them in?*

A. Yes, it would be because you won't lose the interest or be penalized for early withdrawal. Borrowing against CDs is relatively easy. CDs are viewed as your cash on deposit, so often you can borrow a high percentage of their value, even 100 percent. You will be charged a premium over what the CDs are bearing (usually about 2 or 3 percent more); sometimes the lender will have a minimum rate they charge.

Most lenders won't call the CD loan due until you cash in the certificates; but might request that you pay interest on the loan periodically so that a deficit isn't created.

In addition to CDs, other collateral like stocks and bonds could be leveraged to help with a down payment.

Q. *A lender said she would make us a piggyback loan to help with the down payment. This sounds frightening. What is it?*

A. A piggyback loan is more of a financing technique than it is a formal type of loan. It's really a second mortgage behind a first mortgage, that bridges the gap in a down payment shortfall.

For example, if you only have a 10 percent down payment, the lender might take that down on an 80 percent loan (your first mortgage) and make you a 10 percent second mortgage (typically at a higher rate of interest than the first) in order to give you the 90 percent loan-to-value leverage necessary to swing the purchase.

The good news is that you can strive to pay off that second as soon as possible. The interest rate charged should be less than you could obtain from borrowing against your credit card. And (more good news) you can often sidestep paying PMI this way. The interest is deductible; the PMI is not. (You'll find more on this method of financing in Chapter 5.)

Q. *Is it possible for our parents to gift us the entire down payment for a loan? We have great income and enough for closing costs, but no down payment.*

A. It's a little-known fact that a borrower can use a gift of 20 percent or more and sidestep making any down payment on the loan. For example, if your parents gave you a $20,000 down payment for a $100,000 house, you could use your money for closing costs and not have to make a down payment!

Even though Fannie Mae in the secondary market allows the 20 percent gift to be the sole down payment, that doesn't mean that all lenders will be excited about making these loans. (Lenders feel that down payments from the borrower's pocket are security against the borrower walking away from the loan. Additionally, the private mortgage insurer will take a more stringent look at any loan where the borrower doesn't have at least 5 percent down payment into the property.) You may have the best luck first going to a lender who has your (or your parents') banking interest at heart.

Don't be astounded if the lender requests proof of where your parents obtained the funds (from savings, selling an asset, etc.). This is not only to double check that the money came from a legal source, but also that you won't be obligated to repay the funds.

Q. *My mother and I live together and I'd like to purchase a home in my name. Is there any way she can gift me the down payment, and if so, how much would it have to be?*

A. Yes, there is. This is another little-known approach for leveraging a gifted down payment that works only if a relative lives with you.

Fannie Mae, which purchases loans in the secondary mortgage market, allows a resident relative to gift a minimum of 5 percent down payment to the borrower (if you otherwise qualify for a 95 percent loan). The relative must reside with the borrower, but additional gifts could come from other relatives. In addition, the borrower could receive a gift or grant from a church, municipality (like local housing bond programs), or nonprofit organization to use as a down payment and/or closing costs. You would take ownership solely in your name and the giftor would not need to qualify financially.

You need to provide the lender with information to prove that you both live in the property. This can be shown by checking accounts, utility bills or other obligations you pay jointly, or any other assets you have in both names.

The only downside to this type of financing is that qualifying for a 95 percent loan is tougher than other loans, requiring strong, stable employment, cash reserves for two to three months of mortgage payments, and stellar credit.

Because most lenders would feel safer if the borrower had more of his or her own money into the property at closing, this little-known bit of down payment leverage is not widely publicized.

Q. *A guest we invited to our wedding next month called to ask us if we were registered with the FHA's bridal registry. I laughed, thinking she was kidding; but now find out that they do have a program for couples wanting to buy a home. Can you explain how it works, especially if we'll have control over the money once it's deposited?*

A. Just when you think you've registered with all the right bridal registries, another pops up. Only this one's for a mortgage loan, and won't require any merchandise returns!

In late 1996, the Federal Housing Administration (FHA) announced a program to help buyers accumulate home down payments. Even though it's called "Homeownership Bridal Registry Accounts," it can be used by anyone to accumulate funds from relatives or friends—ideal for wedding, graduation, or other special gift occasions.

Here's how it works. Prospective homebuyers contact lenders who originate FHA loans to set up individual federally-insured depository accounts in the parties' names. Funds may be deposited by friends and relatives directly into the account, or given by cash or check to the giftee(s) for deposit.

Depending on how they wish to market the Homeowner Bridal Registry program, lenders can provide information about the program directly to friends and relatives of the potential homebuyer(s) using FHA's promotional brochure or one designed by the lender. In addition, lenders can provide gift cards that reflect the gift-giver's name for the purpose of documenting the gift. Not only will the program help buyers obtain a down payment, the monies will be tracked and accounted for using FHA guidelines, ready as part of the loan documentation when the buyers are ready to apply for the loan.

The funds remain under the control of the individuals for whom they're deposited. The funds can be withdrawn at any time and aren't required to be used to purchase a home. (What a neat way to help pay the wedding expenses!) In addition, engaged couples don't have to be married before they use the monies to close on a home loan.

If you've spoken previously to a lender about obtaining a home loan, call back to ask about the Homeowner Bridal Registry Account. If you need to find an FHA lender, the best source will be to ask people you know for referrals to lenders they've been pleased with. If those aren't possible, other real estate professionals (appraisers, real estate agents, title companies) are also good sources. Display ads in the yellow pages of the phone book under the headings of "real estate loans" and "mortgages" also will state which lenders make FHA loans.

CREATIVE WAYS TO GENERATE CASH AND REDUCE DEBTS

Q. *We not only have too many debts, we're short on cash to close. Do you have some creative suggestions?*

A. You're not alone. Many buyers find they have "too much month at the end of the money"—especially when scrounging up closing cost dollars. Here are some of the more creative ways to create cash and eliminate debts. Good luck!

To create more cash:

- Sell an asset.
- Borrow against an asset.
- Use a relative's asset to sell or borrow against (with his or her knowledge and blessing, of course!).

To acquire a down payment (or in lieu of a second mortgage):

- Use gifted funds.
- Use personal property.
- Transfer or assign the use of an item (like your boat to someone for the summer).
- Barter a service (provide house cleaning/babysitting).
- Use sweat equity (paint the house yourself).
- Use receivables being paid to you (items you've sold "on time").
- Ask a seller to carry a small second mortgage at an attractive rate of interest—you might be surprised at the reception!

To reduce high debt:

- Pay off an obligation or pay it down below the level considered long-term debt (ten months or less).
- Assign an obligation using a letter of assignment (transfer the car debt to your parents—again, with their blessing!).
- Refinance debts.

- Use loan consolidation (after first checking with the lender!).
- Sell or lease out an asset.
- Cancel credit cards.
- Pledge other assets for collateral (in addition to the property).

Remember, before taking any action to restructure your personal finances, consult with your lender first for feedback.

DANGEROUS DOLLARS AND PERILOUS PENNIES ISSUES

Be alert to the fact that Dangerous Dollars issues surrounding The Frugal HomeOwner Law of Buyer Preparation can mount up in a hurry! To ensure that you'll hold tight to your hard-earned down payment:

- Get preapproved for a mortgage (you even can do it online!) before you walk across any seller's threshold. By not knowing if a loan is within your reach, you could stand to kiss your earnest money goodbye, be forced to fall "out of love" with a house you can't afford—or even get sued by a seller for breach of contract.
- Be sure to ask the lender for cost breakdowns between loan programs you're considering. It takes him or her just a minute to do so—a minute spent that could save you thousands of dollars by choosing the best loan.

Prepared buyers can avoid Perilous Pennies situations when they:

- Provide all pertinent financial records and information to the lender on the very first meeting. A frugal homeowner knows that a quick closing means quicker equity!
- Don't change a thing in their financial and employment pictures after their loan is preapproved. The lender is bound to find out and the consequences won't be pretty! Rearranging finances could cost the borrower a higher down payment, a larger monthly payment—or even disqualify them entirely for the loan they need.

CHAPTER 4

The Frugal HomeOwner Law of Logical Home Selection

Choosing the Right Home Puts Money in Your Pocket—From the Start!

The past decade of home buying has placed increased importance on choosing the right home in the right neighborhood. Buyers now spend hours researching neighborhood crime information, teacher-to-student ratios and school scholastic standings, and look outside property boundaries to envision the impact zoning patterns could have on their new home. Whew! It takes a lot of work to choose the best home. But choosing badly can result in lost appreciation or low resale—in general, cash out of the buyer's pocket.

We'll cover questions to help you evaluate the home you're interested in. But keep in mind that even though your heart may lure you to the house where the Italian marble foyer sparkles and the imported ceramic countertops gleam, that's merely the emotional side of the story. Don't make a move until you're thoroughly convinced that the neighborhood is not only safe and sane for your family, but that it's likely to boost your home's equity with strong appreciation for the future. Frugal homeowners know to select the best home with their wallets as well as their hearts.

CHOOSING A NEIGHBORHOOD

Q. *I want to purchase a home in the area in which I currently rent, but the homes are priced higher than I can afford. Any ideas?*

A. You have a classic case of "champagne appetite on a beer income" that plagues many of us! But there are several alternatives you might consider.

First, a larger down payment could allow you to qualify for a larger mortgage. You could either wait to accumulate more down, use a cash gift from a relative, or use other collateral to increase the down payment.

Second, investigate the possibility of buying a condo or town home (only if these are good investments in your area and have sound resale value). They may be more moderately priced than single-family homes, suit your lifestyle just as well, and allow you to build equity.

Third, you could look for a multifamily dwelling (e.g., duplex) to purchase with a coborrower. The lender would use both incomes to qualify which could increase your purchasing power. Scouting for a loan might be tougher because underwriting guidelines for multifamily dwellings can be more restrictive.

Remember that the loan amount you can qualify for also will be based on the type of loan as well as the interest rate. An adjustable-rate mortgage with an interest rate lower than that of fixed rates might help you qualify for more purchase price than you think.

It also wouldn't hurt to check out online rental resources like www.rentnet.com; you might find a landlord willing to sell or allow you to rent with the option to buy.

"Love your neighbours, yet don't pull down your hedge."
—*Ben Franklin*

Q. *The agent we are working with suggests that we walk around the neighborhood. What kind of things should we look for that could impact negatively on the value of homes there?*

A. While many buyers drive around the neighborhood, very few actually get out of their cars and walk around. This means they fail to uncover handyman garages, barking dogs, and other concerns that could impact the value of the house (not to mention quiet enjoyment of the property).

As you stroll through the neighborhood, note if property shows pride of ownership. Have homes been painted and repaired? Are there plantings of trees, shrubs, and flowers? Or is there overgrown grass, yards full of trash, and abandoned cars? Even if the development is fairly new, one or more of these warning signs could mean that property values won't keep pace with the norm and you'd be advised to buy elsewhere.

As you approach the property you're interested in, check out the sidewalk, curbs, gutters, and drainage areas. (It's great if you can check out the property after it rains to make sure drainage is away from and not toward the house.) Newly repaired sidewalks could indicate that an assessment has been levied from a municipality (usually over several years) to pay for the repair. This would add to your annual ownership costs so you'd need to check with city or county records to verify.

It's a good idea to inspect the area during different days of the week, as well as different times of day.

Q. *Would it be okay to talk to some of the neighbors before we make an offer to purchase a house?*

A. It's not only okay, it's a great idea. Neighbors will often be a good source of unbiased information about the neighborhood and the people who live there. Here are some questions to ask:

- Do they feel that the area is generally quiet?
- Would they buy there again? If no, why not?
- Do they think they'd have any trouble selling their house?
- What kind of crime and how much have they seen in the area?
- Have emergency vehicles and police responded well to calls in the neighborhood?
- What about the quality of schools? Did they check them out before they purchased?
- Where do they shop and how close is it?
- Did they find out anything after they moved in that they wished they would have known before?
- Is there an upcoming change in the area that might affect value? Adding a mall or landfill could impact future value.

Checking with several residents can give a well-rounded view of the area, as well as help sidestep any prejudiced remarks.

Q. *How can we check out how much and what type of crime there is in a neighborhood, and why didn't the seller provide this information to us?*

A. While the seller must reveal material facts to you about the property, including its construction and condition, reporting crime statistics is not required by law and is generally not part of the property disclosure. These are usually up to the buyer to search out and analyze because they are subjective. What you consider to be a high level of crime might not be perceived that way by another buyer.

The police department responsible for the area (city or county) has detailed computerized records that are available to the public. By contacting the police department's public information officer (at the non-emergency number) and giving him or her the cross streets where the property is located, you can obtain a detailed report of the type and frequency of crime for the area.

Some police departments even perform a safety check free of charge on a property you're interested in purchasing. This could include making sure doors and windows lock properly, ensuring that there are proper escape routes from the house (in case of fire), giving you tips on cutting foliage to improve line of sight to steps and parking areas, plus making suggestions for burglar-proofing the home.

Don't overlook the fact that community statistics, including crime information, are available on the Internet. Home pages for city and county governments, and large national data providers, are good places to start. You can purchase crime information and statistics at sites like www.crimecheck.com. You'll find a complete list of resources in the Resource Guide.

If you were to make an offer before checking out crime information, you could make the offer contingent on securing satisfactory crime report statistics from the local police department. That way you could back out of the purchase without losing your earnest money if the information was not favorable.

Q. *When we asked the seller's agent which schools were best in the district, she said she couldn't tell us. Isn't this just general information?*

A. General information, yes. Material information about the property, no. And making a determination as to which schools are best is very subjective. When you say "best" do you mean academically, athletically? Conversely, would "worst" mean lower grade point averages or higher disciplinary problems?

You can gather the information on your own. In fact, in doing so you get the answers backed by the statistics you're most interested in.

If time permits, make a visit to the school district's administration office. They can show you information on teacher-to-student ratios, SAT score summaries, and additional statistics tracking how many graduates attend college. Most offices will be glad to give you computer printouts for the information as well so you can take them home and review them with the family. If time is short, information about schools can be found at sites like schoolreport.com.

One last point. Besides the added liability for the agent to interpret "best schools" (what happens if you purchase a property because of the school, only to find that the boundaries have changed before closing?), the seller's agent also needs to keep the client's best interests at heart. If the seller's home is located in an area where the schools are less than perfect, volunteering and pointing out that information to you would not be in the interest of the client he or she represents. (Yet another reason why you need the representation of a buyer's agent!)

PROPERTIES

Q. *Is there a checklist for prioritizing which amenities we want in a home, especially as we can't afford them all?*

A. Figure 4.1 shows a rating system that you may find helpful in determining the features that are really important to you in home selection. By the time you complete the system, you'll know which items you have to have (top priority) and those that you'd like to have but are less important.

Keep in mind that there are very few homes that contain all the amenities you're after (especially if you're on a budget). Ultimately, home selection is about trade-offs.

Q. *We're purchasing a new home and it appears that there's less flash and more square footage in homes than when we purchased our first home in 1975. Is this a national trend and how will it impact prices long term?*

FIGURE 4.1 Home "Wish List"

The first time through this checklist, mark a 1 next to the items you would like to have in a home. The second time through the list, concentrate only on the items you checked before, and add a 2 next to each item that you have to have. Then tally up each individual score. The items with the 3s become the mandatory features; the balance of the amenities are nice, but not necessary.

Final step: Go back through the items that scored a 3 and prioritize them by their importance. That way you'll know which amenities are most important when house hunting.

	Like to Have	Must Have	Total Score	Top Priorities
Type of Home				
1. Condo	_____	_____	_____	_____
2. Town home	_____	_____	_____	_____
3. Detached single family	_____	_____	_____	_____
4. Other (specify)	_____	_____	_____	_____
Type of Neighborhood				
1. Describe (e.g., rural, urban, close to shopping, close to schools):				
_______________	_____	_____	_____	_____
2. Describe:				
_______________	_____	_____	_____	_____
Architectural Style and Design				
1. Describe (e.g., colonial, single level, ranch with basement, new construction):				
_______________	_____	_____	_____	_____
2. Describe:				
_______________	_____	_____	_____	_____
Interior Features				
1. Number of bedrooms				
___	_____	_____	_____	_____
___	_____	_____	_____	_____
2. Number of bathrooms				
___	_____	_____	_____	_____
___	_____	_____	_____	_____

FIGURE 4.1 Home "Wish List" *(continued)*

3. Separate dining room	______	______	______	______
4. Family room	______	______	______	______
5. Office room	______	______	______	______
6. Basement (if applicable)	______	______	______	______
7. Lots of cupboard space	______	______	______	______
8. Lots of closet space	______	______	______	______
9. Fireplace	______	______	______	______
Exterior Features				
1. Size of lot ________	______	______	______	______
________	______	______	______	______
2. Attached garage	______	______	______	______
3. Detached garage	______	______	______	______
4. Storage shed, etc.	______	______	______	______
5. Landscaping	______	______	______	______
Other Features You Feel Are Important (specify): ______________	______	______	______	______
______________________	______	______	______	______
______________________	______	______	______	______
______________________	______	______	______	______

A. What you're seeing is, in fact, a strong national trend. The median size of new houses nationwide today is 2,100 square feet, up nearly 500 square feet in the past 20 years (according to the National Association of Home Builders). More of today's homes are setting aside elegance for comfort and economy in amenities like fireplaces, two-car garages, and central air-conditioning.

While sacrificing luxurious amenities helps offset the cost generated by the additional square footage, it's thought that homes with spaciousness should do very well in the resale market.

"If passion drives, let reason hold the reins."
—*Ben Franklin*

Q. *The home we're interested in is just one of many for sale in the neighborhood. How could we check out what's going on?*

A. Even though you may think the worst when you see many For Sale signs, it could indicate that the location is desirable. The area may have had good appreciation and increase in value, enticing the owners to sell. It also may be an area where schools are strong, amenities great, but where owners are more of the age and demographics of those likely to be transferred. Relocation is more prevalent where owners are upwardly mobile.

It is wise to check facts, however. Ask real estate agents or appraisers to help you gather information regarding the average selling time of properties on the market, and any factors external to the property (such as rezoning, sewer or street assessments) that might fuel sellers.

It also is important to know how listed prices compare to final sales prices. A large number of sellers settling for far less than listed price could point to a hidden motivation and urgency not yet apparent. For example, increasing crime, pending rezoning, or restructured school boundaries might have an affect on the stability of a neighborhood.

If you are seeking a loan when you purchase a property, an appraisal will likely be part of the package. You could certainly make any offer contingent on receiving and reviewing a satisfactory appraisal. Besides stating the appraiser's estimate of value, there also is an overview of what's going on in neighboring areas that could impact the home.

Q. *Is there something wrong with a property if it has been offered as a for sale by owner for six months?*

A. Not necessarily. There could be other factors, not solely negative ones, leading to an unsold property.

First, perhaps the sellers did not aggressively market the property. A For Sale sign in the yard doesn't constitute a strong marketing campaign.

Second, was the property priced right to begin with? An overpriced property will be initially discounted by buyers, even if the asking price is later reduced. Restrictive terms also might have kept the property from attracting offers.

Third, did the sellers have any offers on the property? Perhaps they took the property off the market for a potential offer that never materialized.

Fourth, what type of market competition does the property have? Are there many similar properties for sale in the neighborhood? Depending on the real estate economics of the area, as well as the time of year, six months may not be unusual.

If you still have questions, ask for outside assistance to determine the value and stability of the property. These facts might come from an appraiser, inspector, or other real estate professional. You might negotiate with the seller to help pay for any or all of these items.

Q. *When we first purchased a home in 1970, location was the most important factor contributing to value. Is that still true today?*

A. Property location is still one of the prime ingredients in determining a property's value (though some buyers feel that the quality construction of the home and doing a thorough inspection before purchasing are closely tied to location in importance).

Location impacts the amount of appreciation your home will have, which is particularly critical today because inflation is low. Two identical properties, one adjacent to a park, the other next to a recycling center, could carry different market values based on location alone.

Property location also affects the type and amount of financing you can obtain. A lender may require a larger down payment on a mortgage in an area where appreciation will be less. A property in an area of declining values could be tough to sell if foreclosure occurred. Often forces outside the property may lessen the value as shown in areas of high crime where buildings are defaced and repairs costly.

Private mortgage insurance (PMI), which protects the lender against the borrower's default, will cost more or be tough to get if the area is ill-kept. Homeowners insurance will cost more, too.

Q. *We don't know whether the house is really worth what the seller is asking for it (even though the listing agent says it is). How can we find out?*

A. There are various ways. The listing agent probably did a comparative market analysis (CMA) before listing the property. This compared the property to sales prices and terms of properties recently sold (usually within 6 to 12 months) as well as competing homes currently on the market, plus home listings that had expired or were taken off the market (often because they were overpriced.). These properties were similar in size, style, and amenities to the subject property and helped determine its listed price.

The agent would need to get permission from the seller in order to show you the seller's CMA (because it was prepared for the seller as a client). However, there would be nothing wrong with the agent using information from other sold properties from brokerage files or from the Multiple Listing Service information to show you a range of values in the area. This information is usually accessed through a computer database, and is fairly up to date.

If you're still in doubt, you may want to access online resources like www.experian.com and cswonline.com where, usually for less than $30, you can obtain estimates of value, including demographic information about the area.

Lastly, it's wise to make your purchase contingent on receiving an appraisal for at least the amount of your offer.

Q. *We're moving from a place where homes were cheaper, and even though the agent showed us similar houses here, we're not convinced. Is there any other way we can gather information?*

A. Yes, showing you a sheet of properties is good; but perhaps you need to see the properties in person before you're convinced.

Ask the agent to drive you by (or go by on your own). Notice the age and condition of the neighborhoods as well as the size of the properties. It may be that you could find a similar house in a lesser price range if the neighborhoods were older or the houses had fewer amenities.

Also, use the contrary approach. Ask the agent for a list of properties that have recently sold that are in the price range you want to pay. This should give you a good idea what your dollar can buy at that price.

Make sure that all of the comparable information you look at is on homes that have sold and closed. These reflect what willing buyers paid for properties, not what they were necessarily listed for.

Once you drive by the properties, you should be mentally prepared to either go with paying a higher price, or settle for less house in the price range you want to pay.

If you're still in doubt, check out online sites that compare and contrast home prices in various cities like www.homefair.com.

Q. *How do you determine market value of a property if there are no comparable properties in the neighborhood (if the house is unique in size, design, and style)?*

A. It can be tough to determine the market value of a one of a kind property, particularly if there are no sales similar to it in the neighborhood.

I would suggest that you contact a real estate agent or appraiser to look for comparable properties that have sold outside of the neighborhood. If some can be found, you could get an idea of the range of value by adjusting the sales prices based on location and other amenities. The agent and/or appraiser can give you a general idea of what a garage would be worth, or additional square footage, an additional bathroom, and the like.

Don't overlook Internet resources to help you determine market value.

I have never been a proponent of getting an appraisal before purchasing. The appraiser may actually err on the conservative side and value the property at less than what a ready, willing, and able buyer would actually pay (especially on a unique property).

And as always, make any offer contingent on receiving an appraisal.

"If Jack's in love, he's no judge of Jill's beauty."
—*Ben Franklin*

Q. *A real estate speaker on TV said that buying an overimproved house could be a good buy because the seller would be willing to discount it to sell it. Is this true?*

A. The speaker has an interesting point; but because there are very few absolutes in real estate, the comment is not always true. By definition, an overimproved property is one that has more amenities than the property can financially return in market value. For example, a swimming pool added to a home may be an owner's delight, but a seller's nightmare when the sales price won't cover paying off the second mortgage that financed it!

While it's true that there could be an occasional situation where a seller would take a discounted price just to unload a property, it's unlikely because a majority of sellers refuse to admit that their house is overimproved. These are the sellers who test the market by putting up the For Sale sign one day and taking it down the next—only to put it up again the next month!

In times of low inflation, a buyer has to be concerned with purchasing at the top of market value in an area. Equity won't build quickly so it could be tough to refinance. And, if the real estate market should fall, you could erode part of the money that served as your down payment, especially if you need to sell quickly.

Buyers of overimproved properties need to be especially careful of unpaid improvements that could result in mechanics' liens against the property. The seller might have realized that completing the work was going to put her in a deeper financial hole so stopped short of paying workers for services and/or for materials. On any home where repairs are fairly recent, ask to see paid receipts from the seller and request that the seller provide extended coverage title insurance to protect against unpaid workers and material suppliers.

Q. *There are two adjacent houses with the same floor plan. One has new flooring, appliances, and storage sheds, but is priced $5,000 higher. Which one is a better buy?*

A. Your calculator can help you decide. First, make sure the higher priced house does not exceed the market value for homes like it.

Second, pencil out what each of the added amenities in the more expensive house would cost. Be sure to factor in any labor that you wouldn't be able to do on your own, like laying carpeting. Now, decide which improvements are important to you and/or you'd be willing to pay to have. (Even if you finance the improvement over 30 years, you're still paying for it—with interest!)

If the improvements total the extra that the seller is asking, and you'd pay to have all of those (in exactly that way) added to a house, then the more expensive house is a good buy. But if you wish the carpeting was a different color, or think the trash compactor is something you wouldn't use, then buy the lesser-priced house.

As a rule of thumb, purchasing the least expensive property in a neighborhood gives you the greatest opportunity to make calculated improvements that will increase the resale value.

PROPERTY CONDITION, INSPECTION, AND ENVIRONMENTAL ISSUES

Q. *Our agent brought us the sellers' property disclosure sheet. Some of the items weren't marked at all and others were marked "unknown." What does this mean?*

A. More than 30 states now require sellers to disclose material facts known about the property and its permanent fixtures. Depending on the state, this could include everything from the wiring to the wood burning stove.

The disclosure provides no warranties. It merely states the facts as known by the seller. So when the sellers marked "unknown," it means the information isn't within their knowledge (e.g., they don't know if they have an attic fan because they've never ventured to the attic!)

Have your agent (through the sellers' agent) go back to the sellers to find out why some items were left blank. Most forms have categories like "none/not included," "working," "not working," and "unknown," so there's little excuse for a seller not to check one of the options. While this disclosure is much more than homebuyers have had in the past, it's merely a precursor to a comprehensive home inspection.

Q. *As first time homebuyers who love old houses, are there any red flags that should alert us that a house has physical and/or mechanical problems that could end up costing us a bundle?*

A. Yes, and you're smart to pay attention to them before falling in love with a house. Making any offer conditioned on the house being scrutinized by a home inspector (especially if you purchase an old house) is a must. But let's review some of those red flags that may alert you, even as you walk through the house for the first time.

On the exterior, look at the roof for signs of age or damage (checking especially around chimney and loose shingle areas where water is likely to seep). Check the foundation for cracks and settling (these also can be seen in a basement area). Turn on each and every water spigot to check for leaks and water pressure. (Low pressure can denote a broken or loose pipe somewhere in the water line.)

Inside the house look for water damage on ceilings as well as water damage near kitchen, bathroom, and utility room plumbing. Blistered wall coverings or paint is often an indication that water has seeped under the surface. While you're in these rooms, turn on water faucets, flush toilets, and check for adequate water pressure and leaks.

As you stroll through the house, turn the lights off and on and don't be afraid to test electrical outlets (a night light is great for this!). Glance at window sills to check for water damage or mildew from condensation caused by old or damaged windows.

Next check the appliances that will stay with the home (such as dishwashers, trash compactors, and garbage disposals). Note their ages and quality and turn them on to test them.

Now for the tough stuff (much of which should be rechecked by a professional inspector). Make sure the furnace, air conditioner, air cleaner, hot water heater, and water conditioner are in good working condition. This even means turning on the heat in the summer! Sometimes service companies will leave stickers on the equipment that will indicate when these systems were last serviced and/or when filters were last changed. Ask to see the service company reports.

There's one last place to check (if you're brave!). That's the attic and/or the crawl space to check for dryness, insulation, and insect or rodent presence.

Some possible problem areas such as sewer lines and septic tanks are usually best left to an inspector's eye. But never be afraid to ask the seller or real estate agent questions about the condition of the property. Legally, they are required to give honest and accurate information regarding any known defects in the property.

Q. *The contract on the house I'm buying calls for a home inspection, but how do you tell a good inspector from a bad one?*

A. This is a great question because there are only a handful of states where home inspectors are required to be licensed. This means that you need to evaluate both credentials and personal references.

In your search for an honest inspector, it's important that the person inspecting the house has nothing to gain by finding things wrong. If the home inspector you're interviewing says that he or she does general contracting work as well as home inspection (and/or sells real estate on the side) choose someone else.

One benchmark of quality is using an inspector who is a member of the American Society of Home Inspectors (ASHI). Not only does this society provide continuing education training for inspectors, each society member is required to complete a minimum of 250 paid inspections, pass a rigorous exam, and adhere to a professional code of ethics. You can find them listed in the yellow pages as well as online at www.ashi.com.

When prescreening a home inspector, ask if he or she is bonded, has liability insurance, and if you can see personal letters of reference (not from real estate professionals but from homeowners who have used his or her services). It's particularly helpful if these references span a fairly long period so you can see a track record.

Ask if the inspector minds if you tag along on the inspection. You'll learn a lot about how the house is constructed and pick up some tips for improving and weatherizing the house as well. If you're paying for this service (many buyers do pick up the tab), you might as well get added value for your money.

Besides the major structural and mechanical aspects of the house, ask the inspector to check for urea formaldehyde (you probably remember this as foam insulation used in the ceilings and walls of homes). Although its use is banned, it is usually not a standard item on the inspector's list—so ask.

Asbestos (a fireproof material that was used in building materials like insulation prior to 1975) also is not a standard inspection item. If the house you're considering is older, you might find asbestos problems on insulation that's unraveling from water and heat pipes.

Using a top-notch home inspector who provides you with more than just the basics goes a long way in ensuring that your purchase will be a sound one.

"Don't throw stones at your neighbors if your own windows are glass."
—*Ben Franklin*

Q. *I made an offer on a vacant lot, contingent on a survey. Unfortunately, it appears the neighbor's garage comes across the property boundary. Does it make financial sense to wait and see if this gets remedied?*

A. If you really want the property, there may not be any harm in waiting it out (if your circumstances will permit it). But time is money; and boundary disputes can be some of the most cumbersome to untangle.

The time-consuming part often is trying to convince the encroaching land owner of the error and having him or her move the garage. Sometimes this can be done without court action, sometimes not.

If the problem later appears to be remedied, it would be wise to have your real estate attorney and the title examiner inspect the survey and the release documents to make sure that you won't have any title problems.

Before you decide to wait it out, evaluate if a lengthy wait is in your best interest as a buyer. Consider if you stand to lose out on other properties that are available if you don't act now and if you're willing to wait until lengthy litigation in a court of law is complete. If the seller decides midstream not to pursue a settlement, you'd have no alternative but to walk away. Bottom line is to take the course of action that best benefits your situation.

Q. *On the last house we owned, we tried to file a claim for a faulty cooling system under the home warranty program, only to uncover that the builder was "self-insuring" (and he had declared bankruptcy). Why wasn't this self-insurance aspect pointed out before we purchased? It made the warranty virtually worthless.*

A. What a nightmare for you. But, innocently like most of us, you assumed that all warranty programs are alike, underwritten by a third party. Unfortunately, the term home warranty is used freely and often haphazardly by new-home builders and remodeling contractors, especially when a third-party insurer is not in the picture.

If you had reviewed the policy in depth (even though most buyers don't), you would have uncovered the self-insurance aspect. Here are four additional questions buyers should ask before signing the closing papers:

1. Who is the warranty company and is it backed by insurance? Several strong companies exist, but don't fail to check any company out with the better business bureau.
2. If a dispute arises between the builder and the warranty company, how would it be resolved? A neutral dispute settlement system is one avenue, and its use would be spelled out in the warranty documents.
3. Is warranty coverage transferable? If the homeowner decides to resell the home, it should not affect the remaining portion of the

coverage. This competitive edge may help the homeowner sell the property.

4. What is covered in the warranty and what is excluded? Like many types of insurance, the homeowner should pay particular attention to the exclusions. The more there are, the less effective the insurance will be.

Sometimes the warranty will cover nonoperating system items like roofs and hot tubs. Depending on the age and condition of the item, purchasing a warranty can be cost-effective, especially if replacing some items could prove costly.

Q. *We want to purchase some acreage but are concerned about the soil and water around the site and want to have them tested. Is there information that could help us get started?*

A. No number of booklets or pamphlets can replace a thorough site inspection from a qualified engineer. But information from the Environmental Protection Agency (EPA) could be your first stop for gathering generic information. It has a variety of materials (both printed brochures and more lengthy documents) listed in its National Publications Catalog, plus articles on current issues and trends.

I've found the best way to contact it is through its Web site at www.epa.gov. You can download brochures and articles from its catalog on the Web and choose the ones you need. Or write to the U.S. Environmental Protection Agency, Public Information Center, 401 M Street, SW, Washington, DC 20460.

Q. *Since our area is prone to horrible storms, the joke is that before you buy a home you have to find a company to insure it! Do online resources make insurance shopping any easier?*

A. Absolutely. If you haven't checked out insurance sites online (my personal favorite—and the largest on the Web—is www.insweb.com), you'll be pleasantly surprised. Not only do they let you shop with a myriad of companies, they have handy online calculators to help you determine how much insurance you need. After experiencing online insurance-rate and program hunting, you'll never pick up a telephone receiver again!

"Hope of gain lessens pain."
—*Ben Franklin*

DANGEROUS DOLLARS AND PERILOUS PENNIES ISSUES

Dangerous Dollars can erode your equity overnight because you've violated The Frugal HomeOwner Law of Logical Home Selection. To keep equity intact:

- Thoroughly check out major neighborhood issues like safety, traffic flow, and noise. Don't think that you later can repair your missteps of choosing the wrong neighborhood by discounting your sales price when you sell—you may not be able to give the house away!
- Crunch the numbers on the comparative market analysis (or online comparison resources) you've obtained for the house you're interested in. If the price seems well in the ballpark compared to other homes sold that are similar in size, amenities, and equal neighborhoods, then you're probably making a sound investment.

Perilous Penny issues can start out small and compound over time. Be sure to:

- Check out schools on a wide variety of issues, not merely scholastic standing. Buyers wanting to purchase your home later will be equally interested in teacher-to-student ratios, crime in and around the school, and the quantity and quality of extracurricular activities.
- Spend time talking with homeowners in the neighborhood before you sign a purchase agreement. Most will be more than candid about what "they wished they'd known before they moved in." It also can prove invaluable for reinforcing that you'll be satisfied with this neighborhood and lifestyle—potential insurance that you won't have to walk away from equity later because you purchased the right house, but in the wrong neighborhood!

CHAPTER 5

The Frugal HomeOwner Law of Common Cents Financing

Choose Wisely Using Knowledge, Tenacity, and Logic

If you fail to get the loan, don't blame Fannie!

After being informed by the lender that her pending loan had failed to meet the necessary underwriting guidelines of Fannie Mae (Federal National Mortgage Association) where the loan was being sold, the loan applicant lamented, "I don't care who that Fannie person is, I want a mortgage!"

At one time, we've all felt like that loan applicant—confused, panicked, and looking for someone to blame. Searching for a mortgage can do that. It can turn a perfectly logical, intelligent individual into someone incapable of reciting her own Social Security number!

But if you consider that not properly evaluating financing is one of the easiest ways to overpay for your home (often by tens of thousands of dollars), searching for the best mortgage becomes as much about common sense as it does dollars and cents! Don't overpay in points and costs to obtain a competitive interest rate. Question the type of closing costs you're required to pay. Ask commonsense questions to create cost-effective savings.

The following questions will take you logically and sanely through the underwriting process (with little-known tips for leverage), give you ideas for choosing the best loan, and provide troubleshooting ideas to bring your loan quickly to closing—without having to blame anyone! Not even Fannie!

PROCESSING AND UNDERWRITING THE MORTGAGE LOAN

Q. *It's taken our loan more than three months to close, but now the lender pulled another credit report on us and found a debt that wasn't there when we applied. Can the lender do this?*

A. The lender has the right to check and recheck documentation up to the time of loan closing. In fact, the lender must update certain items (like credit reports and appraisals) in order to comply with guidelines from the secondary market where the loan is sold.

Keep in mind this cardinal rule: After you've signed a loan application on the dotted line, don't change a thing! This includes your debts, your savings, or your employment!

Q. *We were surprised to hear in our loan qualifying interview that if we put just 10 percent down, we'd have to pay for private mortgage insurance (PMI). What is it, and how could we avoid paying it?*

A. Private mortgage insurance protects the lender against the borrower's default, usually on the top 20 percent of the loan. In other words, if you're only putting 10 percent down, you'll be required to offset the lender's additional risk by providing PMI on the mortgage.

You can pay for PMI in a variety of ways, depending on the PMI company that insures your loan. There are up-front premiums coupled with monthly premiums added to your payment, or larger premiums added onto the loan and financed over its life but without premiums up front. The latter method is especially cost-effective if you'll hold the loan or the property for only a short time.

PMI premiums vary between the eight PMI companies currently doing business in the United States as do the type of risks preferred by the companies. Mortgage Guaranty Insurance Corporation, one of the largest PMI providers, allows you to check premiums online at www.mgic.com.

Besides putting more down, you could sidestep PMI by asking the seller to carry a second mortgage for part of the purchase price. This would reduce the amount of the first mortgage below the 80 percent threshold so PMI wouldn't be required.

You might ask the lender to keep the loan in portfolio (meaning in-house, not selling it as an investment in the secondary market). This could allow the lender to be more flexible in underwriting requirements, including waiving the PMI. As a trade-off for holding the loan in-house, the lender might decide to self-insure it, requiring that you pay a bit more interest. However, the interest is deductible where the PMI is not.

Q. *We just received word that although the lender found us acceptable as borrowers, the PMI company didn't like the condition of the property and refused to insure us. What can we do?*

A. While the lender has his or her own guidelines for borrower and property qualification, so does the PMI insurer. Remember that the private mortgage insurer is protecting the lender against the borrower's default. If the PMI company doesn't like the condition of the property, it may be unlikely that the lender will want to take the risk alone.

Several things may help. Have the lender ask the PMI insurer what needs to be repaired and to what degree. You'll need to negotiate who will pay for the repairs (buyer, seller, or third party), as well as the time frame for completion of the work.

If repairing isn't an option, would the PMI company accept any other alternative, such as more down payment, higher PMI fees, etc.? Could the seller carry part of the purchase price in seller financing, eliminating the need for PMI? Or could the lender keep the loan in portfolio to sidestep PMI?

The lender may be willing to shop for another PMI carrier with property guidelines less stringent than the first. Be sure to make this request known to the lender before you give up on purchasing this property.

Q. *The lender said that "compensating factors" could help me obtain the loan I needed. What are they and how do they work?*

A. Compensating factors can be a godsend for qualifying. They are strengths in the borrower's loan application that offset other potentially negative factors (like high qualifying ratios) and help you swing the loan. Lenders use them to sell the fact that although the borrower may not meet all of the underwriting guidelines, he or she does have one or more compensating factors that strengthen the loan application.

For example, if you could show a strong pattern of being able to save, had little or no long-term debt, or were purchasing an energy-efficient home, those would be compensating factors. They also could include a transferred borrower whose spouse would rejoin the workforce, even though he or she had not yet obtained employment.

One last compensating factor is often forgotten, but very important. If you have a history of paying rent close to the amount of the mortgage payment you're seeking, it can help you cinch the loan. The rationale is that even though your qualifying ratios may be a bit high, you've already proven your ability to carry that higher payment.

Q. *The town home we were interested in buying was turned down for financing by the lender because only a small number of units have been sold to owner/occupants. Does this mean that the property might not be a good investment?*

A. The question has two distinct parts: Why would the lender not approve the property and would the property be a good investment?

The lender's concern is that because there are so few of the units sold to owner/occupants, the majority of the units as rentals may tend to pull down the overall value of the property. On-site owners tend to give more TLC to the property, and are less likely to default on loans if it is their primary residence.

Second, guidelines in the secondary market require a certain amount of units be sold before they consider purchasing loans in the project. This could greatly restrict the lender's ability to convert the loan to cash once it is made, and would serve as a disincentive to make the loan.

As far as the property being a sound investment, I suggest that you secure an appraisal, even if you don't obtain financing. The appraiser can give you an estimate of value based on what similar properties in that development and others nearby have sold for, as well as give insight into what has happened with similar town home developments.

You also would be wise to do some investigating on your own to see if the area surrounding the property is converting to homeowners. If the majority remains as a rental area, the property appreciation may be low or the area not the type you're looking for as a resident owner.

CLOSING COSTS

Q. *On the VA loan we recently closed, the lender said we couldn't pay for certain costs. How come?*

A. Here's an exception to the "anyone can pay a closing cost" rule. Based on the type of loan you're using (such as a Department of Veterans Affairs loan), a party may be prohibited from paying a cost. (The rationale with VA loans is that the borrower/veteran has already contributed time to the military and should not be financially burdened with paying certain costs to obtain a VA mortgage. Some of these costs include tax service fees, underwriting fees, termite and roof inspection fees, and express mail charges. In addition, cumbersome costs could overleverage the VA buyer who may be financing 100 percent of the loan.) But that doesn't mean that you can't get creative in other areas. For example, you could negotiate discount points with the seller because the borrower is allowed to pay those on all types of loans, including VA and Federal Housing Administration (FHA).

Q. *We are going after a 95 percent loan and wonder why the lender feels it's important to pay certain closing costs in cash at closing? Our funds are very tight and we need to maximize every cent!*

A. There's method to the madness. The lender feels most secure when the buyer (especially on a high loan-to-value ratio loan like you're receiving) commits financially to the loan by paying the closing costs. This includes the two months reserve payment collected at closing for taxes and insurance.

But that doesn't mean that you shouldn't search for ways to leverage the closing dollars you do have. Ask the lender to specify which costs must be paid in cash at closing and which can be paid by another party or financed into the loan. This will help you prioritize where to put your closing dollars.

Q. *We took your advice and asked to review the settlement statement in depth before we signed the closing papers for our mortgage and were astounded that the lender charged us extra for pictures taken by the appraiser, as well as a hefty fee to receive a copy of our loan schedule printout. We protested the fees (neither of which were included on our good faith estimate) and the lender removed them.*

A. Good for you! As loan fees and profits dip for lenders, some are finding innovative ways to make up the difference! Even though the good faith estimate (an approximation of closing costs you'll need to pay which you receive within three days of applying) can change before the loan closes, reviewing each closing cost for legitimacy is wise.

The appraiser picture fee you refer to is often listed on the closing statement as a "photo fee." You were wise to question this because even if the appraiser has charged the lender extra, the appraisal fee you've paid should more than cover the charges.

The charge for the payment schedule printout often shows on the closing statement as the "amortization schedule fee" and is totally unnecessary. This is merely a principal and interest breakdown of your loan from the first payment to the last. It takes the lender approximately two minutes to print out and would have been free to you had you requested it at the time you applied for the loan. Because it's merely calculating principal and interest, you can figure it yourself or go to many sites on the Internet to obtain a breakdown. Two such locations are www.mortgage-mart.com (click on "calculator") or www.countrywide.com (click on "home loans" then "loan tools").

Unless a borrower can be shown that a charge is for something beneficial and/or required, the charge should be protested.

FINANCING COMPONENTS TO HELP MAKE YOUR FINANCING AFFORDABLE

Q. *My friend has a loan without a monthly impound (escrow) account for her property taxes and insurance. Under what circumstances can this be done and are there legal guidelines that apply?*

A. Because the purpose behind the escrow account is to make sure that property taxes and insurance funds are available when payments are due, waiving the impound or reserve account is done on a case-by-case basis. In fact, the account is neither required by law nor by a majority of the secondary market investors who purchase loans. It's up to the lender to evaluate the type of loan, requirements imposed by investors purchasing the loan, and the size of the down payment when deciding to waive the account. For example, borrowers making a 20 percent or greater down payment (lowering the lender's risk) are much more likely to have the reserve account waived.

Some lenders won't require the account if a fee is paid at closing. If the lender makes this request, object to it. There's more than enough safety with the large down payment to sidestep the impound account requirement—and lots of other lenders willing to do it!

Q. *At loan application, the lender asked us if we wanted to lock in the interest rate. Under what circumstances would a borrower be wise to do this?*

A. Borrowers who are marginally qualified for what they want to buy are always well-advised to lock in the interest rate. Should rates increase, they would not be able to obtain the loan and would need to scramble for alternatives like more down payment or a less expensive home.

If interest rates appear to be on the rise, locking in is also a good idea. Borrowers who don't lock in at loan application should keep checking weekly with the lender to get an idea of where rates are going. Even if you don't lock in at application, most loans (and lenders) allow it to occur at any time during the loan process.

Before locking in the interest rate, ask the following three questions:

1. What is the projected closing date for the loan and how does it correspond to the lock-in period? For example, paying to lock in a loan for 60 days makes no sense if closing is projected for 90 days.
2. If rates fall, can you obtain the lower interest rate? This is available from many lenders (often called "float down") because it makes sense to keep you engaged in closing this loan with this lender and be rewarded for doing so should rates change. Float downs are often limited to once per lock-in period.
3. Can you see a written agreement of just what you're getting with the lock-in (including answers to the previous questions)? As with any other agreement, if it doesn't address a particular issue, ask. It probably means it's not covered.

If you need additional information, there's a free 14-page booklet available from the Federal Reserve Board called "A Consumer's Guide to Mortgage Lock-ins." You can request your copy from The Federal Reserve Board, 20th and C Sts., NE, Washington, DC 20551.

Q. *My son called to say he was thinking about applying for a mortgage with a prepayment penalty in it? Do they still have loans like that—I thought those were long gone.*

A. Your son is correct. Some lenders are going back to prepayment penalties in their mortgages. And it's likely that your son could get a lower interest rate by using a loan with a prepayment penalty.

Lenders used prepayment penalties (often called privileges because paying the fee gave the borrower the privilege to pay off the loan) many years ago to ensure that their profitability would not be sacrificed if the loan was paid off early.

But lender competition in the 1980s drove the prepayment penalty out of loans. Investors who purchase loans have not been happy over lost profit, especially when homeowners used no-cost refinancing to pay off existing loans. A loan paid off earlier than the maturity date means that the lender does not get the full yield anticipated on the investment.

That's why the mortgage industry is introducing prepayment penalties on some of their loans (usually for the first three years of the loan) with the hope of maximizing profit. And they're willing to reward consumers who takc them, often by charging one-quarter of 1 percent less interest on the loan. This could mean approximately $17 per month less payment on a $100,000 loan at 8 percent interest for 30 years.

Before your son takes a loan with a prepayment penalty, there are two questions he should ask. First, how long does he plan to keep the loan and the house? If the answer is less than three years, then there's no way that he could financially benefit, even with the lower interest rate. And if he feels that he might refinance during that time (especially if interest rates were to drop) he would not want a prepayment penalty in his loan.

Second, what are the conditions of the penalty? This would include the amount charged, the duration of the penalty (e.g., 36 months), and any conditions under which it could be waived. These provisions will be covered in the mortgage document and should be thoroughly reviewed with the lender.

Don't forget to tell your son to shop for loan costs. The lower interest rate could blind him to the fact that closing costs or origination fees may be steeper on this type of loan. Have the lender pencil out the costs to see how they compare with other loan programs your son is considering. What he gains in less interest could be offset by higher fees.

FIXED-RATE CONVENTIONAL MORTGAGES

Q. *I am purchasing a home and recently heard about the 10-year loan. What are the benefits of a 10-year versus a 15-year loan?*

A. The 10-year mortgage was first born of the low interest rates of the 1950s. Some lenders are bringing these loans back to entice middle-aged borrowers to refinance old, higher-rate loans, and pay off loans before retirement. These borrowers typically can afford higher payments in return for substantial interest savings. In fact, you might find the interest rate competitive with that of 15-year loans or slightly below.

Let's compare payments and savings of the 10-year loan to that of the 15-year. A $100,000 10-year loan at 7.25 percent interest would give you payments of $1,174 principal and interest per month compared to $927 on a 15-year loan at 7.50 percent. But the 5-year quicker payoff of the 10-year loan would save you $15,981 in interest!

Lenders who do not sell loans to outside investors are most likely to make 10-year loans. In fact, even lenders who don't typically make these loans may negotiate them on a case-by-case basis.

If you don't choose this type of loan up front, you can still create your own 10-year loan by making prepayments to your mortgage. The lender will be glad to run an amortization schedule on your loan, showing what monthly payments (or prepaid lump sums) would retire the loan in 10 years. For example, an extra $260 per month on a $100,000 loan would shorten a 15-year loan at 7.5 percent to 10 years, saving you $24,420 in interest—ideal for a frugal homeowner.

Q. *The lender says I can qualify for either a 15- or a 30-year mortgage, but is the savings worth the difference in the monthly payments?*

A. The issue you're addressing is the very one that keeps many people from going with the 15-year loan—the higher monthly payments. In fact, it's not unusual for lenders to counsel buyers to go with the lesser payment and make prepayments to the principal when they can. The problem is that unless you have an ongoing game plan for prepaying, the money often gets sidetracked into car payments, vacations, and extra trips to the mall.

But let's see if some other numbers can help convince you. It's true that a $100,000 loan at 8.5 percent would cost you $216 more per month for the 15-year loan than for the 30-year loan. But you stand to win big by saving more than $77,000 in interest with the 15-year loan!

Ask the lender to pencil out the figures as they apply to your loan or visit an online calculator like the one at homefair.com. In addition, consider how long you'll keep the loan (and the house), if you can barter a lower rate on the 15-year loan (which also will help the numbers), and whether the higher monthly payment will keep you awake at night. Then you'll know which loan to take.

Q. *The lender says we can't qualify for the $80,000 loan we want, so suggests we use a 40-year loan. We are in our fifties and would retire in this home but are concerned that we won't live to see our house paid off!*

A. Living to see your house paid off is not the issue here—it's the massive amount of extra interest you'll pay if you go with a 40-year loan! Don't go there!

Some lenders are touting the 40-year mortgage as one way to "increase your borrowing power" because your monthly payments would be lower. But the only thing that's really being increased is the lender's profit. Let's look at the numbers.

The principal and interest payment for $80,000 at 8 percent on a 30-year loan would be $587.02 per month. This is $30.77 per month more than the 40-year loan at $556.25 per month.

While qualifying for the lesser payment would help you purchase more house, it could end up costing you $55,673 more in interest over the life of the loan! (This is 480 payments totaling $267,000 compared to 360 payments totaling $211,327.) This might not be such a concern if you were going to be moving again, but using this type of loan on a home you'll keep indefinitely makes no sense.

The bottom line is that saving $30 per month on your mortgage payment could end up costing you more than $55,000 in the long run! Ask the lender to find ways to make a 30-year (or less) loan work for you. This could include using a larger down payment, finding seller contributions to cover some of your closing costs, and/or using some of your cash to pay off existing debts that may limit your borrowing power.

A trustworthy lender will not place you in any loan that's ultimately not a good financial move for you. If the lender isn't willing to explore other options, find another lender that will.

"Think what you do when you run in debt; you give to another power over your liberty."
—*Ben Franklin*

Q. *Because we may be relocating in two years, would a balloon mortgage suit our needs? What factors should we consider with this type of loan?*

A. A balloon is any loan with a relatively short payback period, say three to ten years. The secondary market sanctions seven-year balloon loans with interest rates lower than 30-year fixed rates, and allows the borrower to retain the loan for another 23 years after the loan balloons at a fixed rate one-half percent higher than the FNMA's regular 30-year fixed rate at that time. This means that although you'd have lower mortgage interest initially, your rate would rise should you keep the loan past the conversion period.

Be sure you check out the terms of the balloon. Some programs make the borrower requalify when the balloon is due. Should your income situation change, that could become a problem.

If you're relatively sure that you'll be transferred within several years, the balloon mortgage may work for you. If you sell before that time, the interest you saved offset by the points and fees you would pay would then be your primary consideration, not the fact that it was a balloon mortgage.

Your best bet is to consult several lenders to have them pencil out the figures. Also have them give you quotes on one-year and three-year adjustable-rate mortgages that may be as cost-effective and perhaps more marketable (even assumable) when you sell the property.

FEDERAL HOUSING ADMINISTRATION (FHA) LOANS

Q. *Aren't FHA loans only for low-income buyers?*

A. No. It's a misconception that FHA loans are for low-income buyers. While there are some programs targeted to assist families with low income, the staple program of the FHA, the 203(b) loan is available to anyone who can qualify. In fact, the competitive interest rates, low down payments, and somewhat liberal underwriting requirements of the FHA loan make it an ideal candidate for a high percentage of buyers, not solely those with moderate income.

Perhaps the only drawback is that the FHA sets a maximum loan amount it will lend based both on national guidelines and the median cost of housing in your geographic region. When inflation is strong and home prices rise rapidly, this can prohibit some buyers from financing homes with FHA loans.

It's also a misconception that the federal government makes FHA loans. While lenders make loans, FHA insures lenders against the borrower's default with borrowers paying for that insurance either up front at the time of loan origination, or financed into the loan and added to the monthly payments.

Q. *Who determines the interest rates and points on FHA loans? Are they negotiable?*

A. The government does not set interest rates (or points) for FHA and VA loans. They are negotiated with the lender based on what the borrower can afford and wants to achieve in taking the loan. Generally, a buyer willing to pay more discount points should be able to obtain a lower interest rate loan.

Here's how it works. Discount points are used to increase the financial yield to the lender and can be paid by the buyer, the seller, or a third party. A point is equal to 1 percent of the loan amount. Because interest rates on FHA and VA loans tend to be slightly lower than conventional loan rates, lenders are allowed to charges points as an incentive for them to make FHA and VA loans and to increase its yield on those loans.

For example, if conventional mortgage rates are at 7.5 percent, the lender might negotiate that you pay two points to receive a 7 percent loan. This would mean that two points on a $60,000 loan would cost you $1,200 in cash at closing. If you desired, or could only qualify for a 6.5 percent interest rate, the lender would require more points to make that loan.

Usually it makes sense to pay more points to obtain a lower rate if you will hold the loan for a long time, and pay fewer points (that you couldn't recoup) if you were a short-term property or loan holder.

Even though points are thought to be fixed by the lender, the consumer can negotiate them. It takes a persistent and strong-willed buyer, a favorable loan risk, and a lender eager for new business.

Q. *What does it take to qualify for an FHA loan and is it easier than qualifying for a conventional one?*

A. FHA mortgages are typically easier to qualify for, especially when it comes to self-employed or previously bankrupt borrowers. And qualifying guidelines are generally easier on FHA loans than on conventional ones.

For example, qualifying ratios on FHA allow up to 29 percent of your gross monthly income to apply to your principal, interest, tax, and insurance (PITI) payment. (Conventional loans allow only 28 percent). FHA allows up to 41 percent of your gross monthly income to apply to your PITI plus any long-term debt (debts that exceed ten months in duration). The corresponding conventional ratio is 36 percent.

Down payments are easier, too, requiring a minimum of only 3 percent.

Q. *Compared to other types of loans, what are the financial shortcomings of using an FHA mortgage?*

A. The greatest financial shortfall with FHA loans is the mortgage insurance premium the borrower is required to pay. The fee is based on a percentage of the amount borrowed. And while it can be paid in cash at closing, most FHA buyers choose to finance it into the loan.

Unlike PMI that often can be taken off the loan after a period of time, FHA insurance remains for the life of the loan.

DEPARTMENT OF VETERANS AFFAIRS (VA) LOANS

Q. *How can I get a Certificate of Eligibility to start the ball rolling for a VA loan?*

A. The easiest way is to contact a lender who makes VA loans, get prequalified, and it will be glad to assist you in filling out the necessary forms to obtain your certificate. You need to provide the lender with a DD214 (a synopsis of your military history) issued to you if you were discharged after January 1, 1950, or a form WDAGO, Notice of Separation, if you were discharged before 1950.

If you have lost the necessary document, you can obtain a duplicate from the War Records Department, the local draft board (if you were drafted), or the branch of service from which you were discharged. Also acceptable would be a GSA Form 6954, Certification of Military Service, available from the applicable service department.

Q. *Someone told me that National Guard members could now obtain a no down payment VA loan. Is this true?*

A. It's true that both National Guard and reservist members who have completed a total of at least six years of service are eligible for a VA home loan. The program does not require any down payment (based on your loan qualifications). The only major difference is that more funding fees to originate the loan will be charged.

Q. *Is it true you can finance 100 percent of the purchase price on a VA loan?*

A. A veteran who can qualify can finance up to 100 percent of the purchase price. In addition, the property would have to appraise for the purchase price. It's mandatory that every purchase agreement specifying VA financing contain a clause stating that the borrower can be released from the purchase if the CRV (certificate of reasonable value, aka the VA appraisal) is found to be different from the purchase price. The buyer would still be able to purchase the property, but would have to pay the difference between the appraised value and the purchase price in cash (that difference cannot be borrowed).

Q. *Is there any maximum amount that applies to a VA loan? I got confused when the lender said I could qualify for a $203,000 VA loan with no down payment, but could make a larger loan if I needed it.*

A. Contrary to popular belief, unlike the FHA there is no maximum loan amount for VA loans. However, once a borrower exceeds a loan of $203,000, a down payment is required.

The confusing part about VA loans is understanding the difference between the loan guaranty and the loan size. The maximum current guaranty available is $50,750. Most lenders will make a loan of four times the size of the guaranty without a down payment if the borrower can qualify. This is because the VA guaranty covers the lender's loss on approximately 25 percent of the loan should it default. This is usually more than enough to bail out the lender.

If the lender said you could obtain a loan of $203,000, this follows the lenders' "rule of four" because you qualified for the maximum zero down payment loan of four times the amount of the guaranty ($50,750 × 4 = $203,000).

If you wanted a larger loan, you could obtain one by making a down payment of 25 percent of the difference between the $203,000 and what you wanted to borrow. This is great news for VA buyers who want to purchase a "move up" home, have good income to support a large payment, and want to use their VA eligibility. However, you may need to shop for a VA lender to make this larger loan because it may need to be sold to investors outside of the traditional secondary market.

Q. *We have an outstanding VA loan on a property we now own. Would that loan need to be paid off before we could obtain another VA loan?*

A. Not necessarily. You can purchase again with VA eligibility depending on how much is outstanding through the first purchase, and how much home you can afford.

Let's say you wanted to purchase a new $90,000 home. (Remember, you must use this as your primary residence in order to finance it with a VA loan.) If you have $12,500 worth of loan guaranty outstanding (not paid off) on the old loan it would be subtracted from the loan guaranty amount of $36,000 (for loans of less than $144,000; however, the maximum guaranty increases to $50,750 for loans of $144,000 or greater). The calculations would be $36,000 guaranty less $12,500 loan guaranty outstanding = $23,500 guaranty available for the second purchase. Based on the fact that most lenders will make loans of approximately four times the amount of the guaranty, you could obtain a $94,000 loan with no down payment required!

Q. *Compared to other loans, what are the financial shortcomings of the VA loan?*

A. The greatest financial shortcoming of the VA loan is the somewhat hefty funding fees charged to the buyer. Depending on the amount of the down payment (if any) being made, these fees can both add several points to the amount borrowed and mount up—especially as most veterans finance them into the loan and pay interest on them!

All things considered, a buyer with money for a down payment who wanted to actively negotiate with the seller and/or the lender to obtain the most cost-effective financing overall, would do well to sidestep a VA loan.

ADJUSTABLE-RATE MORTGAGE (ARM)

Q. *Under what circumstances does it make sense for a buyer to use an adjustable-rate mortgage?*

A. An ARM works well for a variety of situations. ARM rates are typically less than conventional fixed-rate mortgages, so borrowers can qualify for more payment. If inflation is low, rates will stay low, too, because interest increases are gauged on the movement of the particular index (indicator of inflation) tied to that loan.

If a buyer will keep the house or the loan only a short time (usually four years or less), an adjustable rate makes sense. This is particularly true because ARMs save buyers the most money in the early stages of the loan; rates start low and hike upward if inflation is present.

Lastly, some lenders can make extra concessions to ARM buyers because more of these loans are held in the lender's portfolio and are not sold into the secondary market. This could mean allowing higher qualifying ratios, waiving the private mortgage insurance, or stretching other qualifying guidelines not allowed by the secondary market.

Q. *How are ARMs calculated? It seems quite complicated.*

A. Calculating how ARMs work isn't as difficult as it seems if you know the components involved and their roles.

The lender (under the guidelines of the investor purchasing the loan in the secondary market) determines which index is used. An index is a benchmark or measure of the economy. Typical indexes include one-year Treasury securities, Treasury bills, and Cost of Funds index (from the Federal Home Loan Bank). You can find up-to-date index rates at www.hsh.com and at www.interest.com.

Next is the margin. It's the lender's cost of doing business plus profit. Margins are determined by the lender; and, as you'll see by the following example, it's worth shopping for the lowest one.

Let's say the lender quotes you an index rate of 4.75 percent and a margin of 2.75 percent; the calculated interest rate would be 7.50 percent. Once the loan is made, the index may fluctuate up or down depending on the economy and the rate of inflation, but the margin remains constant for the life of the loan. Every adjustment is calculated by using the current index and the margin; so it's just as important (if not more so) to shop diligently for the lowest margin because it stays the same as long as you keep the loan.

Q. *I'd like to look at figures and compare several loan programs before I decide on an ARM. What can the lender provide me with?*

A. Under Regulation Z, the Truth-in-Lending Law requires lenders to provide the following information at the time of application:

- An educational brochure about ARMs—either the "Consumer Handbook on Adjustable Rate Mortgages" published jointly by the Federal Reserve Bank and the Federal Home Loan Bank, or a suitable substitute.
- A loan program disclosure for each ARM program in which you express an interest. The disclosure information must reveal that the interest rate or loan term can change, identify the index used and the source of information for that index, plus explain how the index adjusts. A statement must be included advising the consumer to ask about the current margin, interest rate, and discount points.
- A historical example must be given illustrating how payments on a $10,000 loan would have changed in response to historical data for that index. You also should receive information on how to calculate payment amounts on the loan. (Note that this is merely for a $10,000 example. You'll want to magnify the changes based on the size of loan for which you're applying.)
- Using the historical example, a statement reporting the initial and maximum interest rates and payments for a $10,000 loan originated at the note rate (interest rate) quoted.

Be sure to obtain a full set of information for each loan program you're interested in.

"If you would know the value of money, go and try to borrow some, for he that goes a borrowing goes a sorrowing."
—*Ben Franklin*

CREATE ADDED LEVERAGE FOR BORROWERS THROUGH FINANCING

Q. *We have heard of the Community Homebuyers type loans where you can use a minimal down payment. Are there any special requirements to get these?*

A. These Home Affordability Programs are great news for buyers with minimal down payments—both Fannie Mae and Freddie Mac in the secondary market purchase these loans when borrowers have a down payment of only 3 percent.

If there is any downside, it's the fact that income maximums and property purchase price maximums can apply, based on where the property is located.

The positive news about affordability programs is they use competitive underwriting guidelines that allow borrower's strengths to offset risks. Extra leverage to help you qualify would include cash equivalents of more than two months of mortgage payments in the bank at the time of closing, or if you have a low level of long-term debt including car payments, revolving charge cards, etc. Qualifying ratios of 33 percent and 38 percent, respectively, are higher than most other mortgages.

Don't overlook a national homebuyer assistance program called The Nehemiah Program that helps buyers purchase homes for as little as 1 percent total move-in costs. Check out their Web site at www.nehemiahprogram.org and then ask your lender if they're a participant.

Q. *My friend mentioned that I could borrow from my credit card to make the down payment on a house. I already have high credit card debt, so would this work for me?*

A. It depends on how much long-term debt you have in comparison to the amount of your gross monthly income. The money that you borrow on your credit card will have to be repaid; and those monthly repayments will count as long-term debt for the purpose of loan qualification. (You can find more on this type of loan in Chapter 3.)

Q. *We found a seller who will take our small down payment and finance the balance on what we consider to be our dream home. It would allow us to purchase a larger home than we would otherwise qualify for through a lender, and probably refinance three years or so to pay off the seller. Are there any negatives to this?*

A. You are smart to look at both sides of the situation up front. While it is great that the seller will take only a small amount down and carry the balance on time, consider these five areas before you proceed:

1. Will you really be able to afford the property? It's not only a high mortgage payment you'll be faced with, but pricier property taxes and insurance as well.
2. Buyers purchasing with seller financing are often tempted to pay the property taxes and insurance on an annual basis, but if you're already on a tight budget these extra funds required annually or semiannually can take a large hunk out of your monthly income or savings.
3. Will you be prepared to cover the increased costs of maintenance, electricity, and other utilities? You may want to ask the owner for estimates of what she is currently paying.
4. Will you rely solely on appreciation from the property in order to refinance it in the three-year time frame you mention? That's a fairly short time frame and most lenders want a minimum of 10 percent equity in the property (or down payment in cash) before they will refinance. In fact, refinancing guidelines are often more strict than those for new purchasers. Granted, appreciation may increase the property value, but it's tough to say when and how much it will be. For this reason, it's vital to double-check that values in the neighborhood have risen well and at least kept pace with inflation.
5. If you do refinance, is it likely that you'd qualify for the payment at that time (based on where you are financially today)? It may be wise to get a lender's input now as to the feasibility of your plan.

Don't let the enticement of a low down payment lock you into a dream home that could prove later to be a nightmare.

Q. *We are a little short in our down payment and closing costs for a 90 percent conventional loan. Is it possible to have a seller carry financing on part of the purchase price and get a conventional loan for the balance?*

A. What you're describing is called piggyback financing and there are several reasons why it may make economic sense for both you and the seller.

The secondary market will purchase loans from lenders based on first mortgages of up to 75 percent of the appraised value with a 10 percent down payment from you on that loan, while the seller carries 15 percent of the purchase price on a second mortgage. You reduce your down payment considerably and the seller gets the proceeds from the 75 percent loan, less the costs of sale. (This is the same concept to that of the piggyback loan to leverage down payments discussed in Chapter 3, only here the seller, instead of the lender, is holding your second mortgage.) You and the seller would negotiate the terms of the second mortgage (at a mutually favorable rate of interest) and the seller would increase the yield on its investment by receiving interest.

Because the first mortgage is less than 80 percent of the appraised value of the property, private mortgage insurance may not be charged by the lender, but the lender will ask that you financially qualify to repay both the first and second mortgages. Also, some of your closing fees may be reduced because many of the lender's costs (e.g., origination fees) are based on the amount of the first mortgage.

Make sure that you and the seller use attorneys who specialize in real estate to draft the documents on the seller financing. You will live with these terms, conditions, and clauses for the life of the second mortgage, so it's imperative you shop for quality, not just fees.

If the seller won't agree to carry the financing for you, ask the lender if it would make you the extra second mortgage (as covered in Chapter 3). Lenders find it a good way to satisfy borrowers' needs as well as increase their overall yields.

Q. *The only loan I can qualify for (because of some credit problems I had) is called a nontraditional subprime mortgage. Will it cost me more than an ordinary loan? What exactly is a subprime mortgage?*

A. Potentially, yes. A subprime loan is one that has more risks than a traditional loan and therefore does not meet the standard underwriting guidelines for the secondary market where loans are sold. In fact, a subprime loan is one that falls short in one or more of the typical underwriting areas of credit, debt, income, or other potential risk involved in repaying the loan.

Markets for these loans have increased significantly because one set of standard underwriting guidelines cannot fit all borrowers. Things like job loss, death or illness in the family, and divorce can significantly alter a borrower's ability to meet standard qualifying guidelines. Nontraditional loans fill this lending gap by making allowances for credit, income, and loan-to-value ratios.

If your credit is blemished, the lender may assign a credit grade category of A–, B, C, D, or lower depending on the severity of the problems.

The greatest borrower caution is to spend time shopping for points and loan fees and interest rates as they can be markedly higher for subprime loans. After being denied a traditional A grade loan, borrowers tend to take the first loan they can qualify for instead of analyzing what they're truly paying for the loan.

LEVERAGE TIPS AND TECHNIQUES

Q. *The seller of the house I'm buying said if I would give him his price, he would buy down the interest rate for me. Which loans would this work on?*

A. Buying down the interest rate means that additional points can be paid at closing to reduce the interest rate (or note rate) on the loan. A buydown can be either for a short period, called a temporary buydown (e.g., up to three years), or can permanently buy down the rate for the life of the loan. A buydown is prepaying interest for the privilege of a lower interest rate.

For example, the lender might quote a standard interest rate of 8 percent, but say that four extra points could permanently lower the rate to 7.25 percent. In addition to paying less interest, this also could allow you to qualify at the lower interest rate, depending on the loan type.

While buydowns are allowed on VA, FHA, and conventional loans, there are limits depending on the program.

"Necessity never made a good bargain."
—*Ben Franklin*

Q. *What is a lease purchase and could it help me buy more time to accumulate a down payment?*

A. A lease purchase is a true purchase, but with a delayed closing, and is drafted on either a purchase and sales agreement or in contract language by an attorney. In other words, you specify the terms and conditions of the purchase now, occupy the property, and agree to close the sale in the future.

As a buyer under a lease purchase you would want to specify the exact type of loan, maximum loan amount and interest rate, and closing costs you would pay. This means that you ideally should be prequalified with a lender prior to making an offer. At the very least, these conditions could be made a contingency of the contract, and then removed after you have been qualified.

If you need more time to accumulate your down payment, when is it reasonable that you will have it together (in order to schedule your closing date accordingly in the contract)? This is no time to err on the side of overoptimism because you stand to lose not only your earnest money deposit but possibly face a lawsuit if you can't perform under the terms you and the seller agree on.

It's important to spell out the particulars in a lease purchase, including:

- *Services.* When will the charges for water, sewer, garbage, yard maintenance, and so on become your responsibility?
- *Insurances.* When will you need homeowners insurance coverage? Will the seller keep his or her policy in effect (particularly when a lender may require it), and can you add on additional liability and coverage on the contents?
- *Improvements to the property.* Will the seller allow any physical changes to the property prior to closing? This is generally not a good idea because something unforeseen might prevent the sale from closing.
- *Miscellaneous provisions.* Be sure to specify any contingencies relating to the amount, type, and terms of financing you'll require. (That's why it's a good idea to be prequalified with a lender to know where you stand.) It's not unusual for the buyer under a lease purchase to request that the seller contribute a portion of the monthly lease payment to the buyer. This could be used to offset your down payment or could apply to reducing the purchase price (but be sure to specify which).

Q. *Our daughter put down $7,200 on an option to purchase for a two-year lease. During that time the sellers moved out of state, defaulted on the mortgage, and the lender foreclosed. The real estate company sent half of the deposit to the sellers and kept the other half for itself.*

A. I'm sorry this happened to your daughter. Unfortunately, there could possibly be no recourse against the sellers (although a real estate attorney could review the paperwork to tell you what remedies, if any, are available). If what your daughter got was truly a lease option, it's not a purchase contract. It's an agreement that requires the optionors (the sellers) to act only after the optionee (your daughter) gives notice that she wishes to execute her option (at the end of the two-year period). If the option isn't exercised, the optionee cannot recover the money paid for the option right.

Obviously, the sellers didn't act in good faith because the mortgage wasn't kept current and they lost the property. But your attorney may tell you that going after defaulted sellers in another state could turn out to be an exercise in futility!

You might ask a real estate attorney to review the paperwork signed between the buyers and sellers on the off chance that it could be a lease purchase instead of a lease option. A lease purchase is actually a sales contract with a delayed closing and often accompanies a substantial deposit like the one paid. If the sellers defaulted on the terms of a lease purchase, it might provide more legal teeth to go after the sellers. The attorney can help you weigh the cost of fighting the sellers interstate compared to what could be gained financially.

As this unfortunate situation shows, bad things can happen to good buyers. Even though an attorney might have suggested up front that an option to purchase be recorded so that it's of public record (which would be picked up on when the lender ordered the title work as part of the foreclosure), there's very little that can be done to stop this type of dishonest sellers.

Q. *I have a nice sailboat I'd like to use as a partial down payment on a new home. Would a lender allow this?*

A. Possibly. What you're referring to is called trading equity, and there are lenders and loan programs that allow this. It usually requires that you make a 5 percent cash down payment in addition to any personal property you're offering.

To determine what your boat would be worth in the transaction, the lender will subtract any outstanding loan balance on the traded property (along with any transfer costs) from whichever of the following is lower: the appraised value of the property being traded (based on a written appraisal from an impartial third party) or the trade-in value of that property as agreed to by both parties in the sales agreement. Because the boat is personal property, a search of county records will be required to ensure that there are no undisclosed liens.

While these are the typical underwriting guidelines that apply to personal property as down payments, the lender you're using may impose other restriction as well.

Q. *Our friend told us about a lender's program to help us cover our closing costs. But I didn't realize that they would charge us more interest to do so. Does this make financial sense?*

A. It could. You're referring to premium pricing, or overpar pricing. It means that the lender will waive some of the closing costs. As the term suggests, however, you will be paying a premium interest rate for this financing (typically around ⅛ percent more). There are several questions you need answered to determine if it's a good deal for you.

First, how much closing cost money are you short? It makes little sense to pay thousands of dollars in additional loan interest to offset a few hundred dollars of closing costs.

Second, how long would you keep this loan on this house? If you plan to be a short-term owner, paying more interest won't have as great a financial impact. But if you have no short-term plans to sell (or refinance the loan), getting saddled with a high interest rate loan makes less sense.

Before you accept the premium priced loan, look one last time for any other source of alternative funds. Ask relatives, your employer, or even check into a short-term source for the money. Be careful not to borrow against a resource that would count as a long-term debt for the purpose of loan qualifying.

Don't overlook the seller as a potential option. You might be able to get the seller to pick up a few more closing costs, depending on what you've already negotiated. Before you accept this loan, ask the lender if there is any other type of financing with a lower interest rate that requires fewer closing costs. If this lender says no, call other lenders to confirm this fact before committing to the higher interest rate loan.

Q. *We found a home to purchase where the seller was redoing the kitchen but ran out of money. Could we complete the repairs and use our labor as sweat equity to buy the house? Is this a good way to purchase?*

A. Using repairs and sweat equity can assist buyers if handled properly. Once the value of the repairs is determined, it can be credited to you in several ways, either toward your down payment or to reduce the purchase price. One word of caution: If you purchase a property where repairs have been started, be sure to alert the title company and ask if extended coverage title insurance is available. It will help cover any mechanics' liens filed against the property for work and materials for which the seller did not pay.

WHAT TO DO WHEN THE LENDER SAYS NO

Q. *The lender just turned us down for the mortgage we needed. Is there anything we can do?*

A. Absolutely! First, ask the lender specifically why the loan was turned down. Was the problem with you, the borrower, with the property, or with the private mortgage insurer (if applicable)? Is a remedy available with this lender (e.g., a larger down payment, debts reduced, switching to a different loan program)? If so, is this a logical option for you? Ask whether another lender would consider the risk. Why or why not? What would have to happen before a lender would make the loan?

If the problem is borrower-related, here are some options:

- Reevaluate your financial situation (particularly assets, future assets, and existing debts). Has anything changed since the initial qualification? Did you receive a pay raise, were debts paid off or reduced below the long-term debt period, or did you get a debt consolidation loan to reduce the amount of your monthly payments? Remember that verified pay increases that will occur within 60 days after the loan closes can be used as loan qualifying income. Make sure the lender is aware of the positive changes.

- Could the terms of the purchase be changed to make you stronger financially? For example, would the seller be willing to contribute more to closing costs to make the sale fly?
- Seek a less restrictive qualifying program. Underwriting guidelines vary from loan to loan. Shop various programs to see if others would consider the shortcoming as a problem.
- Seek a more flexible lender or a different branch of the same lender (underwriting from one branch may be more strict than that of another within the same parent organization).
- Ask to have the loan held in portfolio, meaning that the lender would keep the loan in-house rather than selling it to outside investors. This may mean that the lender could use different qualifying guidelines, minimize the amount of down payment required, and/or eliminate the PMI.

You may find that the problem was property-related. Lenders want good collateral. But what can you do if the loan was turned down because of the property? Here are some ideas:

- Can the property be repaired? How extensive must the repairs be?
- Who has the most to gain if the repair is made? This person may be willing to pay for repairs, and it may not even be the buyer or seller. For example, it might be a party in another transaction who needs this loan to close to enable your seller to buy their property.
- What time frame would be allowed for completion of repairs? One option may be to close the transaction and hold repair funds in escrow. Generally, a lender requests three or four estimates from contractors, doubles the highest bid, and requires that amount to be placed in escrow.
- Could the buyer use sweat equity in lieu of cash for repairs? A buyer who is a roofer, for example, may use his or her expertise to complete roof repairs.
- Would the lender take the risk if the loan-to-value ratio were lower, meaning a larger down payment? Would the lender be willing to make the loan at a higher interest rate to offset the risk?
- Could the lender hold the loan in portfolio in order to get around some of the stricter underwriting guidelines of the secondary market?

Although PMI guarantees the lender against the borrower's default (typically on the top 20 percent of the loan), the PMI company still will want to approve of both the borrower and the property before insuring. If a PMI company turns down the risk, here are some possible remedies:

- Determine where the problem lies. Is it related to the borrower or the property? Have the lender ask the PMI company representative what, if anything, it would take to change its mind.
- If the problem is borrower-related, ask the lender to hold the loan in portfolio. Sometimes the lender will either waive the PMI coverage or self-insure by asking for a slightly higher interest rate on the loan. (Note this additional interest would be tax deductible, whereas the PMI is not.)
- If the problem is property-related, would a larger PMI premium, greater down payment, or repairs make a difference?
- After you've tried the preceding options, ask the lender to shop for another PMI insurer; there are currently eight PMI companies doing business in the United States. Just as lenders' underwriting guidelines vary, so do the guidelines and risks taken by the various PMI companies. In fact, you even can shop for rates between the companies!
- If PMI is not available, see if you can increase the down payment (perhaps with gifted funds) and/or ask the seller to carry a second mortgage in order to reduce the loan-to-value ratio level to 80 percent or below so that PMI is not required.

Lenders are in the business of lending and really do want to make loans. They dislike saying no even more than the buyer objects to hearing it! It's up to the borrower and the lender to work together as a team to uncover all possible options to get to "yes."

If you're looking for additional information on financing and mortgages, check out my book *All About Mortgages* (Dearborn Financial Publishing, 1999). It's full of additional leverage techniques, especially for marginal buyers.

DANGEROUS DOLLARS AND PERILOUS PENNIES ISSUES

Ignoring the Frugal HomeOwner Law of Common Cents Financing is one of the black-hole areas where Dangerous Dollars can do the most damage in a very short time! You'll be armed against potential losses if you negotiate with the lender for the most attractive interest rate in tandem with a prudent amount of points and fees, keeping in mind what you're financially trying to achieve. This is based on factors such as how long you'll keep the house and the loan, how quickly you want your equity to grow, and what you can afford. Frugal financing isn't the cheapest—it's the most cost-effective for your particular situation.

Perilous Pennies are most likely to slip through your fingers when you don't understand financing and its related costs. To control these seemingly harmless nickels and dimes:

- Check the closing statement prior to closing the loan and ask questions about any costs you don't understand. Compare this statement to the estimate of costs quoted when you applied for the loan. Request clarifications on any discrepancies.
- Ask the lender to explain anything about your loan you don't understand. This is especially important if you have a mortgage with payment adjustments, provisions for balloon payments, or any other time-dated features that require your understanding and attention. Once a loan is closed, it becomes your responsibility to manage its buzzers and whistles. Ignoring these issues will cost you pennies initially, blossoming into serious dollars over time.

CHAPTER 6

The Frugal HomeOwner Law of Negotiating the Purchase

Know the Value of a Sharp Pencil and a Silver Tongue

Remember what we said in the introduction? Not negotiating well is a sure way to part with precious equity even before you obtain it! So using the "iron-hand-in-the-velvet-glove" approach is paramount in creating a win/win negotiation and instant equity when you purchase.

Here's an example. The Petrees are in a bidding war for the house they really want and are willing to give the seller his inflated selling price of $95,000 plus cave in to his demands to pick up $300 of his closing costs.

It's obvious that they've thrown money away in the $300, but that's just the tip of the iceberg. By overpaying for the house, it costs them more money for the down payment on the mortgage, more in closing costs (because most mortgage costs are based on a percentage of the mortgage), *and* thousands of dollars more in interest over the years due to the larger mortgage. All told, overpaying for the house will cost the Petrees more than $5,000 if they own the home for ten years (based on 95 percent financing at 8 percent interest and standard closing costs).

But there's more. Because they purchased at an inflated price, their equity buildup is off to a slow start. If they're forced to sell before the house can realize some significant appreciation, they may have to bring money to closing!—all brought about by not negotiating when they purchased.

You may be saying, "At least they *got* the house." While that's true (and overpaying is sometimes born of necessity in a seller's market where properties are scarce), the Petrees should be aware of and be willing to accept the consequences of overpaying. Unfortunately, many buyers don't realize until too late the potential damaging effect caused by leaving money on the bargaining table.

When negotiating, keep in mind my favorite homebuying adage, "You don't make money in real estate when you sell, you make money when you buy!" Sins like overpaying, overleveraging, and overspending during negotiations will come back to haunt you later in slow equity buildup coupled with fewer selling and repurchasing options. Sharpen that pencil, fine-tune your silver tongue, and apply the following techniques to your negotiations.

OFFERS

Q. *Is there a rule of thumb as to how much lower than the listed price the buyer's first offer should be?*

A. Who said the first offer had to be any lower than the listed price? If a property is listed properly, it should be close to market value. By making a drastically lower offer, you may insult the seller and limit your chance of any further negotiation. A seller may be so enraged by an unrealistically low offer that he or she refuses to see any additional offers from a prospect, or may make a counteroffer back at even higher than the original listed price—just to insult you! This is particularly true if you ask for other concessions from the seller like paying discount points, closing costs, or including personal property in the sale.

If you've seen comparable properties with similar asking and selling prices, and you feel that the listed price is fair, put yourself in the seller's shoes before making an offer. Your first offer will set the stage for future negotiations.

Q. *My parents say to use a small amount of earnest money and make up for it with a strong offer. My feeling is that I'd be better off offering $1,000 to get the seller's attention because I'd get it back if my offer wasn't accepted. Which approach is best?*

A. I agree with you. Buyers today need to make their offers as attractive as possible, especially if multiple offers are anticipated on a property.

Money does talk; all offers being equal, most sellers will be inclined to go with buyers appearing the most motivated. Earnest money (also called a good faith deposit) helps express that motivation. It's also deemed as the first glimpse of the buyer's potential financial position. Logical or not, some sellers feel that a buyer making an offer with a sizable earnest money deposit is more likely to have a stronger financial posture than someone offering a $50 postdated check.

You are correct that you will get your deposit back if your offer is not accepted. And if it is accepted, you'd be parting with it soon for part of your down payment anyway.

Q. *We would have met or even exceeded the amount of earnest money the seller ended up taking with another buyer's offer. Shouldn't sellers tell buyers this?*

A. Some sellers do make it a point to state the minimum amount of earnest money they will consider but are certainly under no obligation to tell buyers that they will accept a certain amount. Conversely, a seller wouldn't discount an otherwise good offer just because a buyer's earnest money was a little less than suggested. Sellers want the best offer and are less likely to counter back on the poorest one.

The seller also may feel that a buyer is less likely to walk away from a contract if a large deposit was put down. At the very least, the seller would get more defaulted earnest money if the buyer backed out.

One technique that may help strengthen your position in the future is to state in the contract that an additional deposit will be made on the seller's acceptance of the contract. This shows that you do have additional funds, but the seller needs to accept your offer first. This amount might be substantially more than most earnest money deposits and even could include mortgage down payment monies.

Earnest money is one of those negotiable items that may not mean much, or it may mean everything (as you found out). In most cases, you should put your best foot forward with enough earnest money to be competitive with other offers and make the seller feel secure.

Q. *We lost our offer to a buyer who gave the seller cash as earnest money. We gave a promissory note, thinking that we would convert it to cash when the offer was accepted. Why didn't this approach work?*

A. A promissory note is a promise to pay. The seller's concern might be that if the promissory note was not converted to cash, the seller would have taken the property off the market for the wrong buyer.

Put yourself in the seller's position. If you received two comparable offers, one with cash/check or one with a note to hopefully become cash in the future, which one would you take?

The psychological impact of cash or a check for earnest money cannot be ignored if you want to compete as a financially strong buyer. First impressions are everything, and this is particularly true where earnest money is concerned.

Q. *What is the standard time a seller has to accept or reject a buyer's offer?*

A. There is no standard time frame for accepting or rejecting an offer on the part of either the seller or the buyer. The person making the offer would specify the time under which the offer was to remain open (either by number of days, hours, or exact date). If there were other properties you wished to make offers on and/or the market was very active, a short acceptance period would be in your best interest.

You also should be mindful of the seller's ability to make a decision. For example, if the seller is not available to read the offer for a time, a short acceptance period would not be in either party's best interest.

A little-used negotiating fact is that you can revoke your offer any time up to the time the seller communicates back an acceptance of the offer. This can prove to be great leverage in getting a timely answer from a seller!

"A quarrelsome man has no good neighbors."
—*Ben Franklin*

Q. *If you're in the middle of counteroffers with a seller, does she have the right to sell it to someone else?*

A. Yes. Even though a seller gives a buyer a predetermined amount of time (e.g., 48 hours) to accept her counteroffer, contract law gives her the ability to withdraw the offer anytime prior to receiving word of the buyer's acceptance. This means that until you notify the seller that you accept her offer, she has the right to either back out or accept another buyer's offer.

Any time an offer is changed (no matter what the degree), it creates an entirely new one that the other party doesn't have to accept. (This is a critical point in real estate negotiating that is often overlooked.) No matter whether it's the buyer making an initial offer or the seller countering back with an amended offer, this provision applies. The bottom line is that until the seller receives word that the buyer accepts the offer, she is free to sell the property to another party.

The contract probably carried the phrase "time is of the essence." This means that negotiations and terms of the contract should be completed in a timely fashion. While you might be given 48 hours to make a decision about the terms of a contract, it's imperative that you respond as soon as possible.

Q. *If a seller receives two offers exactly alike on a property, doesn't he have to take the one that came in first? (Ours was made one hour earlier than the one accepted.)*

A. No. It's up to the seller to determine which offer he or she takes. In fact, the seller's agent (or subagent working on his behalf) must inform the seller of offers rumored to be forthcoming. This leaves the seller open to evaluate all offers and choose the best one for the situation.

Why not suggest that your contract be used as a backup to the one accepted? If the first one does not fly, your offer will take first position with the seller and become a binding sale.

Q. *The agent wrote my offer contingent on me being approved for a conventional loan within 14 days. The lender convinced me that an FHA loan would be better. Then the seller called the deal off, saying the contract called for a conventional loan, not an FHA one. Can the seller really do this?*

A. Only a court of law can decide if the seller could do this, but the point may be legally valid enough to nullify the offer because you were to obtain a conventional loan, not an FHA (Federal Housing Administration) loan.

Your agent was correct to make your offer contingent upon obtaining a certain type of financing. In fact, it's not unusual to see a loan-to-value minimum (e.g., 80 percent loan) with a maximum interest rate, plus a maximum loan repayment period stated (20 years), as a contingency. That protects you from taking a loan that's not in your best financial interest just to satisfy the language of the purchase agreement.

The seller might be concerned that an FHA loan might cost him or her more, or the seller could be looking for a way out of the sale.

Here's how to find out. First, have the lender (or your agent) break down all the loan costs for comparison between the two loans. Next, let the seller know you'd be willing to cover any additional loan costs not previously negotiated between the two of you. Last, evaluate any other differences such as closing time periods or anticipated property repairs and be willing to compensate for those.

Present your case to the seller and see what he or she says. If you've offset all of the differences, a reasonable seller would accept your amended offer. If yours doesn't, he or she probably had other motivation (like another offer in the wings).

Rest assured that if the seller is being difficult at this early stage of the transaction, it may not get better as time goes on. There are many ways to get out of a sale. Unfortunately, this seller might have just found one.

Q. *We made an offer contingent on the sale of our old home; but the seller said he wanted the option to keep marketing the property and would notify us if he got a suitable offer. He will do this by inserting a special clause in the purchase agreement. What is this called?*

A. The seller is referring to a "right of first refusal" clause. It temporarily provides the best of both worlds for you and the seller. Your offer is contingent on the sale and closing of your home (but your offer *is* in a first position with the seller and, as soon as you can remove the contingency, you will purchase the property under the terms and conditions agreed on).

Meanwhile, the seller continues to market his property. And, should another acceptable offer come in, he will notify you (usually in writing) and you will have a specified number of days to either (1) remove the contingency and perform the contract or (2) forfeit the sale with your earnest money being refunded.

One word of caution: It may be important for your home sale contingency clause to specify that you not only sell your home, but net a certain amount of proceeds. Then if the amount is insufficient to purchase this house, you would not be forced to close the sale.

Q. *There were three of us wanting to purchase a for-sale-by-owner property. The seller said the first one to give him a $5,000 deposit would get the house and his attorney would draw up the agreement later. Is this normal procedure?*

A. No, verbal agreements are not normal procedure. In fact, the statute of frauds requires that real estate purchase agreements be in writing in order to be enforceable in most states. The cautions of a verbal contract combined with a hefty deposit could spell disaster. It's possible that by the time you got the contract drawn, the seller could have resold the property (legally on paper) to another purchaser.

One way you could protect yourself in a competitive market is to ask your attorney to draft a generic purchase agreement that you could have ready when you do find a property. You could fill in the information pertinent to that property and have the seller sign it on the spot. (You'd want to clear any unusual seller requests with your attorney before agreeing to them in writing.)

"Silence is not always a sign of wisdom,
but babbling is ever a mark of folly."
—*Ben Franklin*

NEGOTIATION—AN ART YOU NEED TO MASTER!

Q. *We thought we'd test the water and offer the seller 15 percent less than the listed price. The seller was furious and almost refused to deal with us. Was this a remote case or are most sellers like this?*

A. You best can answer your own question by placing yourself in the seller's shoes. If your home was listed for $100,000, how would you feel if someone offered you $15,000 less? Once the seller is insulted, it can be difficult (if not impossible) to gain acceptance on your future offers. Keep in mind that most residential real estate transactions are first emotional, then financial.

The initial offer sets the stage for future negotiation. There is no rule of thumb that a buyer's offer need be any less than the listed price, particularly if the property is priced at market value. If a buyer is serious about a property, he or she should make the strongest possible initial offer, particularly if asking for other concessions such as financing terms and/or delayed closing.

How can you tell if the listed price is within market range? Ask a real estate agent to prepare an overview of properties in the area that have recently sold, their sales prices and terms, as well as what they listed for. This comparative market analysis (CMA) will help pinpoint if the property is listed too high. Additionally, ask the agent to give you comparisons showing the ratio of sales price to list price to help you decide. Knowing that information, you then can structure a competitive, yet fair offer.

"Those disputing, contradicting, and confuting people are generally unfortunate in their affairs. They get victory sometimes, but they never get good will, which would be of more use to them."
—*Ben Franklin*

Q. *We have made several offers to the seller, but every time we present our offer to the husband, he talks to his wife and ends up changing his mind. Are there any negotiating strategies we can use to get this settled?*

A. Sounds like they're playing good guy/bad guy. Onc of the sellers is the agreeable "good" guy, while the missing seller is the "bad" guy at a distance, requesting more than is offered. This flexibility for them encourages you to make offers, but gives them the power to keep renegotiating until they get what they want.

Tell them that you are serious about purchasing the home, but in the interest of time, will present the next offer only if both of them are present. This should help level the playing field a bit.

Q. *I've heard that it's not a wise negotiating approach to have only one last item to negotiate. Can you explain this?*

A. If there's only one more marble left on the table, someone will win it, the other party will lose. That's why seasoned negotiators always have at least two pending items that need to be settled.

For example, if you're down to the wire on negotiating the price, the seller may not relent unless there's something in it for her to win as well. Even minor items like giving back personal property you've already "won" can help offset the difference. If you keep this tactic in mind the next time you're in active negotiations, you'll be surprised at how it evens out the entire win/win process.

Q. *My friend recently hired a real estate agent on an hourly basis to negotiate for him. Why would someone do that?*

A. Negotiations are not only the toughest part of the homebuying process, they're undoubtedly the toughest thing to accomplish on your own. The impact of the third party working on your behalf is powerful and often the only way to put a purchase together—especially if negotiations have dragged on (a fresh face at the bargaining table can bring new perspective to the issues).

A real estate agent working as a negotiator/consultant could be compensated in a variety of ways including hourly, a flat fee, and/or even with a bonus incentive if the contract is negotiated quickly and in your favor. (Depending on the state where the real estate is located, fees may need to be paid directly to the broker employing the agent before being passed on to the agent/consultant you work with.)

Q. *We had seen a for-sale-by-owner property three times. But when we went back to make an offer on it, the sellers had raised the asking price by $4,000. Shouldn't they keep it available to us at the original price?*

A. There's nothing legally wrong with the sellers raising their price. Perhaps they did it knowing that you were going to make an offer. Perhaps they were trying to pad negotiations so they could win by coming down to the original price. Or perhaps they had a market analysis completed on the property, showing that it was priced too low.

Nevertheless, there's nothing that says you have to offer them their new price. You could offer them what you were preparing to offer before the price change. Ammunition such as the loan size you're prequalified for, the amount of the down payment you have, or just that you're sticking by the original price quoted could suffice. If the sellers want to sell, they'll either be reasonable or they won't. In fact, this would be the case with or without the price increase.

Q. *The real estate agents representing the seller and me are having trouble convincing the seller to budge off his list price of $95,000* *down to my offered price of $92,000. But won't a lower sales price save him something in costs?*

A. You are correct. Let's say that the seller has agreed to pay $8,852 in costs based on paying the real estate commission, one discount point, title insurance, and other miscellaneous closing costs. Your offer of $92,000 won't be a true $3,000 reduction.

Here's why. Because the sales price is lower, all costs based on the price will be lower. The commission will drop by $210, the discount point will be less because your loan amount is less, and other costs calculated using the sales price (like title insurance) will be cut, too.

What appeared to be a flat $3,000 discount off the listed price was only $2,662 after the costs were reduced. So in essence your offer is $93,338. By having your agent pencil out the costs particular to this seller, plus emphasize that their equity would be free to work for them in other ways, it might help convince the seller to take less.

Q. *Does offering personal property in a sale always help attract a buyer?*

A. While personal property can help sweeten a purchase, it can just as often cause financial headaches for sellers, especially if buyers are seeking a new loan.

With new financing, an appraisal is ordered. Because most loans are sold to the secondary market, FNMA and FHLMC guidelines are used to evaluate the appraisal. A portion of those guidelines speak to abnormal concessions in the sale, including personal property listed on the purchase agreement (particularly if it has substantial value). This means that the appraiser may lower the appraisal amount to subtract for the value of the personal property.

Adjustments for personal property are based on the fact that the lender is making the loan tied solely to the value of the real estate. If this were not true, personal property could vanish or lose value after the sale closed, leaving the lender with weakened security in the loan.

There are several ways to financially handle personal property in the purchase. First, the seller is allowed to contribute up to 3 percent to the buyer on 90 percent loan-to-value ratio loans, and up to 6 percent if the loan-to-value ratio is 80 percent or less. You could decide to sell the personal property on your own and assist the buyer by paying additional closing costs instead.

Second, on sales where the buyer will be applying for a conventional loan, you could negotiate the sale of the personal property on a side agreement with the buyer. This should not affect the appraised value of the property, and would save you from having to move the personal property.

It is not wise to use a separate agreement to sell personal property if the sale is being financed with VA or FHA financing. This is considered a side agreement and is illegal in government insured and guaranteed loan programs.

Regarding the personal property as a negotiating tool, you may have good luck including it in a full price offer. Tell the buyers up front that you would consider parting with the personal property if a full-price offer were received. This will allow you to evaluate the merits of the entire offer and use the personal property as extra leverage for negotiating.

Q. *We were negotiating offers and counteroffers with the seller but hit a roadblock when the appliances came up. Now he won't return our phone calls. What can we do?*

A. If you really want the house then you need to decide what lengths you're willing to go to get it. I would suggest two avenues. First, call back (even if you have to leave the message on an answering machine) and let him know that the offer you last made gave him "X amount of time" to accept or reject your offer. (This time frame should have been stated on the face of the offer.) That's why you'd like a response as soon as practicable. (Technically, you can revoke the offer any time up to the point that he communicates back to you that he's accepted it—but I sure wouldn't use this "ace" if you think he's upset!)

Second, decide if you want to change your mind about any or all of the appliances you were negotiating. If you won too much in the last round (or the round before), his pride may be hurt and that's why he's stalling. This is a prime reason why it's dangerous to have one last issue to negotiate—someone wins, someone loses. Find something he can win with—either part of the personal property or another entirely new point (like you agreeing to pay for the title insurance).

Neither you nor the seller should be set on winning all the marbles—or the appliances! Find a happy medium where you get what you really want (the house) and the seller can save face by winning on a few of the last issues.

Q. *I had no idea how many buyer closing costs were negotiable! I asked the seller to pay for most of them and he agreed. Why don't people know more about this?*

A. Perhaps sellers are keeping it a secret! Seriously, besides the ability to ask for what the buyer wants, two additional roadblocks keep most buyers from negotiating closing costs—the brick wall of traditional real estate practices and the impact of preprinted agreement forms used to write up the purchase.

Depending on where you live in the United States, buyers traditionally pay certain costs and sellers pay others. For example, in some states, sellers typically pick up the cost for the standard title insurance. That's not based on law, it's based on practice over years and is now seen as normal for that geographic area. In other states, title insurance could be deemed as a normal closing cost for buyers to pay.

Also, a preprinted purchase agreement form may emphasize the traditions of an area by spelling out which party pays for which cost. What buyers and sellers forget is that most everything in real estate is negotiable—even the wording on preprinted forms! To change who pays for what, merely mark out the wording, replace it with new, have both parties initial it and it's complete!

Q. *Our purchase agreement said that "the seller will pay for all repairs noted during the home inspection"; and it appears that the house needs $2,000 worth of roof repairs that were caused by a severe storm. The seller wants to renegotiate with us, saying we'll be the ones to benefit from the repaired roof. Is this common?*

A. It's rare to see a purchase agreement that would not specify a maximum amount for repairs. This amount could be a percentage of the total repairs or a flat amount. But if you were the seller, why would you agree to repair a home not knowing what it would cost? Doesn't sound like the seller's agent employed the best counsel or the most favorable purchase agreement where his client was concerned!

Look through your agreement for the home inspection clause. If there is no ceiling on the amount of repairs and the clause states that the seller will pay for all repairs, then there is no legal need for you to renegotiate with the seller.

If you do feel a twinge of guilt and want to chip in, wait until you get close to closing. If the seller knows that you'll contribute, who knows what other costs and issues he'd find for you to help him out with!

One last point: Try to find out if the seller was reimbursed by his insurance company for the damaged roof and/or any other storm loss. This could be why he's willing to pay in full for repairs that need to be made.

Q. *We are several weeks away from closing our home purchase and the seller continues to lie about how much she owes for mortgage payments and improvements recently made to the house. The latest is that we may need to help pay some of these costs if we want the house. How can we work through this?*

A. Before you decide to pick up more closing costs, you first need to separate yourself emotionally from your feelings about the house and look at the true costs involved in purchasing this property. Given the scenario, the seller may need more than just payment of closing costs to bail her out.

Because you are obtaining new financing, it's up to the seller to pay off the outstanding mortgages. If she can't, she technically can't sell under the terms of the agreement and your earnest money should be refunded. Also, your lender will not grant the new loan unless it will become a new first mortgage. Until those old loans are paid in full, that can't happen.

The purchase agreement states which costs you are to pay and which costs the seller will pay. You are under no obligation to renegotiate at this late date.

There's one more thing to be concerned about. Given the situation, the materials and labor used for improving the house may not have been paid for. If undetected, this could cause mechanics' liens to attach to the property even after closing.

There are several things you can do right now. First, whoever is doing the closing can tell you how short the seller's equity will be to pay off the debts. You should consider this a conservative guess because amounts tend to increase the longer you wait until closing. This information can help you decide if paying additional monies is worth it.

If the sale does go to closing, make sure that the title company knows about the remodel on the property. Extended title insurance may be available to help cover additional risk and ensure that those bills have been paid.

Last, if your purchase agreement provides for an inspection, be sure to do it. This can help you uncover any other "surprises" before you close and own them yourself!

> "Many a man's own tongue gives evidence against his understanding."
> —*Ben Franklin*

Q. *When the purchase agreement was drawn up, we failed to address who would pay several hundred dollars worth of closing costs. How can we negotiate these at this late date?*

A. Unless you want to pick up the total tab, you have no choice but to negotiate with the seller. Before you do, grab a copy of the purchase agreement to double-check if any of the costs in question could fit into any of the miscellaneous categories covered. That could attribute a cost to one or both parties.

Another fair way to approach allocation of expenses is to determine whom they benefit. For example, if the costs help the seller transfer title, the seller might be convinced to pay them. But if the costs are related to your ability to obtain financing, you may have little (if no) negotiating room because the purchase agreement has been agreed to.

You could ask the seller to split the total with you. Another strategy is to determine what half would be, and then you contribute a bit more than half. For example, if $150 each would cover the costs, it would show good faith for you to go the extra mile and pay $200.

Depending on the type of loan you're obtaining, the seller may be restricted from paying some closing costs. For example, FHA loans may prohibit the seller from paying some closing costs, and there are some closing costs the buyer is prohibited from paying as well.

It's best to clear this up immediately so that it won't get in the way of the actual closing—where, if you really want this house, your bargaining power is likely to dissolve.

Q. *The seller of the home we're buying refuses to let us make improvements to the house until our loan is approved. If we're actually making the house better, why should she have a problem with this?*

A. What you're considering is not only dangerous for the seller, but dangerous for you as well. Until your loan is firmly approved and closed, many things can come up to shift the tide.

Let's paint a worst-case scenario. You make the improvements but can't get the loan. Will she agree to reimburse you for the money you've spent? What about your time in making the repairs? Will that be compensated, too? You may improve someone else's property for nothing if the details aren't spelled out in full.

Even though the property would be improved, the seller has much to lose as well. If the sale fails after the changes are made, the seller may not like what you've done. If the improvements aren't paid in full, mechanics' liens could attach to the property. This would mean that the seller would have to pay those bills in order to get clear title to the property. The property might appear to be improved, but the changes could add more headaches than benefits if the sale doesn't go through.

The seller would be wise to consult her attorney before allowing what you suggest. If you're allowed to proceed with the work after loan approval (and before loan closing), there will need to be a lengthy agreement as to the quantity and quality of the improvements as well as control of the payment for them.

With so many variables, both you and the seller should proceed with caution. Until loan closing occurs, there are no guarantees that the house will be yours.

Q. *We were leisurely structuring an offer to present to the seller when another buyer jumped ahead of us and got the house. What market tricks can we learn so this doesn't happen next time?*

A. Your unfortunate experience takes the homebuyer term "buyer beware" and expands it to include "buyer beware of other buyers!"

There are several reasons why buyers appear more competitive today. First, a shortage of hot properties during peak buying times can create a buying frenzy. Everyone wants a home in a great school district, a low-crime neighborhood, and/or one that requires very little fixing up. In fact, a majority of buyers today want turnkey ownership where all they have to do is bring their toothbrush and move in!

If there's a shortage of desirable properties, competition between buyers heats up. Buyers become more willing to pay a premium to get what they want. That could translate into not only a full-price offer, but one that exceeds the seller's listed price (especially in a bidding war situation between prospective buyers).

Second, in purchasing real estate, timing is everything. In previous markets you might have had the luxury of viewing a home several times, or even taking your relatives to see it before you actually made an offer. But in today's market (especially if the home is a "hot" property or one-of-a-kind home), if you snooze, you stand to lose!

Third, today's real estate market rewards buyers who are financially prepared to speed through the homebuying process. Being financially preapproved has leveled the playing field for a majority of buyers. If all of the buyers making offers on a property are equally financially qualified, the best offer (as interpreted by the seller), gets the property. This requires making your strongest offer first.

Remember the three steps you can take to strengthen your position with the seller:

1. *Be financially preapproved.* Visit the lender before viewing property. Some lenders give you a certificate you can show to sellers and/or attach a copy to any purchase agreement you make.
2. *Be honest with the seller about your interest in purchasing the property.* This doesn't mean that you can't negotiate a fair purchase and terms; but your honest feelings may help cinch the purchase. Sellers often choose between buyers of equal strength and similar offers based on the level of personal interest the buyer shows in the property.
3. *Make sure you fully communicate the desired outcome to your real estate agent.* If he or she is a buyer's agent negotiating on your behalf, outline to the agent just how much you want this house and what you're willing to do to get it. As a trained professional, your agent then will evaluate the best tack to take in price, terms, and negotiating tactics to help you realize that goal.

TITLE INSURANCE AND ITS ROLE IN THE PURCHASE

Q. *We are paying cash for a home where the seller has agreed to make repairs prior to closing and we want to safeguard against problems cropping up after we move in. What can we do?*

A. There are several steps you can take, but they must be in place before closing. First, have the seller agree that funds should be held back at closing until all final inspections can be made. Typically, one-and-one-half times to two times the highest estimate of the repairs is a reasonable amount. (Don't forget to have the purchase agreement amended or an addendum added to spell out exactly what you decide, including the quality of the finished product and what will happen if the funds are short to pay the expense.)

Second, make sure that all contractors and material suppliers are paid. This can be handled by the closing attorney, but make sure that he or she knows well before closing that it may be a concern.

You don't mention title insurance, but this is very important especially because new construction has occurred on the property. The title officer can counsel you about types of extended policies that might suit your needs.

THE PROPERTY WALK-THROUGH

Q. *I was planning to close the purchase of my home via the mail until the agent called to ask how I wanted to handle the property walk-through. Is this important?*

A. The property walk-through prior to closing a sale can be an important part of the homebuying process. It helps give you peace of mind that the property you are purchasing is in the same condition with the same amenities it had when you first viewed it.

Here are some of the things you can check. First, are the mechanics of the home in order? This includes checking the plumbing for leaks and the electrical system for operation, as well as the heating and cooling systems. Be sure to turn on the heat in the summer, and the air-conditioning in the winter.

Next, are the flooring, paint, cabinets, doors, and windows in approximately the same shape as you remember? Move area rugs to view all portions of the floor, as well as any large pieces of furniture that may obstruct your view.

Last, take a copy of your purchase agreement with you to verify which fixtures (items attached to the property) as well as any personal property you negotiated will stay with the home. If there are any items that require a transfer of title, make sure that happens at closing.

If you choose not to be present for the walk-through, you could give your power of attorney to someone to view the property for you. This might be any attorney you are working with or perhaps a real estate agent (if one chooses to take on the responsibility and the liability on your behalf).

ROADBLOCKS TO CLOSING THE SALE

Q. *It's taken forever for the sale of our property to close and now the lender is requesting that a second appraisal be completed before closing. Why is this?*

A. I only can guess that it's been six months or more since the original appraisal. In today's market where values are fluctuating, it's in the lender's best interest (as well as the borrower's) to make sure that there is adequate collateral in the property before making the loan.

The appraisal request also could be made by the private mortgage insurance (PMI) company. They insure the lender against the borrower's default, usually on the top 20 percent of the loan. If the first appraisal is old, or if the PMI company has questions about the value of the property or its neighborhood, a second appraisal could be required.

Q. *Two weeks from closing, the seller notifies us that his assumable loan requires $7,000 more to assume it than we thought—and than we have. What options do we have? We really want the house.*

A. Here are four suggestions:

1. You could ask the seller to carry back a second mortgage for the $7,000 difference, especially as he made the error in the assumption amount. Perhaps you could make minimal payments with a balloon payment sometime in the future.
2. Perhaps some of the closing costs could be renegotiated so that the seller pays more. These could include assumption fees or

closing fees. This could slightly reduce the amount of cash you would need to bring to closing, but won't be enough to solve the entire problem.

3. If your offer was written conditioned on "assuming an existing loan of approximately $______," you might ask the seller to come down a bit on the sales price. Your attorney could tell you whether you'd still be obligated to buy if the loan amount was radically lower than what the seller represented.
4. Perhaps you could use a combination of these alternatives. For example, if the seller would lower the price to meet half of the $7,000 difference ($3,500) and then carry the remaining $3,500 on a second mortgage, you could bridge the gap and the sale could close.

Q. *I am $400 short to cover my closing costs and there's no more room to negotiate with the seller. How can I find more cash in the next two weeks to close on the 15th?*

A. You may be able to shave dollars off the money you need by closing the loan at the end of the month instead of in the middle. Interest is paid in arrears on a mortgage, so the lender must charge you the interest at closing to cover the days between your closing date and the end of the month. For example, if you're closing on August 15, you'd be charged interest from that date through August 31. Then you'd skip a payment in September (because you'll pay interest in arrears on your loan) and your first official payment will be due on October 1.

This means that you'll pay less prepaid interest by closing late in the month—(that's why most loans close then!). And because most lenders use 15 days' worth of interest when estimating your closing costs at the time of loan application, you may not need as much for closing costs as your good faith estimate shows.

Before you panic, contact the lender (and the seller) to see if there's any harm in changing the closing date. Then get an exact (or pretty close to it) figure of what you'll need to bring in for closing. Make sure the seller agrees in writing to the extension.

Don't forget that any earnest money you paid also will be a credit on your closing statement.

Q. *The sellers are going to stay in the house after closing. What issues do we need to address, especially of a financial nature?*

A. You are thinking ahead to realize that you're dealing with more than just a loan payment. In fact, in several parts of the country, occupancy doesn't occur until 30 days after closing. There are several major issues you'll need to address.

First, make sure everything is spelled out in writing. You can do this as an addendum to the purchase agreement and call it "Occupancy after Close of Sale." If a real estate agent was involved in the sale, he or she can help draft this. If not, it's best to have an attorney do it—this is no time to scrimp on legal services.

The agreement should include the date when you will occupy and when and how utility obligations will be prorated, paid, and transferred. You also need to address how the mortgage payment will be made. It's probably best that you control it, collecting rent monies from the sellers and making the payment yourself. Adding a stiff daily penalty if the rent is late is incentive for the seller to pay on time.

Remember that even though the property is currently owned by the sellers, they will be tenants after closing. It may be in your best interest to request a security/damage deposit, refundable when they move out and a house inspection reveals no damages. The rationale is that the sellers would be expected to pay this for any other rental they found.

Additionally, address who will provide casualty insurance on the property and in what amount? Make sure that the lenders are shown as the loss-payees for the proper time periods.

Be sure to do a walk-through inspection prior to closing the loan. This is to verify that the property is as you remember it, but also for the sellers to log any items of wear and tear that might later be held against them as excess damage as tenants.

The most dangerous part of delayed occupancy is what to do if the seller's home is not completed by your occupancy date. How will you get them out? An attorney can provide contract provisions in the agreement, calling for stiff financial penalties (e.g., double rent paid daily plus payment of all attorney's fees) that could act as motivation to the seller.

Protect yourself financially and up front in the contract and things should turn out okay.

DANGEROUS DOLLARS AND PERILOUS PENNIES ISSUES

Where The Frugal HomeOwner Law of Negotiating the Purchase is concerned, you'll cut a wide swath into Dangerous Dollars by leaving money on the negotiating table. Position to win big when you:

- Decide what it is that you want to win, what you're willing to give up, and structure your negotiations accordingly.
- Never have "one last issue" to negotiate because someone will win, someone will lose—and you don't want to be the latter!

Those Perilous Pennies can grow into Dangerous Dollars when negotiating. Avoid this by:

- Being a good negotiator. You stand to win thousands just as easily as you can a hundred. Go for the gold!
- Sacrificing the small stuff (appliances, small closing costs, etc.) to get what you really want. These are often emotionally-based items that become more trouble than they're worth over time. Use them as leverage, but back off fighting for them when you see that although they can help you win a temporary battle, they may end up costing you the war! In other words, don't sweat the small stuff.

THE ECONOMIZING OWNER'S CREED

To Refinance, Repair, or Prepay— Financial Management's the Way!

• • • • •

"The art of getting riches consists very much in thrift.
All men are not equally qualified for getting money, but it
is in the power of every one alike to practice this virtue.
. . . Trivial loss, nor trivial gain despise;
Molehills, if often heap'd to mountains arise;
Weigh every small expense, and nothing waste,
Farthings long sav'd, amount to pounds at last."

—*Benjamin Franklin,* Poor Richard's Almanac, *1749*

I don't care what Ben proclaimed—it's downright tough managing all those issues like whether it will pay to remodel the outdated kitchen or how low you should let interest rates drop before you refinance—tough decisions for sure.

But Economizing Owners have the answers, or at least know where to find them! They spend time weighing the pros and cons of whether to improve or move, use only the best materials and craftspeople when they make home repairs, and know when it does and doesn't pay to prepay a mortgage. They spend the extra effort it takes to understand home financial management because they know the end result—maximizing their equity nest egg to its full potential. Flexibility like that comes in handy when funding a child's college education, adding on a family room—or knowing there's extra financial padding to fall back on should Social Security come up short at retirement.

Economizing Owners develop peace of mind through hard work and diligent equity management. Dig in to learn the tough lessons so you can subsequently reap the rewards. See how large that molehill can grow!

CHAPTER 7

The Frugal HomeOwner Law of Cost-Effective Home Management

Focus on Your Objectives

Congratulations, Bargain Buyer! You've used your financial savvy to purchase a home that will be an intricate part of your financial future. But that doesn't mean that you should put down your pencil just yet. In fact, you'll need a mountain of checks, a financial calculator, and the patience of Job to financially manage your home potentially for decades! But because financial management is one of the most abused home ownership areas, directing it well is vital to affordability and profit.

The National Association of REALTORS® estimates that today homeowners move every 11.7 years on the average. This is up from the average 7.5 years from several years past. It means that owners are moving less often, are happy staying put (for the most part), and will spend more time concentrating on managing their investment rather than recycling their equity.

That's why you've graduated to the next phase of home ownership—being an Economizing Owner. You'll tackle Perilous Pennies issues like monitoring your utility bills and weatherizing your home when appropriate, retiring private mortgage insurance (PMI) from your loan, and being sure that you are not paying excessive property taxes based on the assessed value of your property.

Dangerous Dollars issues you'll need to master include keeping abreast of federal tax changes as they impact home ownership, knowing when it would pay to remodel your home, and foreclosure alternatives should you fall dangerously behind on your mortgage payments.

And once you reach the lofty pinnacle of Economizing Owner status, what then? You guessed it—psychological and financial rewards for keeping ahead of the game and ahead of the tax collector, and for carefully socking away those leftover pennies for a rainy day. Economizing Owners—start your calculators!

PROBLEMS AFTER CLOSING

Q. *When the sellers told us, "We don't use the outside faucet much, it leaks," they really meant that it flooded the basement—and it did, costing us nearly $2,000 in damage! Should we sue?*

A. It's doubtful that you could get to first base in a court of law because the sellers did alert you to the leaky faucet. It was up to you to pick up on that cue and investigate further (although I didn't either when I purchased a rental house, only to find the tenants standing in three feet of water).

A majority of states now have property disclosure laws that require sellers to provide you with data regarding property condition (to the best of the seller's knowledge). But it's your duty to uncover how defects might affect the value and desirability of the property.

Many purchase agreements state that if the buyer waives the right to a property inspection, he or she assumes the property "as is" and the seller has no further liability as to repairs.

Chalk this experience up to the value of reading between the lines, asking questions, and making a property inspector part of your team next time you buy.

Q. *I closed on a home last week only to find that the new Kenmore refrigerator included on the purchase agreement had been replaced with one on its last legs. Can they do this?*

A. It appears not only that they can, they did! The best way to dissuade sellers from taking advantage of buyers is to specify the brand, model, and serial number of all appliances included. Sellers won't usually be so bold as to remove something that has been carefully identified on the agreement.

You could locate the sellers and ask them to make restitution, such as paying you the difference between the value of the refrigerator they took and the one they left. (Good luck!) You could threaten to take action to make them perform under the contract. Your position may be weak because they could say that the refrigerator was not identified clearly enough, and they misunderstood.

The bottom line is that you may end up spending more time and money to set things right than the refrigerator is worth. This is a lesson learned, and keep it in mind next time you buy.

Q. *The seller repaired the roof before closing (as agreed), but our agent said the closing agent forgot to take the costs ($2,500) out of the seller's proceeds. What do we do?*

A. Take a copy of the purchase agreement (where it states that the seller would pay for the repairs) and make a personal visit to the closing agent. If the agreement states that the seller would pay for the repair, the closing agent should have picked it up as a debit to the seller at closing.

The closing agent will attempt to rectify the problem. He or she will probably first attempt to have the seller write a check to the closing agent to forward to the roofing company. If that proves futile, it's possible that the closing agent's company will cover the expense because it was an omission on their part. Most closing agents do an excellent job of being thorough, but they are human and errors can occur.

Delaying action here could cause a mechanic's lien to be placed on the property by the roofing company. That is their right if not paid for material or services that improve the real estate.

Copy the agent and the seller on any written communication you have with the closing agent. He or she was working to carry out the agreement between seller and buyer. If an oversight was made, the errors and omissions insurance carried by the company may cover the loss.

Q. *After moving in, we found that our house (purported by our buyer's agent to have 2,400 square feet) only had 2,150 square feet. It seems the agent took this information off someone else's old listing and didn't measure the house himself! We figure we may have paid more than $20,000 too much at today's prices. What should we do?*

A. Sounds like the agent fell short on the job. Cases like yours can get very complicated because there are several issues you'd need to prove in a court of law, including that you've been financially damaged by the missing square footage. This can be tough to prove because you did fall in love with the house and might have paid the same price for it all over again even knowing the true square footage.

But there is one issue that could be easier to prove—the fact that the agent did not exercise what's called *due diligence* in representing your interests. In other words, that he was derelict in his duties.

As a buyer's agent, the agent was bound by law to uncover and check facts, negotiate on your behalf, and take care to paint a thorough picture of the property to you. Taking someone else's word for the amount of square footage could be seen as a violation of these duties and penalties under state licensing law, including the loss of the agent's real estate license, could apply.

Running the facts by a local real estate attorney couldn't hurt. He or she can give you information about what you'd need to show to prove financial damage, what you could stand to win, and what it could end up costing you if you don't set the record straight.

In addition, if the agent is a member of the National Association of REALTORS®, you could file a formal grievance against the agent through the local Board of REALTORS®. This brings the matter to a panel of the agent's peers who often are more critical than any court of law. The address of the Board nearest you could be found in both the business pages as well as the yellow pages of the phone book.

MANAGING YOUR MORTGAGE LOAN

Q. *I just received a check from my loan servicer for $435 for "overpayment in escrow account." What's going on? I've never gotten money back before.*

A. Under the federal law called RESPA (Real Estate Settlement and Procedures Act) impound accounts are limited to no more than is necessary to pay the annual taxes and homeowners insurance plus one sixth of the anticipated annual charges as a cushion.

While this law has been in effect for many years, it was the focus of several HUD (Housing and Urban Development) surveys in 1994 and 1995. These surveys found that between 10 and 18 percent of escrow accounts were overfunded. In addition, it was found that lenders were calculating the two months' cushion on each separate impound account (such as one for insurance and another for taxes) rather than on the combination of accounts in the borrower's name.

Lenders use a rule of thumb to calculate impounds: At least once a year, the balance should fall to a level no greater than the two-month cushion immediately after payment of the charges. The check you received was part of this overage, which is sent to you on an annual basis.

One final note of interest. By law, lenders are not required to have reserve accounts for loans. It's totally up to the individual lender. You might keep this in mind as leverage the next time you apply for a mortgage.

Q. *Is there a law requiring the lender to respond to the letter and cancelled checks we want to send to prove we've made payments? Is there a procedure to use?*

A. Section 6 of RESPA gives you certain consumer rights regarding mortgage payment procedures. If you send a qualified written request to your loan servicer concerning your loan, the servicer must provide you with a written acknowledgment within 20 business days of receipt of your request. A business day is any day, excluding public holidays (state or federal), Saturday, and Sunday.

A qualified written request is written correspondence, other than notice on payment coupon or other payment medium supplied by the servicer, that includes your name and account number and your reasons for the request. Not later than 60 business days after receiving your request, the servicer must make any appropriate corrections to your account, or must provide you with a written clarification regarding the dispute. During the 60-day period, your servicer may not provide information to a consumer credit reporting agency concerning any overdue payment during that period.

Send your request by certified mail (return receipt requested). In the letter, note your account number, the names of the those on the mortgage, and your current address. Send copies of canceled checks (both front and back) to verify the payment dates. Also ask for suggestions as to how you can avoid the situation in the future.

Q. *Our mortgage has just been sold to a new investor. We've heard so many horror stories about this and wonder if there are guidelines that lenders have to follow?*

A. Guidelines do exist to protect you when your mortgage is sold to a new investor. Just because the maintenance or servicing of your loan has changed hands, there should be nothing that adversely affects you or your mortgage.

By law, the original lender should send you a "goodbye" letter at least 15 days before the date your next payment is due. The letter should state who your new servicing company will be, where it is located, the name and phone number of a contact person or department, and where you should send your next payment. You also should receive a welcome letter from the new servicer outlining the same information.

It is very important that you receive both letters and that they are on the company's letterhead. If you receive only a letter from the new servicer, be sure to call your original lender to verify that your loan actually has been transferred. Several fraudulent operations have recently attempted to intercept mortgage checks by claiming to be the new servicing company.

If your payment is made through automatic checking withdrawal or electronic transfers each month, you will need to cancel your present arrangement and fill out new forms. As this records change often takes time, you may need to send a check directly to the new company before the first withdrawal is received by the new servicer. Your welcome letter can help you determine this.

A free booklet entitled "When Your Loan Is Transferred to Another Lender" is available from the Mortgage Bankers Association of America. You can request it by writing to 1125 Fifteenth St., NW, Washington, DC 20005.

Q. *Our mortgage loan was recently sold to another company, and our payment was late because we didn't know where to send it. Now they're asking us to pay a late fee. Can they do this?*

A. No. Federal law protects the consumer against situations such as yours when lenders sell the servicing rights to loans. If a borrower sends a payment on time, but to the wrong company, late fees will be waived for up to 60 days after the loan transfer. Make a note of your circumstance on the face of the next payment coupon—but take a photocopy of that note before you send it!

Q. *My mortgage was sold to another investor three months ago and I just received a note saying next month I need to increase my* *monthly payment to cover "a potential shortfall in the escrow account for taxes and insurance." Can they do this without warning?*

A. What you are describing is not unusual. When a new loan servicer takes over a loan, they analyze the escrow account to ensure that there are sufficient monies to pay the insurance, taxes, and any other premiums paid through the account (such as mortgage life or disability insurance). If it appears that there will be a future shortfall, most servicers will increase the monthly payment immediately. There is no formal period of notice required.

It's likely that this increase would have happened no matter who owned the loan. However, it is your right to have a written explanation as to what the anticipated changes are and how the servicer reached the conclusion to increase the payment.

If you happen to receive a note stating that your insurance and/or taxes are due, call your new servicer to make sure that company has the documents and funds they need to make these payments. If the transition between servicers is still taking place, they may ask you to assist by sending copies of the due notices you received. Phasing in changes sometimes takes upwards of 60 days between companies.

Q. *We thought that the newly adjusted payment on our adjustable-rate mortgage (ARM) seemed a little high, so we had the lender check it and uncovered several errors in the calculations. How can we make sure it's correct in the future?*

A. You can guarantee accuracy to your adjustable mortgage by doing just what you did this time—double-checking the figures. Audits within the mortgage industry have uncovered that a high percentage of ARMs do contain innocent adjustment errors—many in favor of the borrower. There's a great online resource at www.hsh.com to assist you in determing if your ARM adjustments are correct.

Each loan has its own set of variables including which index the loan is tied to, the date the loan is to be recalculated, and how the interest rate is to be rounded off (whether to the next ⅛ or ¼ percent). This information is found in the loan documents signed by the borrower at closing.

For example, if most of your lender's loans are using the one-year Treasury bill index (at 5 percent on the day of calculation), it may be overlooked that your loan is tied to the 11th District Cost of Funds (which was only 4.5 percent). After adding the loan's 2.5 percent margin (the lender's costs of doing business and profit) to the index, a one-half percent interest rate error has occurred. This $42.45 per month payment difference adds up to more than $500 annually!

Warning signs that indicate you may need a review of your ARM include loans with frequent adjustment periods using complicated formulas, loans written prior to 1986 when guidelines were very loose, or any loan that has recently been sold to another investor.

Here are the steps to take if you feel your payment is incorrect. First, contact your lender in writing (a letter sent registered mail, return receipt requested is advisable). There should be both an address and a phone number on the adjustment letter you received. If a person's name is included, use that as well.

Let the lender know what part of the loan adjustments seem off and where your loan adjusted in the past. For example, if you know that your loan uses the Cost of Funds index and that the adjustment date is January 1, list that information. Ask to have the loan recalculated and request that a copy of that calculation be sent to you. Request that all supporting information and figures be included. Lenders are required to respond to your request in 30 days or less on this type of inquiry.

Last, ask for the name of a company representative you can talk to if you have additional questions. Depending on how clear the information is when you receive it, this may be necessary.

"In this world nothing can be said to be certain, except death and taxes."
—*Ben Franklin*

PROTESTING YOUR PROPERTY TAXES

Q. *Our property taxes escalated right through the ceiling this year. We're on a fixed income and have no idea how we're going to pay them. Do we have a right to protest them?*

A. Not only do you have a right to protest your property tax bill, if you do you'll join tens of thousands of people across the country in this action! There are three steps to gathering information for your protest:

1. Review your tax bill for (a) the description of the property and (b) the assessed value based on the description. Often the descrip-

tion is in error (such as the size of the lot), which causes the corresponding tax to be wrong as well.

2. Note whether you've made any capital improvements to the property in the past year that could account for the rise in assessed value. Most assessors only review properties every few years, so it's possible that the remodeling or renovating you did previously is just now being taxed. (This is one reason why, when a buyer purchases a home, property taxes usually rise in the next year or two because the assessor now has a sale that often can be used to justify a higher assessed value.)
3. Locate information about how your assessed value and corresponding tax can be protested. (This information will be in detail on your assessment notice or contact the assessor's office for information.) Most counties/municipalities have a detailed procedure you must follow for your protest to be filed and heard. This includes a deadline for filing the protest. (Don't assume that any extension will be available—it won't.)

Make sure you're well armed with information to back up your protest. Make a visit to the county to research properties like yours, what similar homes have sold for, as well as other homes assessed lower than yours. Information is power.

"Beware of little expense; a small leak will sink a big boat."
—*Ben Franklin*

REMOVING PRIVATE MORTGAGE INSURANCE

Q. *How can PMI be removed?*

A. PMI removal is regulated by federal law on mortgages originated on or after July 29, 1999. If a homeowner has a good mortgage repayment record, the property value has not declined, and there is at least 22 percent equity in the property as shown by a fee appraisal, the PMI must be removed. Additionally, the consumer can ask to have the PMI removed if an appraisal can prove that there's at least 20 percent equity in the property (which has been the course of action prior to federal legislation).

The exception to both of these guidelines are properties owned in any state that already legislates the removal of PMI. Those states will have two calendar years from the law's effective date to comply with the new federal law. In addition, community homebuyer and other types of highly leveraged loans (including FHA) will not be affected by this law.

Consumers have long fought the battle to have the removal of PMI federally regulated. Be sure to exercise your right to remove PMI from your loan as soon as you can.

Q. *We thought we had 20 percent equity in our property, so we got an appraisal to prove it to the lender. But now the lender and servicer are saying that they won't accept the appraisal and are requiring that it be redone. Is this fair?*

A. Fair may not enter into it. It may be lender guidelines. Refusing to accept an appraisal might happen for several reasons.

It could be that the lender and servicer have not used the appraiser before and therefore don't have the appraiser approved to do business with them. These requirements can be imposed by not only who made the loan, but who purchased it as an investor.

Second, they might not agree with the value shown on the appraisal. This can occur if there has been recent downturns in value in a market and/or especially in a certain neighborhood.

Contact the servicer directly to inquire why the appraisal was unacceptable. If it's a problem with the appraiser, there may be nothing else to do but allow one of the lender's certified appraisers to redo the appraisal. (Yes, you will be stuck paying the additional cost.)

If the property value is in question, you and the appraiser may need to come up with new comparable properties sold in your area to state a stronger case.

The lesson here is that while it's commendable to work toward removing the PMI on your loan before you reach the 22 percent mandatory removal, make sure you do so playing by the mortgage servicer's rules.

RENTING OUT A PORTION OF YOUR HOME TO GENERATE CASH

Q. *I'm looking for additional cash and thought about renting out a room I have at the back of my house. It's in a separate area of the house and has its own bath and small kitchen. Wouldn't this also be* *good when I go to sell my house next year because it could be listed as income property to attract more buyers?*

A. Be careful. Some people do rent out rooms in their homes, but that does not make it legal or classify your home as a rental property.

Your first concern is zoning regulation. Depending on how your property is zoned, it may be illegal for you to rent out a room in your home. A call to city/county zoning officials can determine how your property is currently zoned, if rezoning is possible/probable, and the steps it would require to do so.

Because the house is configured with a separate bath and kitchen does not mean it's conducive to becoming an income property. Factors like separate entrances and parking availability also enter into the picture.

If you do consider rezoning the property, be sure you explore the downside as well. Down-zoning the property to rental status may actually make your property value slip, especially if it's close to an area of upper-value single-family homes. Your property insurance may increase because you are no longer a single-family residence. And when a buyer goes for financing, single-family loans may not be available, requiring a borrower to use a larger down payment, find less-liberal financing terms, and pay higher interest rates.

Talk with both a real estate agent and an appraiser about any changes you're considering before you take action. Based on your neighborhood, the value of your property, and the market trends, turning your home into a rental property may not be worth the little extra cash flow it could produce.

"Light purse, heavy heart."
—*Ben Franklin*

LATE PAYMENTS AND DELINQUENCIES

Q. *We got one of those second mortgages (up to 125 percent of the property value) but can't make the payments and are two months behind. We're considering selling the house and bringing a check to closing, borrowed from our parents. At least we could take the loss on our income tax. What do you think?*

A. The 125 percent loan you're describing seems to be getting quite a few homeowners in trouble! Lenders are making these loans in the hopes that (1) appreciation will continue to increase the market value of the property; and (2) the homeowner wouldn't need to sell the house until the debt was paid down.

Taking on more debt just to sell the house doesn't make much sense as the IRS won't allow you to take a loss on a personal residence.

Here's a three-step systematic approach to find the best solution for your problem.

1. *Contact the lender on the second loan.* Inform it of the problem and ask if there's anything that can be done. This could include interest-only payments, partial payments, or adding a few payments to the back of the loan. If your cash flow problem is short term, the lender may be willing to work with you. (But act immediately—don't let the situation get any worse before calling.)
2. *Evaluate your housing needs and alternatives.* Ask yourself where you would live if you didn't own this house? Would a rental be less expensive? If you did keep the house, how long would it take before you might accumulate equity or be able to sell without bringing a check to closing? Money from your parents might be better spent making up the payment shortfall instead of bailing you out of the loan. If you could hold on until appreciation generates more equity, you might be able to pay them back from the proceeds of the sale.
3. *Find a way to generate more income (the toughest option).* By solving this problem, you'll not only be able to make your mortgage payments but eliminate some stress as well. A recent Mortgage Bankers' Association survey found that not only were late payments on the rise, but mortgage foreclosures as well. And the primary culprit is too much consumer debt coupled with underemployment.

Hopefully processing through these suggestions can lead you to the best option.

Q. *I had to move for my job. I can't sell my old house for what I owe against it, and the rent I could get wouldn't cover my mortgage.*

I'm considering giving the property back to the lender. Would this go against my credit?

A. Don't do this in haste. What you're talking about is a deed in lieu of foreclosure (also called a friendly foreclosure) and is not to be taken lightly. It means that you release your interest back to the lender instead of going through a formal foreclosure action. Not only can the lender object to taking the property back, doing so might have a similar impact credit-wise to a full foreclosure, remaining on your credit report for seven years. This would hinder another purchase of real estate as well as obtaining additional credit, rental approval, and possibly other employment you might seek.

The first step is to contact the lender to see if something can be worked out. Lenders do not want the cost of foreclosing if there are other remedies available because it costs them approximately 15 to 20 percent of the loan's remaining balance to do so. They might suggest decreased payments for a time (e.g., interest only), or help you identify ways to structure your finances to make things work.

If the property has a conventional loan with PMI to protect the lender, perhaps the PMI company will help you subsidize the payment until you can sell, or agree to cover any sales loss to the lender if you do sell.

Consider selling the property using a lease purchase. This would allow the buyer to occupy the home and make the payment, and close the purchase at a predetermined date in the future. The occupant you find should be qualified to buy, but merely needs time to close. He or she might be receiving proceeds from another home sale, waiting for two years of employment history, or other some other logical delay.

Although it's not high on your priority list, it may be necessary to pay the difference monthly between what the property rents for and your mortgage until you can sell. This is one reality of owning real estate that no one likes, but sometimes it is the best alternative.

Q. *Our equity line of credit payments are behind and we were going to use our income tax refund to catch up. Now the lender has attached our bank account, but we need that money to pay our first mortgage. Can the lender do that?*

A. Depending on the documents you signed at loan closing, yes. Many equity lines of credit do permit the lender to attach any other account or asset within their lending institution if payments fall behind. This is to prevent the owner from having assets available while failing to make payments to the lender.

You should inform the lender immediately of your intent to catch up the payments. If the money isn't available now, perhaps you could secure a loan against your tax refund (or pledge it as collateral).

Don't forget that just because the equity line is not your first or primary mortgage, it does not mean that its terms and repayment conditions are to be taken lightly. The equity line lender also has the right to call the loan in default and foreclose for nonpayment.

Q. *Our high-rate second mortgage is behind. Even though we're trying to work out repayment terms with the lender, it is calling us constantly, bordering on harassment. What are our rights?*

A. Consumers of all products and services are protected against creditor harassment under the Fair Debt Collection Act. The Act would apply to all types of situations where credit has been extended.

There are two free booklets I would recommend:

1. The "Fair Debt Collection," published by the Federal Trade Commission, Pennsylvania Ave. and 6th St., NW, Washington, DC 20580 (or gather information online at www.ftc.gov), covers common questions and answers about the law and explains what a debt collector can and cannot do.
2. "Fair Debt Collection Practices Act," published by the Federal Reserve Bank, P.O. Box 66, Philadelphia, PA 19105-0066, outlines violations under the law and describes how and where to report violations.

Until the problem is remedied, it's a good idea to keep a log of your contacts with the lender, noting what was said, in case you do decide to file a complaint.

Q. *We have fallen behind on our mortgage payments because my husband has been out of work. We contacted the lender and were amazed to find that the FHA has several alternatives to foreclosing on the house, including financing our late payments into a new loan.*

How does this work and would it be preferable to foreclosure?

A. Most anything is preferable to foreclosure! The alternatives you're talking about are available through HUD on their FHA loans. They were developed to combat rising foreclosures.

HUD offers five options for handling mortgage delinquencies (including various incentives to lenders ranging from $100 to $1,000). The one you're asking about is called mortgage modification. The lender agrees to add your back payments, interest, and penalties into the loan and amortize it over the loan term. HUD requires that the new payment be lower than the present payment. This is accomplished by lowering the interest rate and/or extending the loan term. While you're paying more over time because your loan balance is higher, the lower payment should make it easier for you to keep current.

The lender may be choosing this option because it believes your husband's employment situation is temporary. But before agreeing to this, you might inquire if the lender would be willing to waive your payments for a time in lieu of rewriting the loan. Used for situations like yours, when a homeowner suffers an involuntary reduction in income or increase in expenses, the lender can postpone payments for up to 18 months to help the owner get back on track.

"Great estates may venture more, but little boats should keep near shore."
—*Ben Franklin*

TACKLING REAL ESTATE TAXATION ISSUES

It's critical that homeowners consult with their own tax advisers regarding how these and other tax issues impact their particular situation.

Q. *Can a buyer get any tax benefit from paying discount points on a home purchase?*

A. Yes. Discount points that you pay to purchase your residence are deductible as interest on your income tax return in the year they are paid. In fact, you can deduct any discount points paid by the seller to help you finance your home as well (but they must be subtracted from the sales/purchase price). The IRS requires this because seller-paid points are seen as an adjustment to the purchase price of the home.

Here's an example. Let's say that the seller agrees to pay two points (a point being equal to 1 percent of the amount financed) for you to obtain an $80,000 mortgage and you agree to pay two points as well. That's $1,600. If your purchase price is $101,600, the seller's true net (with the points the seller paid subtracted out) would equal $100,000. Your net purchase price would be the same at $100,000, but you get to deduct the entire $3,200 in mortgage points—the $1,600 you paid plus the $1,600 the seller paid. The rationale is that the purchase price you paid reflected both sets of points. What a bonus!

A few of the IRS rules that apply include computing the points as a percentage, payment must be part of an established business practice and not excessive, and the points must be paid directly and only for the purchase of a residence. Check with your tax adviser to see if this IRS rule applies to your situation.

Q. *What are the biggest benefits to homesellers with the Taxpayer Relief Act of 1997?*

A. There are several exciting and relieving benefits to homeowners under the act, especially when you sell.

Gone is the over-55 rule allowing you a one-time exclusion of up to $125,000 of profit on your personal residence when you sold it. Now all homesellers, no matter what their ages, can exclude up to $250,000 of gain ($500,000 for a married couple filing a joint return) every time they sell their principal residence. They can take this exclusion if they meet the following criteria:

- They must have owned the home and occupied it for a combined total of two years during the past five-year period (occupancy doesn't have to be for a consecutive term).
- They can file for this tax break only once every two years.

What if you have gains greater than the applicable $250,000/$500,000 when you sell? You could reduce the amount of that gain by deducting any capital expense you've added to the property. For example, the cost of that second bathroom added or that concrete driveway you poured would be deducted from the gain before any tax is figured.

Q. *What if you sell before the two-year time period elapses? Is the tax break lost?*

A. The tax break would still apply if you could prove that your employment changed, forcing the move; you moved for health reasons; or other unforeseen circumstances (which are itemized in the IRS code).

If one of these criteria is met, you would only be able to exclude the fraction of the gain equal to the portion of the two years you did meet these requirements. For example, if I was single, lived in my home one year, and was then relocated with my job, I could potentially exclude up to $125,000 of my gain ($250,000 total exclusion for single person divided by two years time = $125,000 per year exclusion).

Q. *What happens if you previously used the old one-time $125,000, over-55 exclusion? Does the new tax break apply if you sell you current home?*

A. Yes. Those lucky folks who previously took their one-time exclusion when they sold their primary home, now get to benefit by taking the new tax break if they sell again. Now that's frugal and fun!

Q. *What happened to the old rollover rule that required you to reinvest in another residence within a certain time?*

A. The rollover rule is gone. Tax is now forgiven each time you sell (if you meet the guidelines), instead of the tax on the gain merely being deferred as before. There now is no need to roll over the gain.

Q. *What if a seller rented out the principal residence? Would that violate the tax break guidelines?*

A. No, it wouldn't; but you'd still have to meet the owning and occupying guidelines for two of the past five years to claim your exemption.

Q. *If we sell our home at a loss, is that deductible?*

A. No. Just as under the old tax law, you cannot deduct the loss on the sale of one's residence.

Q. *Did the Taxpayer Relief Act of 1997 change the amount of capital gains tax payable on the sale of income property, like rentals?*

A. Yes, it did. For sales closed after May 7, 1997, the top capital gains rate has dropped to 20 percent, and just 10 percent for taxpayers in the lower 15 percent tax bracket. But the holding period for long-term capital gains treatment has been extended to 18 months. Property held from 12 to 18 months will be taxed at 28 percent, and properties held for less than that period will be taxed as ordinary income.

Q. *Now that I can sell my home and don't have to pay tax on up to $250,000 of gain (I'm single), is it necessary to keep home purchase/sale records?*

A. Absolutely! Just because Uncle Sam changed the tax laws in favor of the homeowner doesn't mean that recordkeeping flew out the window! Federal guidelines require that you maintain records showing the purchase price and any improvements to your residence for as long as you own the property, and keep those records for three years after you file the income tax return reporting the home sale.

For example, if you sell your residence in 1998, you will report the sale on the return you file on April 15, 1999. That means that you should retain records until April 15, 2002, showing the original price and any improvements.

You're also forgetting that even with the exemption, you'd still have to pay tax on any gain that exceeds the $250,000 when you sell. However, capital improvements (a new roof, driveway, etc.) that you add to the home can help reduce the amount of gain you'd realize as well as the corresponding tax you'd pay. Without good recordkeeping, these improvements could be tough, if not impossible, to prove.

The great news about favorable tax treatments for homesellers is they are more than worth the time and effort it takes to keep adequate records.

DANGEROUS DOLLARS AND PERILOUS PENNIES ISSUES

Dangerous Dollars come in a variety of forms where The Frugal HomeOwner Law of Cost-Effective Home Management is concerned. The following will help you to cover a majority of these financial leaks:

- Become thoroughly versed in tax law as it applies to home ownership (or as well-versed as any non-IRS mortal can be). That way you'll be able to maximize your tax deductions, receiving full value for Uncle Sam's home ownership rules.

- Understand the ins and outs of your escrow account for property taxes and insurance, your legal rights when dealing with your lender, and what to do should you fall behind in your mortgage payments.

Mismanagement in any or all of these areas could end up costing you the property—far too dear a consequence for not being informed.

You may feel that Perilous Pennies issues revolving around home financial management have only a meager impact. Just think how they can mount up over the years! Don't forget to:

- Remove the private mortgage insurance on your loan as soon as possible. Even though it's only a meager $30 per month, those perilous pennies mount up in a big way over the life of your loan. Remember, it's your federal right!
- Keep good tax records right from the start of home ownership. Heaven only knows when you'll need to piece together information about the points you paid when you refinanced, the cost of that new family room addition, or perhaps for documenting your home ownership records for that pesky IRS audit—the ultimate motivation for sound recordkeeping!

CHAPTER 8

The Frugal HomeOwner Law of Sound Equity Decisions

You've Worked Hard for Your Home—Now Manage It!

The closing gavel has rapped, the keys and the electric garage door opener are slid across the closing table to you—the house is officially yours! You breathe a sigh of relief. It's over.

No, the really big job is just beginning. You must now become an active asset manager of perhaps the largest savings account you'll ever control—your home equity. By definition, equity is the difference between what your house would sell for and the mortgages you have against it (plus the costs of selling the house, of course). Equity requires that you care for it (watch out for that refinancing); maximize it (how much extra equity could you grow by prepaying your loan?); and, if need be, have the courage to let it work for you in important ways like providing the kids' college tuition.

Many of the equity management questions in this chapter reflect how tempting it is to be teased relentlessly by low interest rate equity loans to buy this or do that. But an Economizing Owner knows better than to fall prey to using equity for anything other than the most financially sound investments. She knows how tough it is to replenish it once depleted, and weighs each equity management option with the greatest of care. It's much like nurturing a child. You need to encourage growth, yet be firm enough to control and discipline it when necessary.

Let the questions that follow give you peace of mind that *The Frugal HomeOwner* is your equitable partner in your home's equity management!

"There are three faithful friends, an old wife, an old dog, and ready money."
—*Ben Franklin*

BUILDING EQUITY—HOW TO PICK UP THE PACE

Q. *The next time we buy a house, is there any way we could build equity faster? My husband is transferred often and it's tough for us to build much because we move every couple of years. Any suggestions?*

A. Many upwardly mobile homeowners are in your shoes. But by choosing the mortgage with the shortest term, it's amazing how much faster the equity will add up.

Here's an example. Let's assume we're comparing two $100,000 7 percent loans—one for 30 years and the other for 20. Because you were in your last home two years, we'll use that as the time frame.

You'll pay $665.31 in principal and interest for the 30-year loan, compared to $775.30 for the 20-year loan. That's a monthly difference of $109.99. For many buyers, this is where the shopping ends because it's tougher to qualify for the larger payment and they feel that the higher payment could strap them should they fall on financial hard times.

But it's more than just monthly payments. In two years time, the 20-year loan is paid down to 95.1 percent of its original balance, or to $95,100. But the 30-year loan is reduced to only 97.9 percent of its original balance, or $97,900. That's a difference of $2,800. So the $2,639.76 we thought we were spared with the lower monthly payments, is more than offset with the loss in equity buildup. And as the loans mature, the greater that savings gap becomes. Five years into both loans, the 20-year loan balance will be at $86,300, while the 30-year loan will still be at a whopping $94,100—$7,800 more equity for an 8 percent difference in equity buildup in just five years!

Don't forget that you should be able to capture a lower interest rate from the lender on the shorter-term loan. And if you're interested in taking a 15-year loan, the savings should be even greater.

PREPAYING YOUR MORTGAGE LOAN—THE GOOD AND THE BAD

Q. *I just received some inheritance that would pay off my 7 percent mortgage. How can I evaluate if this is a good financial move to make?*

A. On the surface, paying off a mortgage sounds like the answer to anyone's prayers. But, like any other business decision, it should be done only after evaluating the answers to questions like these:

- Is the payment a financial burden? Have you ever missed a payment or made several payments after the due date? It's wise to eliminate the debt if it's a struggle to pay, could hurt your credit, or you risk losing the property.
- Do you have substantial financial reserves that could carry you through a financial downturn (most financial advisers suggest six months of living expenses)?
- Do you have other high interest rate loans or credit accounts that should be paid off first? It makes little sense to pay off an interest-deductible mortgage when you're paying higher nondeductible interest.

But you may decide not to pay off the loan based on answers to these questions:

- Where could you invest the money that might make better investment sense? Would an investment generate enough return to help offset the current mortgage payment?
- What are the long-term cash needs for the family's future including college tuition and retirement?
- How long do you plan on keeping the property? Retiring a mortgage at 7 percent may not make financial sense if you're going to buy another house and replace the loan with a higher-rate one.

Last, don't forget the peace of mind afforded when a home is free and clear. That may be tough to financially factor in, but shouldn't be discounted.

Q. *We have a new 30-year $100,000 (8 percent) mortgage and have made a commitment to prepay a certain principal amount every month. Is there a system that can help us do this?*

A. There is. People who find a system and stick to it (not just when they have extra funds) are much more likely to reap the benefits. By applying a meager $25 a week extra to your mortgage, you can pay it off a decade early and save more than $62,000 in interest. Now that's frugal!

One system I find effective is to obtain a printout of your mortgage payments (1–360), broken down into principal and interest amounts. (Your lender, real estate professional, local bank, or a site on the World Wide Web, like www.countrywide.com can do this for you.)

Let's use your $100,000 loan with monthly payments of $733.77 as an example. The first number on the amortization printout is the payment number (#1), followed by the interest due for that month ($666.67), the amount applied to principal ($67.10), then the loan balance ($99,932.90). To prepay, merely add the next month's principal payment ($67.55) to your regular payment of $733.77 so that your loan balance is actually $99,865.35! Figure 8.1 has a chart showing payment breakdowns.

FIGURE 8.1 A Systematic Plan for Prepaying Your Mortgage

Loan amortization chart and prepayment schedule for a $100,000 loan with 30-year term at 8 percent interest

Month of Loan	Principal and Interest Payment	Interest Portion of Payment	Principal Portion of Payment	Loan Balance
1 (Jan)	733.77	666.67	67.10	99,932.90
2 (Feb)	733.77	666.22	67.55	99,865.36
3 (Mar)	733.77	665.77	68.00	99,797.36

By merely adding the next month's principal payment to your current month's (principal and interest) payment, you'll not only develop a commitment to prepaying your mortgage, you'll always know the outstanding balance.

Q. *How can I alert the loan servicer to the fact that I'm making a prepayment on my loan? There's no box to check on my payment coupon, and they keep missing them.*

A. You can "invent" a prepayment box on your payment coupon, or make the prepayment on a separate check. (Be sure to mark on both the coupon and your separate check, "prepayment to principal only.") Not only will that be tougher to miss, it will give you a running record of your payments if the servicer does miss it!

Q. *We decided a year ago to make prepayments to our mortgage. When we tallied up the checks at the end of the year, they had waited two months to credit the first ones. We want to sue!*

A. While it's unfortunate that you didn't get immediate credit for prepaying your mortgage, I doubt it's financially worth suing the lender over. What you want is the credit to your principal payment.

To that end, contact the lender via certified mail. Inform them of the incident, and ask to have the loan recalculated based on the date of your checks. By law, the lender must respond to your inquiry in writing within 60 days. In addition, ask the following questions (ideally these questions should be asked when the loan is originated and clarified once again before prepaying):

- When can prepayments be made and what is the suggested way to do this (i.e., separate check or itemization on regular payment coupon)?
- Is there a minimum prepayment amount? (Some loans require that you make a minimum prepayment amount. In fact, they could have been holding your checks until that amount was reached.)
- Will you receive both a receipt back for the prepayment as well as an annual printout showing the principal reduction on your loan? (You may have to make multiple requests and/or pay a small fee for this service, but it would be worth it.)
- Can you have the name of a real person and a phone contact (preferably an 800 number) you can call if the situation either isn't rectified and/or happens again?

Q. *I recently refinanced my 9 percent $85,000 loan into one at 7 percent. Now that my interest rate is lower, will it make sense to prepay the loan like I did before?*

A. Your question brings up the point that there's less savings in prepaying a lower interest rate loan; but even though you'll save less, you'll still save.

Here's an example. Prepayments of $75 per month on your old 9 percent loan would save you more than $60,000 in interest over the life of the loan. But the same monthly prepayment on a 7 percent loan would reduce that savings to less than $40,000.

Does this mean prepaying is less valuable? Not really. What you're saving is not taxable, so your yield is actually greater than 7 percent, somewhere closer to 9 percent. Not a bad yield for such a low risk.

Don't forget that the extra equity you're growing by prepaying can provide added leverage in the future. It can mean a larger down payment when you purchase again or the ability to qualify for a larger home—all silently compounding right now in your equity nest egg!

Q. *We paid off an FHA loan and were shocked that they charged us an extra month's interest just because our final payment was made after the first day of the month. What is this penalty all about?*

A. It is FHA policy that mortgages insured on or after August 2, 1985 can be prepaid by a borrower on the first day of any month without prior notice to the lender. If a lender receives the balance due on a loan on any other day of the month, the lender may either prorate the interest on the loan or may charge interest through the last day of the month. HUD reports that most lenders choose the latter.

No other loan types calculate interest this way—only FHA. But this newer policy is still less restrictive than the payoff guidelines for older FHA loans.

Payoff for FHA loans insured prior to August 2, 1985, can only be done with 30 days notice to the lender. If the payment is not received by the lender on the first day of a month, the lender has the option of either prorating the interest on the loan or charging interest through the last day of the month, according to HUD.

These payoff guidelines have come under much scrutiny from consumers and real estate agents alike. They feel it is unfair for homesellers to be penalized, especially when they may have closed on the last day of the month, but had the loan payoff tied up in disbursing settlement monies. Real estate professional groups are attempting to have this restrictive policy reversed.

Q. *I have an FHA mortgage that I'm considering paying at the end of this year. I read that FHA mortgage insurance premiums might be refundable. Is this true?*

A. There is a lot of confusion about FHA mortgage insurance refunds. This is caused in part because there are actually two different types of refunds, based on how the mortgage insurance premium is paid and when the loan was originated.

The newer type of premium refund applies to loans originated after September 1, 1983. The borrower must have paid an up-front mortgage insurance premium at settlement and did not default on mortgage payments. Upon final payment of the loan, the FHA Commissioner determines how much premium is refunded, based on the number of months the loan was insured. The mortgage company usually initiates the paperwork on the borrower's behalf.

Unfortunately, it sounds as though your loan falls into the second category of FHA mortgage insurance called Distributive Share. The premium refund guidelines changed in 1990 for loans in this category, originated before September 1, 1983. Unless HUD (Department of Housing and Urban Development) processed a loan's FHA insurance termination before November 5, 1990, it's doubtful that there will be any premium refund.

Before you throw up your hands in despair, contact the lender where the loan is held to have it give you an opinion. Based on when the loan was originated and if any up-front premium was paid, a refund could be available.

If you'd prefer to go direct to FHA, you can write to Housing and Urban Development, Attn: Mortgage Insurance Division, 7th and D Sts., SW, Washington, DC 20410-3000 or contact it online at www.hud.gov. Be sure to include your FHA case number (if available), your full name, and when and where the loan was originated.

By the way, don't fall prey to anyone who calls asking to "obtain your refund" for you (for a small fee, of course). This is a scam that does exactly what you can do as an independent citizen.

"Gain may be temporary and uncertain, but ever while you live, expense is constant and certain."
—*Ben Franklin*

REFINANCING YOUR MORTGAGE LOAN

Q. *Refinancing options seem cumbersome and I can't believe that people always make the right decisions. What would you consider to be the biggest mistakes people make when refinancing?*

A. I believe that the two greatest motivating factors in improper refinancing are need and greed. These include setting unrealistic goals and wanting to win all of the marbles, often losing in the process.

Here's an example. A homeowner says, "I'm not going to refinance until fixed rates hit 6 percent with no points." Unless you have an idea that an interest range and costs associated with that rate are in the realm of possibility, don't wait for a miracle to happen. Ask several lenders how probable it is for interest to fall to the interest rate you have in mind (with no costs involved) before you decide to wait.

The second mistake in refinancing is getting too greedy. A homeowner rationalizes, "Once rates start to drop, they are going to continue to drop. I'm going to be smart and hold out to refinance until they hit bottom!" If you have these powers, we'd love to use your crystal ball! Think of refinancing as 50 percent skill and 50 percent sheer luck—it's a gamble. Set a goal of what you want to financially achieve by refinancing. Once rates and points are at that level, lock in your interest rate and go for it. A lender can show you on paper what you stand to gain and can advise you when that's achievable.

Here are some questions to ask yourself:

- How long will I keep the property (hopefully, long enough to recoup your costs of refinancing)?
- What types of situations are anticipated in my personal and economic future (e.g., needing equity in three years to send a child to college, possible expenses for personal health care, or nursing home care for an elderly relative)?
- If I pull cash out, will it be used for a sound reason that will make economic sense (e.g., adding on a second bath in lieu of moving to a more expensive home)?

- Are there any benefits in keeping the existing loan on the property (e.g., easily assumable loan, flexibility with seller financing)?

Ask the lender:

- Would a new loan require additional costs of private mortgage insurance (PMI) or escrow accounts for taxes and insurance that weren't previously required?
- How does the lender's new loan compare to the competition based on interest rate, points, and closing costs? There also are fluff fees (also called garbage fees, these differ from lender to lender). In most cases, if you knew you could negotiate them, they could be dropped!
- If I do want cash out, which is better for my situation: a new refinanced loan or an equity line of credit?
- If my interest rate is lower, how will paying less interest affect my tax picture?

Don't be swayed solely by the attractiveness of the lower interest rate. After all, you're dealing with your potentially largest savings account—your home equity!

Q. *Is there a rule of thumb for deciding when it pays to refinance your mortgage?*

A. As a rule of thumb, it may pay to refinance your mortgage if you can reduce the interest rate *and* will hold the property long enough to recoup the costs of refinancing.

If you want a more exact figure, you can access excellent calculators online to compute your savings (one of my favorites is www.homefair.com). Or you can calculate it the old-fashioned way with this formula: Take the amount of the current monthly mortgage payment and multiply it by the number of months you plan on keeping the property (e.g., 5 years would equal 60 payments). We'll call this answer *A*. (Don't multiply by the number of months left on the loan because this may not represent how long you'll keep the property.)

Next, multiply the new lower mortgage payment times the number of months you'd hold the loan. We'll call this answer *B*. Subtract *B* from *A* to give you answer *C*. *C* represents your savings before the costs of refinancing.

Calculate the actual costs of refinancing. (You may need to call a mortgage lender for exact amounts or access one of the online lender sites for an estimate.) These costs could include any points for originating the new loan, appraisal costs, closing costs, penalties for prepaying the old loan, and any additional income taxes over the loan term because you'll have less interest to deduct. This total becomes *D*.

To find what you'd save by refinancing, subtract *D* from *C*. This will represent your net savings over the life of the mortgage. You'll find a worksheet in Figure 8.2 to help you pencil out these numbers.

It is wise to shop first for new financing with the lender who holds your current loan because it may be eager to keep your business by offering reduced points, fees, and/or a competitive interest rate.

FIGURE 8.2 Refinance Worksheet

Present monthly payments	$	________	
Number of months to pay*	×	________	
Total payments	$	________	*A*
Payments at the lower rate	$	________	
Number of months to pay*	×	________	
Total payments	$	________	*B*
Difference in total payments (*A* minus *B*)	$	________	*C*
Refinancing costs:			
Prepayment penalty (if applicable)	$	________	*D*
Closing costs for new mortgage, including points	$	________	*E*
Added income taxes over loan term figuring reduced deduction from lower interest payments	$	________	*F*
Total (*D* plus *E* plus *F*)	$	________	*G*
Net savings over life of mortgage (*C* minus *G*) =	$	________	

*Be sure that the number of months to pay is for the period the borrower expects to own the property, not the number of months remaining on the loan.

Q. *We called a mortgage person we've worked with before to find out if it would make sense to refinance our first mortgage. He said that unless we could shave 2 percent off our existing interest rate, he wouldn't recommend it. Frankly, we were a little disappointed because he neither asked what we owed nor tried to give us an estimate. This 2 percent savings rule is contrary to what we're hearing now. Who is correct?*

A. *You* are! The 2 percent refinancing rule is dead and buried. In fact, lowering the interest you're paying by as little as 1 percent or less may be enough to make refinancing affordable.

Besides calculating the monthly difference between the two payments, you'd need to factor in how much you'd pay for refinancing costs as well as how long you expect to keep the loan.

Suppose you want to refinance your 8.5 percent $100,000 15-year loan into a 7.5 percent 15-year loan that you'd keep until you'd sell the house in two years. Monthly you'd save $57.74 on your payment. Don't forget the $1,000 in closing costs the lender said he'd charge you on the new loan. To determine your breakeven point, divide the $1,000 by the monthly savings. You find that you won't break even on the new loan until the 18th payment. So unless you're willing to keep the loan for at least 18 months, refinancing won't make financial sense.

It's unusual that the mortgage professional you talked to didn't offer to run the numbers for you. The 2 percent rule could have been his company's rule of thumb (used to protect consumers from overleveraging); but even so, it doesn't make good business sense not to give you the facts you were asking for, even if they couldn't (or wouldn't) make the loan. His nonresponse could be a blessing in disguise!

Ask the next mortgage professional you work with to run a complete comparison of exactly what you stand to gain by refinancing. This is especially true if you're going from an adjustable-rate loan into a fixed-rate or a 30-year loan into a 15-year loan because there are other variables between the loans to consider (such as the difference in equity buildup between loan terms).

Q. *When I refinance my mortgage, can I deduct the points paid that year as well?*

A. No, deducting points for refinancing are not figured the same as when you purchased. While you can deduct the points you pay to refinance, they must be amortized (which means prorated over the years of the loan) and deducted that way. For example, you would deduct a pro-rata share of the cost paid each year for 30 years. Certainly not much of a financial help.

Q. I was surfing the World Wide Web and ended up applying to refinance my mortgage. They faxed me the rates and points I would qualify for. But now I'm wondering if I should go through with it.

A. Online mortgage applications are sweeping the country. In fact, I've had a favorable experience refinancing my home that way. I spent time checking out various Web sites, shopping for rates and points, and was able to take my time in making a decision. I, like you, only shopped online—I bought the loan over the phone with a real person more than two thousand miles away!

While technology is making Web-transmitted information safer, some homeowners are concerned that their personal information will fall into the wrong hands. (But this is equally true dealing face to face with any lender that's untrustworthy!) To eliminate the concern, many lenders use their Web sites to present the information/loan options and then follow up with faxed or e-mailed information to the consumer. In my case, the formal loan application was faxed to me, I faxed back the documentation (income tax returns, asset verifications, etc.) and a local title company closed the transaction. I've yet to meet the lender face to face, but did take the time to check it out (both with the better business bureau in its area and with two business references they provided me).

Online information has given the mortgage shopper new freedom to search for the best financing and costs even with lenders thousands of miles away. But the ease and convenience should never replace good old common sense. Know who you're dealing with, its track record, and your rights as a consumer—online or off.

Q. *I've heard you can refinance your house in a week without some of the customary paperwork. How would I find a lender that would do this?*

A. Just as all loans are not created equal, lenders aren't either! The speed of your refinance is based on many aspects—some dealing with lender policy, others dealing with you as the borrower.

You often can shave days or weeks off the refinancing process if you use the lender holding your current mortgage. You have a track record with a lender who knows the property and would like the opportunity to keep your business. To assist repeat customers, more lenders are using streamlined refinance processes, requiring no formal appraisal and no credit check, relying primarily on the fact that you've paid your current loan on a timely basis. Saving you time and expense can give you the incentive to keep your loan with that lender.

Questions to ask when screening a lender include:

- Do you use any streamlined process for refinancing? What does it entail?
- If you require a formal appraisal, how long is it estimated to take and at what cost? (Even if the lender doesn't require a formal appraisal, make sure you're not charged a fee similar to obtaining one!)
- How long would it take to close the type of loan I need? (Make sure you ask the lender if its refinancing volume is increasing or shrinking as this makes a difference as to how long it will take. But remember that the big picture of affordability is what you're after—not merely saving a fcw processing days. You'll need to shop for rates, points, and other closing costs depending on what you want to achieve financially by refinancing.)

You may find lenders promising to cut you a check for your equity virtually overnight. Be careful that you're not overpaying for the speed of this process with what the industry calls "garbage fees"—extra processing and delivery charges that vary from lender to lender and loan to loan. Question the rationale for each and every fee shown on the good faith estimate of costs provided to you by the lender at the time you apply for the loan. And question the costs again before closing. New fees could have slipped in during loan processing. Unless the lender has a very good reason for the additional charges, stand your ground and refuse to take the loan. With all the loan competition and low interest rate money in the marketplace, it makes no sense to overpay just to expedite the loan.

Q. *My wife and I are considering refinancing for the second time, but wonder if it wouldn't be better to sell now instead as we'll be needing a larger home soon. How can we decide?*

A. Looking down the road to your future home needs is wise. Unfortunately, many homeowners don't do this and it ends up costing them thousands to refinance and then pay duplicate costs with the new loan they get.

Financial considerations aside, here are some timing questions you should answer before you decide to refinance or move.

First, is the type of home you're interested in available now? If the selection is sparse, you could be paying a premium to buy. If a different time of the year and/or a more favorable buyer's market would increase availability for the type of home you want, waiting may make sense.

Second, is the timing right for your family to move? There's a certain element of stress in moving your family, not to mention placing your old home on the market. If the market isn't right for selling your home and you'd have to sacrifice the price and/or if the kids will have to change schools midterm, staying put may make short-term sense.

The last consideration is your current financial picture. A mortgage on a new house means not only a possible increase in a mortgage payment (if you move up in price), but going through the financial hoops of credit checking, verification of employment, etc., as well. While any or all of these might be required for a refinance, the process might be more streamlined than getting a new mortgage on a different house. If your credit is a bit shaky or you've recently changed jobs, waiting to move may make sense.

Q. *I guess I was pretty naïve to think that just because the interest rate was lower on my 90 percent loan-to-value refinance, it wouldn't hurt me if I decided to resell. But it did, and now the closing agent is asking me to bring a check to closing! Can they do that?*

A. They not only can, they are. After all, you've already received the money advanced from the refinance. If it's any consolation, many people have commented that because the interest rate is lowered with a refinance, we start thinking lower interest means less debt. As you painfully learned, a 90 percent loan at 6 percent is still a 90 percent loan. This is the very reason that homeowners should look to the future (or as far as they can in that direction) to see the likelihood of a move. You basically ended up using your precious equity to pay two sets of closing costs (one for the refinance, one for the sale). It was a dear price to pay, and a mistake that I'm sure you won't repeat.

Q. *Is it true that you don't have to live on a property financed with a VA loan in order to refinance it?*

A. Yes. While the borrower's intent must be to reside on the property when the VA loan is first obtained, the VA interest rate reduction loan refinance program does not require that the veteran live on the property in order to refinance it.

Because the idea behind refinancing is to assist the veteran in a lower interest rate, the refinance must lower the loan's interest rate. There is no appraisal or credit check required. The new loan can include the financing of points and funding fees, along with the loan balance. In fact, the veteran could negotiate with the lender to finance the closing costs into the loan, and raise the interest rate to compensate. (You'd only want to consider this if you'd be holding the property and the loan only a short time.)

Q. *If I refinance to cash-out my wife's equity per the divorce settlement, will I be limited to a certain size conventional fixed-rate loan? (I've heard the terms cash-out and limited cash-out.)*

A. The term cash-out refinance refers to one with a maximum loan-to-value ratio of 75 percent (25 percent equity). Limited cash-out is a refinance with a maximum loan-to-value ratio of 90 percent (10 percent equity).

But because many peoplc arc asking questions similar to yours these day, Fannie Mae (who buys loans in the secondary market) has clarified the two refinance situations as they apply to divorce situations. Fannie Mae will allow a borrower acquiring sole ownership under a divorce to use the limited cash-out refinance as long as he or she will not be receiving any cash from the transaction (proceeds going to the other spouse). This would allow you the higher maximum loan (90 percent).

The lender would require documentation to support this treatment such as a copy of the divorce decree or the property settlement agreement.

If you want to put cash in your pocket from the refinance (in addition to paying your wife her equity), then you would only be able to receive a 75 percent loan.

Q. *We've been holding off refinancing our 10 percent mortgage until our credit was back in shape. But now we can't decide if we should choose a 15-year mortgage at 7 percent or go with a higher* *payment for only ten years. (We have ten years remaining on our $51,000 loan with payments of $645 principal and interest.)*

A. You are wise to refinance. But don't take the 15-year loan. It will actually set you back in savings.

While you would obviously pay less if you went with a new 7 percent 10-year mortgage ($71,040), you would NOT save money if you went with a new 15-year mortgage ($82,440). Let's look at the analysis.

With a 7 percent 10-year loan, your monthly principal and interest payments would drop to $592. And with the 15-year loan your monthly payments would drop even more to $458 per month. But when you add five additional years of payments with the 15-year loan, it adds $11,400 more to your cost.

You need to consider that because you've paid five years on your existing loan, you've whittled down a fair amount of interest. That's why the new 10-year loan makes the best economic sense.

Q. *We currently have a 20-year loan with a payment that's a stretch for our income. We don't know whether to refinance into an $85,000 loan with a few points, or take a higher rate of interest. Which makes the most sense?*

A. Paying higher points to secure a lower rate of interest depends on several things. First, how long do you intend to keep the property? Obviously, paying hefty points up front to secure a low interest rate loan won't be as valuable if you keep the property for only a short time.

For example, let's say that the lender gives you a choice of an $85,000 20-year loan at 7 percent with two points (that means paying $1,700 at closing) or 7.5 percent with no points. Which is a better deal? It depends on what you want to accomplish and how long you will own the property. The difference between interest rates of 7 percent and 7.5 percent is just $25.75 per month principal and interest; but it would take 66 months to recoup the $1,700 in points at the rate of the $25.75 per month difference. Paying points at settlement also means you have lost the use of that money, including the potential to invest it.

Because your focus is to make your monthly payment more affordable, you may want to pay the points up front to get the payment lower if you estimate you will keep the loan and property for approximately six more years.

Q. *We were about to close on the refinance for our mortgage when the lender called to say that the insurance company we chose didn't have the proper rating. Isn't insurance coverage all the same?*

A. It's not just the coverage the lender is concerned about, it's the rating of the insurance company. The lender has the right to specify that you use an insurance company with a specified rating, such as Class A or above. They apparently feel that the company's rating has a bearing on how solvent the company is and how fully the claim would be satisfied if a loss occurred.

Have the lender specify exactly what type of rating they're looking for before you start shopping new companies.

Q. *We recently refinanced our mortgage with a new lender and are confused about our homeowners insurance policy.*

We negotiated with the lender to waive having to pay insurance premiums monthly with our loan payment. We also did some comparison shopping with insurance companies and found a lower premium. But at closing, we were required to provide not only a binder, but a receipt showing that we had paid a year's premium in advance! This held up the closing by two days because our insurance carrier is out of the area and the lender's home office insisted on reviewing the binder.

Was the lender getting back at us for not including our premium monthly in our payment?

A. It wasn't a vendetta on the lender's part, it was a sound financial move. If you look at the situation from the lender's viewpoint, requiring the advanced insurance coverage makes sense.

Because it has a lien on the property, its financial interest needs to be protected. If it didn't require the paid binder at the time of closing, it would have no way of knowing whether the property was insured. Should a loss occur before the homeowner acquired coverage (or if the owner failed to provide coverage), the lender would lose.

Before advancing funds to you (called funding the loan), most lenders review the binder, the type of coverage, the coverage amount, and the rating of the insurance company.

Don't forget that if this new loan paid off an old one, there may be insurance refund monies coming from either the lender (from your impound account) or the old insurance company (if you had prepaid the premium). This could help lessen the blow of having to pay the new annual premium up front.

Q. *I'm considering a biweekly mortgage when I refinance. Are they new and exactly how do they work?*

A. Biweekly mortgages are not new. In fact, they have been around for nearly two decades (born in Canada to combat the high interest rates of the early 1980s).

The biweekly concept is simple. The borrower pays one-half of the required regular monthly payment every two weeks, meaning 26 one-half payments per year. The effect is that the loan pays off approximately 12 years early, saving tens of thousands of dollars in interest. This happens because the principal is reduced every 14 days (instead of 30). Further, one full month's extra payment (two one-half payments) are added to a normal payment year because biweekly (half of 52 weeks in the year) is more than the 24 payments of a twice monthly payment (two times 12 months).

But as with all loan types, there can be negatives to biweekly mortgages. First, most lenders require that the payment be paid through direct withdrawal from your checking or savings account. This means that the borrower parts with one-half of the payment every other Friday while the lender gains the use of the money. It's obvious that borrowers considering this type of loan should definitely be paid on a regular, consistent basis!

Second, because the lender is making less profit from the interest, this loan may cost more in terms of amount of down payment required, points, or other closing fees.

Third, once the loan is closed, the loan payment terms cannot be changed. That means that if times got tough and you couldn't make a payment, you could potentially be in default in two weeks' time.

Because of these reasons, most borrowers prefer to go with a traditional 30-year fixed-rate loan and opt to make an extra monthly payment each year and/or make monthly prepayments to the principal when possible. This gives the borrower more control than being locked into the regimented payment schedule of the biweekly mortgage.

Remember to compare the 15-year loan program before you decide. Although the payment will be higher than with the 30-year loan, you will have a quicker payoff period and your payment will be due only once a month.

A lender will be glad to do a loan comparison of the 30-year fixed, 15-year conventional, and the biweekly mortgages, or you can access any of the mortgage calculators online like the one found at fellow columnist Peter Miller's site at www.ourbroker.com.

Q. *Our lender wrote asking if we'd like to save thousands on interest by paying our loan every two weeks. It would cost us a fee of $375. Should we do it?*

A. Absolutely not. Lots of homeowners are receiving letters just like that asking to convert your monthly mortgage into a biweekly loan (with one-half of the payment paid every other week, reducing the principal by an additional month's payment every year).

You don't need the lender to set up this type of prepayment program. In fact, you're pouring $375 down the drain to do so. An additional downside is that once set up, you must adhere to the biweekly schedule.

Design your own prepayment schedule. It can be an extra principal payment each month, each quarter, or annually after you receive your income tax refund. You can prepay while controlling your own cash flow—all without extra fees and obligations.

EQUITY LINES OF CREDIT

Q. *We don't have much equity but wonder if it wouldn't be a good idea to use an equity line of credit to pay off my student loan of $10,000 at 8 percent interest. How could we weigh the issues?*

A. There are a lot of variables that should go into making your decision. Let's tackle them one at a time.

First, the most obvious concern is that the equity line of credit is a second mortgage that, if you can't make the payments, could foreclose on your home. That's a bit more severe than going into collection with the student loan creditors (even though that also would be posted against your credit record).

Many equity lines of credit do not use fixed interest rates. Most are based on adjustable rates that could start low, but eventually far exceed the 8 percent you are paying for your current student loan. This adjusting payment could be tough to budget as well.

And don't forget that the equity loan may have up-front fees (or fees added to the loan) that could lessen its desirability.

You might decide that instead of paying off the student loan with cash from your home that you try to budget prepayments to reduce the student loan debt. Prepaying in the early stages of the loan will do much to decrease the principal balance quickly and reduce the amount of interest you pay overall.

Q. *We need approximately $70,000 to add on a master bedroom and bath and expand our garage. But the lender said we'd be better off doing an equity line of credit now with an introductory rate of 5 percent and then refinancing once the remodeling is complete. We currently owe $55,000, and the property should be worth approximately $150,000 after the improvements. Does it make economic sense to do it this way instead of refinancing right now?*

A. Depending on the costs to set up the equity line as well as the projected costs to refinance, it may very well make economic sense.

Here's why. Funding the improvements using the equity line allows you to not only pay less interest initially, but requires that you only make payments on the outstanding balance. For example, if the contractor bills you $15,000 for improvements the first month, the equity line payments would be based only on that balance.

If you refinance now, your loan would be based on the property's current value, not the improved value. That could mean you'd be short of the total funds needed. Even if you were to obtain all you needed by refinancing, your payments would be higher than the equity line because you'd be borrowing more up front rather than as you need it, probably at a higher interest rate. And with the anticipated amount you'll need for improvements (plus being able to pay off your current loan of $55,000), the refinanced loan could require private mortgage insurance because you'd need a loan that exceeded 80 percent of the property's value. This, too, would increase your monthly payment.

Before you make a decision, be sure to ask what the lender will charge to originate the equity line, as well as the total estimated costs to refinance once improvements are complete. If those costs don't exceed the savings you'd realize by the lower interest rate and lesser payments on the equity line, then it would pay to structure the loans as suggested.

You'd also be advised to have a firm commitment on the future refinance barring anything changing in your financial picture. Some of the downsides of most equity lines is that they must be paid off when the property is sold, usually won't allow other loans to be placed with them, and the low introductory rate of interest (like you're promised) will expire typically in less than a year. Once the low interest rate expires, the new rate is often based on the prime rate plus 2 percent. If you later found you couldn't qualify for a refinance, you'd be saddled with higher payments on a large balance and realizing no savings, only more costs by taking the equity line of credit route.

"For age and want, save while you may; No morning sun lasts a whole day."
—*Ben Franklin*

IS HEAVY MORTGAGING SOUND FINANCIAL LEVERAGE?

Q. *Several people have told us that it makes the greatest financial sense to keep our house heavily mortgaged and reinvest the money in other investments. But we're in our late 50s and really like the idea of having our home paid off (which it will be soon).*

A. Then do it. It makes me crazy when I hear someone prescribing a one-size-fits-all financial remedy for home ownership when they certainly wouldn't do the same for any other investment!

Yes, it makes sense to have a larger mortgage than other types of debt that are nondeductible. Perhaps it makes sense to use your home as financial leverage for life events you haven't saved the cash for (like for a child's education or medical emergencies). It may not be financially prudent to prepay a mortgage if you have the need for another when you move and/or if you can invest the cash in another investment that will yield a higher return over the long run.

It's up to each homeowner to weigh the house as an investment coupled with his or her risk threshold. There are plenty of people like you who would not sleep at night if their mortgage payment was sky high, especially as they near retirement.

If you've done a good job in overall financial planning, just turn a deaf ear to anyone pretending to know how you should or shouldn't leverage with a high mortgage. Let them be the one who doesn't sleep at night!

Q. *We received a flyer in the mail stating that we could obtain up to "125 percent of our equity" in an equity loan. What is this and would it make sense?*

A. 125 percent mortgages are all the rage right now—a second mortgage is added to your first and can total up to 125 percent of your property's value.

Why are lenders making 125 percent loans and who's being approved for them? They're being made in the hopes that (1) appreciation will continue to increase the market value of the property; and (2) the homeowner wouldn't need to sell the house until the debt was paid down. Most lenders require that borrowers have stellar credit. And because a strong credit picture is exactly what the borrower wants to keep, lenders feel that there's a better-than-normal chance that these loans will be repaid.

Unfortunately, it's not a perfect world. Buyers get transferred unexpectedly and have to sell. Families have financial problems and feel the crunch of higher payments.

So how could you best evaluate if a 125 percent loan is good for your situation? First, is your home in a stable neighborhood with above-average appreciation? If so, this will do much to help your home's value rise above the heavy debt.

Second, is it likely that you'd keep the home (and the loan) long enough to whittle the debt down below what the property could sell for? In fact, to be truly on the safe side, you should add an estimate of sales costs (say 10 percent) to that number (because that would come out of your equity). And be sure to make this calculation based on the lowest—not highest price your home might bring.

If you are interested in taking this plunge, make sure that you shop diligently for interest rates because (unlike first mortgages and refinances) rates easily can be in the 10 percent plus range. If you read the questions earlier in this chapter dealing with people behind on their payments, you saw at least one 125 percent mortgage fatality! Know what you're getting into, and why, before you take this route.

DANGEROUS DOLLARS AND PERILOUS PENNIES ISSUES

The murmur of equity eroding in your home can be barely audible, or as obvious as a parade of bagpipes, when dealing with The Frugal HomeOwner Law of Sound Equity Decisions. To guard against losing Dangerous Dollars down the equity drain:

- Refinance only when it makes financial sense (to lower an interest rate, pay off nondeductible consumer debt, and/or to shorten the life of the mortgage). Avoid refinancing to purchase personal property (like boats, cars, or motorcycles) that will be worn out long before the loan is repaid!
- Prepay your mortgage prudently! This means retire nondeductible consumer loans first and avoid prepayment when you'll only keep the loan for a short time. Be sure to set up a methodical system for repaying your loan and tracking the payments, no matter if you'll make extra principal payments monthly, annually, biweekly, or sporadically.
- *You* are the only one who can determine if it's personally prudent for you to leverage your equity to the hilt! Don't let anyone else convince you to take a bad financial step.

Where equity is concerned, Perilous Pennies issues come in a variety of passive and active forms. To plug up those slow—yet steady—equity drains:

- Know the refunds you're entitled to when you pay off or refinance your mortgage loan. These could include private mortgage insurance premiums (on conventional loans), mortgage insurance premiums (on FHA loans), and/or impound account balances should your new loan not require that you pay your taxes and insurance with your monthly payment.

CHAPTER 9

The Frugal HomeOwner Law of Prudent Home Improvement and Maintenance

Measure Twice, Cut Once

Have you ever driven down a neighborhood street and nearly run off the road when you saw a house that looked as though ten different contractors, with ten different ideas, simultaneously made improvements without even bothering to ask what the game plan was?

I know you have. And often homes like these are owned by very well-meaning, hard-working people who want to make improvements but just don't know how to go about it. They don't have a game plan, they don't use expert craftspeople, and they try to do it all on a shoestring budget. In short, they have ignored the frugal carpenter's and seamstress's creed: Measure twice, cut once. Further, more often than not, this slipshod approach comes back to haunt them when they can't find a buyer, let alone recoup the cost of the improvements. Statistics show that overimproving a home in the wrong type of market and/or neighborhood is one of the biggest ways to flush equity right down the drain!

Conversely, Economizing Owners think through home improvements before they ever pick up a hammer. They know the financial impact the renovation or remodel will make, how much it will return when they sell the house, and the cost of those improvements, almost down to the nickel. In other words, they financially "measure twice, cut once."

Just as the legendary Bob Vila wouldn't think of beginning a project that couldn't return him added equity, we'll learn what other experts say about sprucing up to sell, remodeling to stay, all done in the manner of frugal home ownership.

NEIGHBOR MAINTENANCE

Q. *What can you do about a neighbor who builds an unsightly (and potentially illegally constructed) fence? It's hideous and is bound to bring down the property values in the neighborhood.*

A. A real estate attorney would be best suited to give you that type of advice. But you may have ammunition in zoning regulations.

Call the city and ask to speak to the zoning department. Based on where the property is located (and any other covenants or restrictions for that area or subdivision), you can discover a wealth of information.

For example, what are the construction requirements (types of materials that can be used, maximum height and width permitted, minimum setback required from the street)? The fence may have violated any or all of these specifications. If so, the building inspector may require that the fence either be repaired to meet the guidelines, or torn down.

A building permit may be required for the fence, which the neighbor may or may not have. A call to the building inspector will check this out. If no permit is on file, the inspector will more than likely make a visit to the property.

There's only so much you can do about eyesores on abutting property. If the homeowner is within the law regarding construction requirements and permits, your hands may be tied.

"For want of a nail the shoe was lost;
for want of a shoe the horse was lost;
for want of the horse the rider was lost,
being overtaken and slain by the enemy,
all for the want of care about a horse-shoe nail."
—Ben Franklin

REPAIRING YOUR HOME

Q. *We live in a home where water seeps into the basement during the rainy season. The first contractor we called said we only needed to dampproof the foundation. The second contractor we spoke to said we'd be much happier with waterproofing. What's the difference (other than quite a lot in price)?*

A. If you're like many homeowners, keeping water and moisture out of a basement or crawl space (especially during certain times of the year) can be a problem. In fact, basement/foundation water is the second most common homeowner problem, second only to roof leakage.

Besides properly grading around the house and adding drains to divert the water from the foundation, sealing the foundation from the outside is a solution. While more expensive than applying coatings on the interior of the foundation, it provides a more long-term solution.

But (as you found out), not all coating systems are made equal. In fact, they are categorized by whether they provide dampproofing or waterproofing. Dampproofing only resists the passage of water. Most homes, even new ones, receive only dampproofing usually with an asphalt emulsion. Waterproofing, on the other hand, actually resists water flowing under pressure (like ground water) that often can be very forceful and damaging. Materials used for waterproofing include cement coatings and polymer modified asphalt, and are more expensive than those used for dampproofing.

Your best bet is to have several contractors evaluate how severe the problem is as well as the depth of the water table, and then give you an estimate of how long various remedies should control the problem. You then can compare the solutions to what you want to achieve (e.g., short- or long-term ownership, how much you want to or can spend, etc.) before taking the most effective course of action.

Q. *What should you do when a repair person comes to your door promoting discounted repair services that are available for only a short time? Are these always a bad move, especially if they provide references?*

A. While not always a bad move, remember the homeowner's motto regarding home improvement companies and services: "If it sounds too good to be true, it probably is!" It's best to do nothing until you've had time to evaluate the service, the contractor, costs involved, and references.

The first question raised should be why was the offer only available for a limited time? Be careful of products that could be seconds or left over from another job. The tight time pressures also leave you with limited time to check out the contractor, particularly references of past satisfied customers. Reputable companies who rely on repeat and referral business know the value of personal references and would welcome extending you the time to check out references.

Here are some red flags to check out before choosing a home repair company to work with:

- Check the company's licensing and credentials. Ask to see a contractor's license (if applicable), verification of his or her worker's compensation policy as well as proof of liability insurance coverage. In fact, it's a good idea to call the insurance company to see if the policy is still in force. Just as would be required if you were working with someone in a credit situation (which you are), ask if the company is bonded and to see verification. If you still have questions, ask for a bank reference for the company.
- Check out the company with the local better business bureau (BBB). It can tell you if there's anything derogatory on them. If the company has recently come from another locale, call the BBB in that area.
- Be cautious working with someone who only provides references for out-of-town work they've done. The same is true if they have no local phone other than the motel down the street! Your best bet in sizing up repair and home service companies is to speak directly to others who have recently used this company and this service. Seeing yard signs announcing that "Ajax Concrete has recently poured a new driveway for this homeowner" is weak at best because some unscrupulous companies actually pay homeowners to place advertising signs like that in their yard.
- Run, don't walk, away from the person requiring all cash up front or even a deposit. (Would *you* demand to be paid before you had rendered a service?) If they feign that it's to cover the purchase of materials and/or supplies, consider if it's wise to do business with

a company who is so financially unstable. Many of the signs of trouble are there initially if you pay attention to them.

- Be wary if the time for completing the job seems unrealistic (either too short or too long). If you've done your homework and secured a minimum of three bids for the job (if it's on the small-dollar side) and six bids if it's larger, you'll have a fair idea of the time frames involved.

There are very few instances when you wouldn't have ample time to first check out a company and/or be able to find another company to provide the service.

REMODELING DOLLARS AND CENTS

Q. *A group of people at a party were talking about home remodeling. Someone asked what we thought the home of the future would look like because knowing that would help homeowners make prudent remodeling decisions. What do homebuilders think the future will bring?*

A. While it's probably impossible that any industry would have a meeting of the minds about change, some homebuilders are reporting trends that may appear as changes in years to come. These include technology built into the home, more flexible use of interior space, plus returning to the look of neighborhoods of the past.

Technology will perhaps play the most extreme role in changing new homes. A built-in central control unit could regulate most lighting, heating, and cooling functions in the home programmed in by times of the day, days of the week—even seasons of the year. For example, if you desired lower lights starting at 6 PM, you'd program the control unit to lower the lights and draw the blinds—even close the shutters! Or perhaps you'd like to wake up to sunlight streaming into your bedroom. Again, just program the bedroom blinds to open at the desired time, simultaneously turn up the heat to warm the bathroom—even start your coffee to brew.

Technology could become instrumental using voice-control activation. You could verbally command the front door to close, lock, and activate the central alarm system—without getting up from your armchair!

Consumers are leaning toward more open, flexible space within the home. Great rooms—combinations of dining, living, and kitchen areas larger than we've seen to date—may be popular, allowing the family additional togetherness, while pursuing separate activities in game, computer, and craft alcoves. One strongly proposed interior addition is what we've traditionally called the "mother-in-law apartment." This can accommodate elderly parents, provide separate space for kids who stay (or return) home, and give guests their privacy. Complete with its own minikitchen, the extra refrigerator and microwave included can help take pressure off the central kitchen area.

Outside things may not appear to be too different from today; but a closer look at the materials used may change your mind. We'll see a much greater use of molded plastics—everything from foundations to sturdy, long-lasting fences. Helping to protect our natural resources, wood and similar products will be used more sparingly for decorative purposes, not as primary materials (like exterior siding) as they are today.

Outside will find many more walkways and bike paths. In fact, as walking becomes more important for health, energy efficiency, and to cut down on pollution, developments are returning to broad sidewalks where homes sit closer to the street. Especially apparent in planned communities (like Seaside, Florida), sidewalks and front porches on homes may become a requirement of construction and zoning in some developments. They allow greater opportunity to meet neighbors as they stroll by and create a friendlier environment with the hopes of deterring crime when you know who does and does not live in the community.

While home design and construction always will focus on the size of the household, its space needs, and the demographics of the buyer, consumers continue to want what they've always wanted—flexibility, comfort, and efficiency in their homes.

Q. *My husband and I would like to do some updating to our kitchen and add a second bathroom to our home. But our concern is that we might be transferred within the next 18 months or so. Does it make sense to put money into the house, and if so, how much of our investment could we expect to recoup if we did have to sell?*

A. You are in luck. According to the 1997 "Housing Facts, Figures and Trends" survey compiled by the National Association of Home

Builders (NAHB), updated kitchens and bathrooms are the two rooms most likely to add value to your home.

The NAHB report analyzed data from *Remodeling* magazine's 1997–1998 Cost vs. Value Report. Based on national averages, a minor kitchen remodel (a job costing approximately $8,400) returned 102 percent of that cost to the homeowner if the home was sold in the first year. Improvements included replacing cabinet doors, oven and cooktops, laminate countertops, sink, faucet, and flooring, and repainting.

A bathroom addition (added to a home with currently one, or one-and-a-half baths), recouped 90 percent of the homeowner's investment. In the survey, the bathroom was finished with ceramic tile and a linen closet for a total job cost of approximately $22,500.

Major kitchen remodeling ranked third in adding resale value, recouping 90 percent of the improvements' cost. In addition to the items in the minor kitchen remodel, major remodeling included adding an island, custom lighting, plus a built-in microwave. A sample of this survey can be found in Figure 9.1.

Statistics are great; but as the survey was based on national averages, you must factor in particulars about your home and neighborhood before you decide. If your home is smaller than the norm in your area, is in a less-than-desirable location, or is already priced on the high side of your market, making improvements may not add anywhere near the value shown in the survey. In fact, additions could actually overimprove the home, making it tougher to sell at the price you need to recover your investment.

Take into consideration how long homes in your area take to sell. While market conditions could change before you list the house, needing top dollar out of your home could extend the marketing time, even then with no guarantees. Talk to a real estate agent who specializes in marketing homes in your area as well as a homebuilder who constructs homes similar to yours. These local market professionals can help you decide how many resale dollars a kitchen remodel and bathroom addition can put in your pocket.

Q. *Are there some general guidelines for remodeling a home? We don't want to make improvements that won't pay over time.*

A. Most professionals will tell you to avoid high-cost remodeling if you live in an area where the value of homes has dropped or it appears

FIGURE 9.1 Popular Remodeling Projects Cost versus Value

Updating and remodeling kitchens and baths will add the most value to your home. In some instances, these projects could possibly return more than 100 percent of the cost if the home is sold within a year. If the home is kept longer, returns should increase, according to *Remodeling* magazine.

National Averages

	Job Cost	Added Resale Value	Percent of Cost Recouped
Minor kitchen remodel Replace cabinet doors, oven and cooktop, laminate countertops, sink, faucet, and floor, and repaint	$ 8,395	$ 8,579	102
Bathroom addition Add a second bath to a house with 1 or 1.5 baths	11,721	10,820	92
Major kitchen remodel Redesign kitchen, replacing all of the above, plus add built-in microwave, custom lighting, cooking island	22,509	20,340	90
Master suite In a house with 2–3 bedrooms, add a 24′ x 16′ master suite with walk-in closet, whirlpool tub, separate shower	37,388	35,527	87
Two-story addition First-floor family room and second floor bedroom with full bath	56,189	48,943	87
Attic bedroom In a 2–3 bedroom house, convert unfinished attic space with bedroom and shower/bath	23,002	19,839	86

(continued)

FIGURE 9.1 Popular Remodeling Projects *(continued)*

	Job Cost	Added Resale Value	Percent of Cost Recouped
Family room addition Add a 16′ x 25′ foot room with skylights, hardwood tongue-and-groove floor	$32,558	$27,904	86
Bathroom remodel Update existing bath with new tub, toilet, vanity, medicine cabinet, lighting, tile	8,563	6,582	77
Deck addition 16′ x 20′ deck of pressure-treated pine including built-in-bench, railings, and planter	5,927	4,356	73
Replace siding 1,250 square feet of new vinyl or aluminum siding and trim	5,099	3,593	71
Home office Convert existing room into office with custom cabinetry and rewiring for electronic equipment	8,179	5,679	69
Replace windows 10 new 3′ x 5′ aluminum-clad windows with trim	5,976	4,042	68

Source: *Remodeling* magazine, 1997–1998 Cost vs. Value Report.

that homes in the area could devalue. This could be due to changes in zoning nearby, alterations in traffic patterns, etc. The idea is that you don't want to make costly improvements if the area won't hold its value.

Even if the area does have stable values, be sure not to overimprove the home to a much higher level than other homes in the neighborhood. It's best if your home's value is just a little below the best in the area. That way you'll have room for appreciation to strengthen your property value but won't be putting money into improvements that the market won't return when you sell.

Be sure to evaluate how long you think you'll stay in the house. It makes no sense to invest time and money in remodeling if you plan on moving before you derive personal satisfaction from the work. Ask a real estate professional to show you properties that include the improvements you're considering, and then ask for a market analysis of what your home is worth right now. Economically, it may make more sense to sell now and purchase a home that's exactly what you want—without adding the expense and the headache of remodeling.

Tips to help you get good return on your investment if you do remodel include making sure the work is done professionally using quality materials. Second, respect your floor plan and the layout and size of your lot. Appraisers add little value for rooms that lack function and/or appear to be added on as an afterthought to the general floor plan. Examples of lack of function could be an attic bedroom with no access to a bath or rooms too small to be useful.

Last, be sure to update without resorting to fads. Improvements need to outlive the latest trend and be serviceable long after they're paid for.

Once you pencil out the improvements you want to make, consult with a lender to see if it will be cost-effective to finance these changes, and with an appraiser to see if they're good additions for the type and style of your home.

Q. *Are there reference materials to help us select a good contractor to remodel our home?*

A. There's an excellent free publication to help you ask questions to find a contractor who's right for you. It's published by the remodeling industry association, and focuses on how to determine your needs as well as the financial and legal responsibilities a contractor would have to you. If you use a contractor who is a better business bureau member, he or she has already agreed to arbitration in case of a dispute.

The booklet is free of charge and is titled, "Selecting a Professional Remodeling Contractor," published by the National Association of Remodeling Industry, 4301 N. Fairfax Dr., Arlington, VA 22203.

"The use of money is all the advantage there is
in having money."
—*Ben Franklin*

Q. *Would FHA finance renovation work in a home I want to buy?*

A. There is an FHA (Federal Housing Administration) program known as 203(k) that will finance both your purchase and the renovation costs into one loan.

You need to be an owner/occupant but the loan is applicable to single-family homes and multifamily buildings (up to four units) where you would reside in one unit.

Here's how it works. The loan value is based on the postrenovation (appraised) amount but can't exceed the maximum FHA loan amount for your area. For example, you could finance repairs for electrical and heating and cooling systems, or a new roof. In fact, the work repairs can be quite broad—including the cost of new landscaping, fencing, or a patio or deck.

There are no mortgage payments during the time the work is being completed up to a period of six months (only payments for property tax and homeowners insurance).

Owner occupants make the standard down payment for FHA loans, which is approximately 3 percent down, up to the maximum loan allowable for an area.

The trick in working with this type of loan is finding the most knowledgeable lender. It's best to first try the lender who makes the most FHA loans in your area because paperwork on this loan is deep and time consuming.

Q. *We live in a nice neighborhood and are just about the only house on the block without a pool. How could we tell if adding one would be a wise financial move?*

A. As you probably could guess, it's impossible to tell if adding a pool can positively add to the value of your home. Other considerations like size and style of your home, its amenities, and exact location and market conditions at the time of sale come into play.

Because you know that your home is in the minority of those without pools in your area, the possibilities are strong that you're making a good financial decision.

Before you call in the contractors, take one more step to double-check the financial advantages. Call a real estate agent and/or an appraiser who specializes in selling and appraising property in your area.

Give the professional facts about your home's size, amenities, location, and the improvements you're considering, and he/she will share statistics with you from similar properties that have sold and approximately what value the pool contributed.

While you may not be able to determine dollarwise exactly how much the pool addition netted in the sale, the marketing time and sales prices should indicate if it added to or hindered those sales.

A last source of information would be to check the property assessments from the county assessor's office. While assessed value is not market value, the assessor can give you an indication of how pool improvements have faired in your area on properties similar to yours.

If you are a family with small children, be sure to consider the personal issues before tackling the financial ones—swimming pools are the leading cause of death to children under the age of five.

WEATHERIZING TIPS

Q. *My husband and I are debating whether just adding extra insulation without any upgrades will make a difference in our utility bills. What do you think?*

A. Insulation may make some difference (especially if you live in an area where you have either strong heat or cooling demands, or both). But maximum energy conservation comes by coupling added insulation with investments in storm windows and doors, caulking and sealing around chimneys, and proper weather stripping. These latter items are inexpensive and can be installed quickly and easily.

The most important places to insulate are the attic (where heat is wasted in the winter and where the sun penetrates to run up the air-conditioning bills in the summer), exterior walls, and crawl spaces and basements. Standard R (which stands for resistance—to the flow of heat) factors should be at least R-30 in ceilings, R-11 in exterior walls, and R-19 in floors.

Your local utility company may provide a free assessment of which weatherization applications may be most cost-effective. If they don't they may be able to recommend several general contractors who can assess your needs.

"Men take more pains to mask than mend."
—*Ben Franklin*

Q. *The cost to air-condition our home is going through the roof! Are there any no-cost, low-cost ideas you could share to trim our bill?*

A. It's amazing how making a few changes can help whittle down those high summer air-conditioning bills. For example, close doors to seldom-used rooms and turn off air-conditioning to these areas. Keep windows near your thermostat tightly closed and be sure to block out daytime sun with blinds and shades. And make sure to keep lamps or TV sets away from the thermostat as well. The extra heat can cause the air-conditioning to run longer than necessary.

When you have a choice, use the range top or microwave instead of the oven. And just as grandma used to do, try to cook early in the morning before the heat of the day. Turn off the oven before the cooking is completed; in most cases, the existing warmth will complete the cooking cycle.

Be sure to dust and vacuum vents frequently and don't forget to replace the air conditioner or furnace filter as grime tends to impede air flow. Also, make sure that your air conditioner is professionally serviced at least annually. That small cost leads to one of the very best ways to keep utility bills under control for the long run. Invest in a programmable thermostat, especially if the house is vacant during the day.

LEAD ISSUES

Q. *Our friends recently had blood tests run on their child and found that she had high levels of lead in her blood that might have been caused by loose paint chips when they remodeled their home. We've never paid attention to lead-based paint issues, but this has been a wake-up call. Where can we find information about locating and removing lead-based paint in our home?*

A. Remodeling a home has been found to be one of the most dangerous times to uncover lead issues in the home because lead dust becomes airborne and inhaled. In addition, young children who touch paint surfaces and then put their hands in their mouths are at higher risk because their nervous systems are still developing and their bodies absorb proportionately more lead. National statistics find that 1 out of every 11 children in the United States have dangerous levels of lead in their bloodstreams.

The National Safety Council hosts a National Lead Information Center that not only distributes information, but can direct you to lead inspectors and risk assessors in your area. By calling 800-LEAD-FYI (available 24 hours a day), you can obtain an information packet containing information on how to locate and assess lead-based paint in your home, how to protect children from it, and tips on how to significantly reduce lead hazards in your home.

If you find you have questions not covered in the materials sent to you, you can call the same number again (during the hours of 8:30 AM and 5 PM EST, Monday through Friday) to speak directly to an information specialist.

Q. *I just inherited an old house and am concerned that the plumbing might contain high levels of lead. Should I worry about this?*

A. High levels of lead in drinking water have been linked to central nervous system, brain, kidney, and blood disorders. High concentrations of lead are especially dangerous to children because their tissues are more sensitive to damage and their lesser body weight causes higher concentrations in their system.

In an effort to control lead in drinking water, materials containing lead have been banned from use in public water supplies since 1986. Additionally, lead-based solder was banned in home plumbing applications in 1988.

These changes have decreased the amount of lead in drinking water, but homes built or remodeled prior to this time are at higher risk. Increased lead occurs in the water supply when plumbing fixtures, pipes, and lead-based solder are corroded by water, releasing lead into the system. Particularly high levels of lead in drinking water are found in homes where corrosion occurs on copper pipes connected with lead-based solder.

For your peace of mind, have your water tested by your county health authorities. After the analysis, they can advise you of any additional steps you should take.

There is no way visually to check the lead level in your water. This must be done by a chemical test. Should you suspect that lead is present in your water, the county health department can give you information on how to have your water tested in your area.

If you want further information on lead and your drinking water, free brochures are available from the U.S. Environmental Protection Agency. "Is Your Drinking Water Safe?" and "Lead and Your Drinking Water," can be obtained by writing the Public Information Center, 401 M Street, SW, Washington, DC 20460.

DANGEROUS DOLLARS AND PERILOUS PENNIES ISSUES

According to the Frugal HomeOwner Law of Prudent Home Improvement and Maintenance, Dangerous Dollars can haunt you right up to the closing table, causing you to part with thousands of dollars. To avoid financially fatal errors where improvements are concerned:

- Remodel your home only after researching what the cost of the improvement is likely to add to the market value of your home. Sure, some things are great to improve just because you want to—but don't expect a buyer to compensate you for them when you sell!
- Have most major repairs and all remodeling jobs performed by professional craftspersons. Never fall prey to scam artists, quoting you prices "good only 'til Friday." They're likely to skip town with your good faith deposit—leaving you with neither faith nor repairs!

Home improvement and maintenance Perilous Pennies can slip carelessly through your fingers unless you do the following:

- Constantly monitor your utility bills and make corresponding cost-effective weatherizing improvements.
- Prioritize and focus improvements and upgrades in rooms that have a high priority to buyers, such as bathrooms and kitchens.

THE CREED OF THE SAVVY SELLER

Well Begun Is Half Done

• • • • •

"So much for industry, my friends, and attention to one's own business; but to these we must add frugality if we would make our industry more certainly successful."

—Benjamin Franklin

Come on, Ben. What could be an easier way to make money than to sell a house? After all, the homeowner's already done the tough stuff—bought the house, made the mortgage payments, paid the property taxes. All that's left is to find a buyer, attend the closing, and pick up a proceeds check, right?

Wrong. The reality is that there's a big difference between being a seller and being a Savvy Seller. Sellers plant a yard sign, place an ad, and wait for the house to sell. But Savvy Sellers know that while it may look easy, it takes a well-orchestrated approach to price the house right, work only with preapproved buyers, all the while keeping in mind the primary mission—to meet your financial objectives in owning the house in the first place! Whew, Ben was right. It does take more of that frugal stuff to make homeowning more successful, and it makes one tired just thinking about it!

That's why we end *The Frugal HomeOwner* with tips to give you one last chance to meet those financial homeownership goals. A misstep here could not only cost you time and effort, but precious home equity that once lost, will be forever missing from your sale proceeds check. And that means fewer of those green things with Ben's face staring back at you!

Ready, Set—keeping the Creed of the Savvy Seller ringing in your ears, "Well begun is half done"—Go!

CHAPTER 10

The Frugal HomeOwner Law of Seller Preparedness

It's about Price, Preparation, and Planning

Doesn't it seem like yesterday when you were picking up the keys to your castle, wondering which corner of the living room would best showcase the baby grand piano?

And now you're thinking about selling. That's great, but don't forget the Law of Seller Preparedness that reminds us that "it's about price, preparation, and planning" when selling a home.

First, price. Yes, it's important to price the property properly (we'll give you a myriad of ideas for doing that). But even though the house is priced right, it doesn't necessarily guarantee that you'll (1) attract a buyer who will make a full-price offer; and (2) obtain the largest net proceeds from that full-price offer. In fact, a less-than-full-priced offer might actually net you more due to lower closing costs, fewer points, or a buyer prepared to offer you other financial trade-offs. As a Savvy Seller you'll need to learn how to evaluate each offer based on what you stand to net (or hire an agent to do that for you).

Second, preparation. It takes a lot of work to prepare a house for sale. As a Savvy Seller you must be willing to spend the time, effort, and money getting it in tip-top shape; hire someone who will; or be willing to settle for a little less equity as a result. (Note this is the same reason some should never attempt a for sale by owner. It takes an inordinate amount of time to do it right, even if you're going to use the World Wide Web to assist in the process.)

Third, planning. Just as you found in buying a home, selling also requires a plan. Are you willing to sidestep waiting for a full-price offer so that you can sell the house and move for your promotion? Is it important for you to sell before school starts so the family can move together? Making these decisions up front helps you best evaluate offers as they come in, avoiding missteps that could cost you money.

Don't forget to journey back to the buyer chapters in this book. A little trip down memory lane can help make you a more empathetic seller.

If you're ready to manage the tips and traps you'll face as a Savvy Seller preparing to sell, then why not begin visualizing the sweet reward you're headed for—the sound of hearing that equity jingling merrily in your pocket!

FOR-SALE-BY-OWNER EMPOWERMENT

Q. *How much of the information we'll need as for-sale-by-owners can be obtained from the Internet?*

A. A lot! Cyberspace offers for-sale-by-owners a wealth of information—everything from being able to expose the house to millions of potential buyers to ordering your own home inspection!

Using the Resource Guide at the end of this book, you can do an online search by category of information needed (e.g., "pricing property") or use a search engine to gather a broader category of information (e.g., "legal issues when you sell your home").

Besides gathering current information about the real estate market from sources like www.inman.com or frugalhomeowner.com, an ideal beginning point as a for-sale-by-owner is www.owners.com. Not only can you place your property in an online listing from the site, but you can shop for marketing items you'll need like signage, marketing materials, and information packets.

But there's one caution to using Web-based for-sale-by-owner services—don't start having so much fun online that you forget that your original mission was to sell the house!

Q. *We've been working for about a month to sell our home. Yesterday my wife got a wild idea to change the position of our yard sign—and the phone rang off the hook. What happened?*

A. Congratulations! Your wife's idea is one of the oldest, yet potentially most effective, strategies for breathing life into stalled listings. Studies have shown that by changing the position of the yard sign, you can attract more attention to a property.

When a yard sign sits on a property for a month or more, it becomes part of the landscape of that property. This defeats the purpose of the sign, which is to attract interest. By changing both the physical location of the sign (from one corner of the property to another), as well as the direction the sign is facing, it looks new again. In fact, after changing the position of a sign, I've had potential buyers call to inquire, "When did this property go on the market? I just noticed the sign today!" Remember, it takes just one person—the right person—seeing the sign to get your house sold.

Q. *As for-sale-by-owners, we decided to work with a buyer's agent and pay him a fee (even though he didn't legally represent us). Now the buyer says the agent misrepresented the property (failure to tell the buyer about a leaky roof that we told the agent about) and wants to sue us. How can we be held responsible for something the agent did?*

A. When buyers are upset, they often want to get everyone involved. It sounds as though you haven't spoken to a real estate attorney. He or she would probably tell you there is little to worry about because the agent was legally representing the buyer and owed the duty of full disclosure to that buyer—especially after you shared information about the leaky roof with the agent.

A buyer's agent is responsible to his client for representing the property and uncovering facts about the property as well (even material facts and defects that you failed to uncover).

You were wise to tell the agent about the leaky roof and equally wise to know who was and wasn't represented. Both of these facts will help cement your position should the buyer try to involve you in the dispute.

"He has lost his boots but sav'd his spurs."
—*Ben Franklin*

Q. *My husband and I used a real estate agent to purchase the home we currently own. Now that we're ready to sell, we find that we don't need the full array of services typically offered by a real estate company. Would it be okay to call the agent to see if she would, for a fee, do the things we need done (like qualifying prospective buyers and double-checking the price we feel is fair market value)?*

A. Absolutely. I'm receiving a lot of questions lately just like yours. Many sellers feel that while they'd like to use a real estate professional, they don't need the full menu of traditional brokerage services to market their homes. These sellers are often business professionals who know how marketing works, what it takes to showcase a home to prospective buyers, and often have bought other properties. This new trend termed "unbundling services" allows consumers to purchase what they need, when they need it, in a type of à la carte approach, often paying a flat or hourly fee rather than a percentage of the sales price. (Visit www.realestatecafe.com to see the approach one company takes, as well as www.frugalhomeowner.com for other information about the fee-for-service approach.)

Contact the real estate agent you used previously with your request. Outline the services you need and ask how much the agent will charge to provide them. Frankly, the greatest challenge may lie in determining a fee structure for the services you're requesting. Traditional brokerage business prided itself on "full service" and just now is realizing that the one-size-fits-all real estate brokerage needs to adapt to consumers' needs.

The fact that you were pleased with her services before is a good indication that she can assist you again.

"An honest man will receive neither money nor praise that is not his due."
—*Ben Franklin*

HOME IMPROVEMENTS PRIOR TO SELLING

Q. *Our home is very small, and we are in the process of painting and doing some remodeling in order to put it on the market. I'm concerned that some of the repair work my husband wants to do (like reroofing with cedar shakes) will actually overimprove the house and* *we'll never get our money back. Is there any survey or resource I can show him to help change his mind?*

A. One of the best resources I've seen is a 1997 survey done in conjunction with the National Association of Home Builders called "Housing Facts, Figures, and Trends." It outlines what homebuyers want in a home, based on two categories: first-time buyer and move-up buyer. This would be a great initial point of discussion because the survey breaks the homes down into not only the features required by these different buyers, but then expands into the effective life of each component in a house. For example, the cedar shakes you mention are said to have a life expectancy of between 15 and 30 years and are not features typically requested on first-time buyer's wish lists! This justifies what you expected that adding this feature is, in fact, not cost-effective given that your home would probably attract a small family just starting out.

A copy of the survey can be ordered through the National Association of Homebuilders at www.nahb.com for $35.

Q. *In trying to price our house it looks like we can't get back all the money we recently spent on landscaping. Is this universal or does it differ by area?*

A. It's tough to say. Property location as well as the type, size, and price of a property have a bearing on the value of the amenities. Buyers purchase from the standpoint of market value, which is dictated by what a ready, willing, and able buyer will pay for a property. This means that amenities can have different "market value" to different buyers.

A fountain might be an important amenity to a purchaser of an expensive house, but of lesser importance to a starter-house buyer. The latter might prefer more interior space, such as a second bathroom or larger kitchen, for their buying dollars.

A buyer in a certain area might consider mature landscaping the norm and not be willing to pay extra for it as an amenity.

Don't forget that some improvements add little, if any, market value. Sellers are sometimes amazed to find that costly improvements such as a spa or hand-rubbed woodwork bring little or no increase to market value to certain properties and may actually be overimprovements.

As you found, adding expensive amenities should be thought of as personal conveniences to the individual owner that may not be recaptured in the sales price.

Q. *Why do some subdivisions go to such detail in restrictions as to tell you what color you can repaint your house? We're getting it spruced up to sell and are amazed to find that our hands are tied on this issue. Is this normal?*

A. It's becoming more the norm. Just as zoning requirements give uniformity to an area, so do limitations on exterior paint colors and property uses.

For example, historic neighborhoods might initially put restrictions in place in order to keep the flavor of the area uniform. Over time, it not only helps preserve the heritage of the architecture, but increases the property values as well. If you put yourself in the position of someone who owned a landmark property, you can see why you wouldn't want neighbors painting their house a distracting color that would detract from the elegance of the neighborhood.

A majority of new developments today have similar restrictions designed to exercise an element of quality control. Now you can see why it's important to ask the developer, the title company, and/or the real estate agent with whom you're working to show you printed information on the conditions, covenants, and restrictions affecting the property.

OBTAINING AN APPRAISAL BEFORE SELLING YOUR HOME

Q. *My wife and I are debating whether we should get an appraisal before we put our house on the market. Is it a good idea?*

A. No, not usually unless your home is unique and you would not be able to find other sold houses with which to compare it. In fact, an appraisal prior to finding a buyer may actually be a detriment. What if the appraiser has few comparables to use in the appraisal, causing it to come in unrealistically low? What if you order a conventional loan appraisal, only to find that the property sells with FHA (Federal Housing Administration) financing, requiring that a second appraisal be done? Because market value is determined in part by what a ready, willing, and able buyer will pay, part of the equation is missing until the buyer makes an offer.

Market value is determined by comparing a house to what similar properties in similar neighborhoods have sold for. This comparative market analysis (CMA) can be done by a real estate agent, or you can do one yourself using online resources like www.cswonline.com or www.experian.com. The CMA will pinpoint a range of value for the property, approximately how long it should take to sell, and the types of terms (e.g., financing options) expected for the property.

Unless a property is unique, a CMA usually gives the seller enough information to begin marketing the property.

HOME INSPECTIONS

Q. *We ordered a home inspection before we listed our house because we wanted to close the sale quickly once we found a buyer. Now that we have a buyer, she demands her own inspection even though the lender will close using the one we purchased. How can we convince her that our inspection is good enough?*

A. You probably can't and shouldn't. Even though your intentions were good in wanting to get the inspection out of the way, you may have lost sight of who the inspection is really for—the buyer.

Put yourself in the buyer's place. If a seller already had an inspection in hand when you made an offer, you might wonder if he (1) was worried about what an inspection would reveal; (2) chose an inspector he knew would be lax in finding problems; or (3) might have paid the inspector off!

While it's predicted that in the future technology will speed up the closing process (including appraisals, inspections, and title work), most buyers today still want to order and review their own home inspection. This is also a risk reduction tool for you as the seller. Should the buyer later uncover a major property defect after you'd convinced her to forego her own inspection, it could look even more like a cover-up.

Let the buyer spend several hundred dollars on her own inspection. The time it takes to obtain the results is in both of your interests in the long run.

AGENT DUTIES, RESPONSIBILITIES, AND SERVICES

Q. *We're thinking about putting our house on the market and wonder if it's worthwhile contacting a real estate agent. What exactly would an agent do to earn the commission?*

A. A good real estate agent is worth the commission many times over. When you hire an agent, you receive assistance in three primary areas: property evaluation, marketing, and contract negotiation.

The agent will assist you in determining the proper list price for the property, as well as inform you how to prepare the property for showing. This would include suggesting minor repairs and cosmetic fix-ups that would be important in attracting a buyer.

The agent can determine how best to advertise the property, prescreen buyers, and qualify them financially. This frees the seller from being housebound, waiting for the prospect who fails to keep an appointment. It also assures the seller that only qualified buyers are touring the property.

When the offer is made, the agent's services really pay off. The agent will help the seller evaluate the strength of the buyer and the offer, analyze the terms and conditions of the contract, and bring the sale to a successful closing.

If you're confused about which of the many brokerages would be best to sell your house, screen several with these questions:

- Have you sold properties like this before?
- Do you have a marketing plan so that I will know what to expect?
- What steps do you take to make sure that prospective buyers are prequalified and prepared to buy?

If you don't feel comfortable with a particular agent or brokerage, don't do business with them. Building strong communications between the seller and the company is vital to a successful sale.

Q. *We've talked to four different real estate firms. Three of the market analyses showed a similar price, but the fourth was considerably higher. Is there any harm in starting at the highest price and working down if we have to?*

A. If three out of four comparative market analyses were close, it leads me to believe that the fourth was not a true reflection of market value. Unless there was additional information known only by the fourth company, the approximate value indicated by the other companies is probably closer to what a ready, willing, and able buyer might offer.

Although it is unethical, agents have occasionally been known to "bid" for listings. It's important that your house be competitively priced the moment it hits the market. An overpriced property will be quickly forgotten by buyers and real estate agents alike. Statistics show that not only will an overpriced listing take longer to sell, but the sales price will usually be lower than true market value. Don't waste your time (or the agent's) in being unrealistic about the listed price.

Q. *We are considering listing our unique house with a real estate company that has an impressive Web site and does international marketing. Does the World Wide Web really generate real estate sales?*

A. As with other advertising tools, the World Wide Web does generate some real estate sales. Reports from brokerages find that it's especially effective in reaching relocating buyers, international buyers, and answering questions about services, schools, and leisure activities in communities. This could be good if your house is one of a kind, requiring a special type of outside buyer.

But a Web presence is just one part of any marketing campaign a brokerage would use. First, focus on finding a company and a listing agent that specialize in marketing property like yours. Ask for documentation on the number of these houses sold, personal references from sellers, and marketing plans they've used to generate sales. The agent should be able to tell you why a certain strategy is used—what works/what doesn't—and design a personalized marketing plan to generate buyers.

It's possible that the brokerage's strategy would include marketing on the Internet. If so, visit the site yourself. If you were a buyer, what would be your response to what you see?

The bottom line is that cybermarketing should not be a brokerage's sole strength. No amount of international exposure will compensate for personal attention and contact from the agent. Information sharing and communication between the seller and the agent are still foremost in putting sales together.

Q. *The agent taking our listing asked us to sign a paper agreeing that it was okay to advertise the house on the Internet. I guess I assumed this was part of the service, but still wondered why she asked us to sign something separate. Is this normal procedure?*

A. With more brokerages and Multiple Listing Services (MLSs) placing their properties online, it's a good business practice to ask the seller's permission to do so. This written permission can be incorporated into the listing agreement you sign or on a separate addendum like your agent used.

Just as one seller might not desire a yard sign, another might not want the sale of his house broadcast across cyberspace. Because you are the agent's client, she not only wants to keep you informed of the marketing channels she'll use, but make sure placing the house on the Internet is in your best personal interest.

A seller recently wrote to say that his listing agent launched his house on the Internet, complete with picture. The first the seller knew about it was when his boss asked him if he was moving. The seller was forced to confess that he was in the running for another job out of state. To make a long story short, he not only ended up losing his current job, but failed to make the final cut for the out-of-state job. This nightmare is just one lesson in why it's important for the agent and seller to work as a team, focusing marketing activities on selling the house with the seller's best interest at heart. Ask your agent about the pros and cons of placing your property on the Internet to make sure that it suits your selling needs.

Q. *Our listing agent is rude, unprofessional, and has even falsely advertised our property. We'd get rid of her, but we're afraid that she'll do something to kill the pending sale we have going. What can we do to make this more tolerable?*

A. Contact her broker about her demeanor and then dump her! Don't worry about hurting anyone's feelings—if things keep breaking down, it's likely that the sale might fall, too!

The broker is responsible for the salespeople and probably is not aware that you're having trouble with the agent. There can be occasional personality conflicts in business dealings, but what you're describing is not normal.

If you brought the advertising error to her attention and it is still not corrected, the broker needs to know this as well. The broker is legally responsible for all advertising done by the brokerage and its agents. Uncorrected advertising can violate federal law and cause potential penalties under state licensing law governing real estate licensees.

The broker could select another agent to work with you, or choose to work on closing the sale herself. (Obviously, the second agent would also get paid from the brokerage fee you're already paying, and it would be up to the broker to determine how much.)

In today's competitive market, no broker/owner wants to think that the firm's representatives are providing anything but the highest quality service and you should settle for nothing less. You are doing yourself, the broker, and the real estate industry a favor by bringing your dissatisfaction to the broker's attention.

Q. *Are guaranteed sales programs a good idea for sellers who need their house to close before they can purchase another house?*

A. A guaranteed sales program usually states that the real estate company will market the property for a certain number of months. If the property has not sold by the time the listing expires, the company agrees to buy out your equity and own the house. They, of course, would charge a fee for doing this and it would be charged against your equity at closing.

This could be an acceptable way to go, especially if a seller is forced to move quickly to another area. But be sure to ask certain questions before signing on the dotted line. First, make sure you understand the contract in its entirety. Because you'll be purchasing another property, now is a good time to find a real estate attorney who can handle both transactions for you.

You'll need to determine what the length of the listing is and how it compares to the market time for houses like yours. For example, if the CMA shows sales of houses like yours are taking six months, you don't want the guaranteed sale to kick in after only three months.

Is the listed price competitive in the marketplace and will it be reviewed periodically (so you could consider a price reduction, if necessary)? What will the guaranteed sales fee be and is it in addition to the brokerage commission? Be sure to get a marketing plan in writing, spelling out how they plan to market the property during the listing. This is important so that you know they are actively marketing the property, not just waiting until the guaranteed program kicks in.

Ask the brokerage what percentage of their transactions are with the guaranteed sales plan and request names and phone numbers of past clients who have used this service. The brokerage may say that it can't give out that information, but they can if they have those former clients' permission. This request should meet with little resistance—a satisfied client is their best form of advertising.

As a final precaution, ask the agent for a net sheet, showing approximately how much you'd make from the guaranteed sale. If the costs are high, you may be wise to go with a standard listing right now before you commit to the guaranteed sale.

Q. *The agent informs us that before the lender will provide loan information to him, we need to send a check for $25. Is this normal?*

A. What you are describing is becoming more of a normal occurrence with lenders. The payoff letter, formally called an estoppel letter, provides the seller with not only the amount of the outstanding loan, but reflects the interest rate on the loan, any delinquent payments owing, and whether the loan can be assumed.

Lenders feel that preparing such a document (and updating the same prior to closing) bears a certain amount of extra administrative cost. That's why more lenders are beginning to charge for its preparation.

I suppose you could refuse to pay for the document; but even if the lender did agree not to charge you, the delay in receiving it would undoubtedly cost you more in headaches and marketing time than the $25 fee.

Q. *What determines the practice of a marketing fee being charged when a listing is canceled?*

A. The listing agreement dictates the complete agreement between you and the brokerage firm. If your agreement does not contain any provision for paying a cancellation fee, a brokerage would be hard pressed to force you to pay one.

Brokerages put this cancellation fee into the agreement because it's costly to market properties, only to lose the business opportunity when a seller backs out. An unscrupulous seller also might use the brokerage to generate market exposure and then pull the listing.

As with any broker/seller relationship, a cancellation fee is a negotiable item in the listing contract. But you need to negotiate it before signing the listing, not after.

Q. *My house has been listed for five months and is one of the nicest in the neighborhood. Now the agent wants me to lower the* *price in order to attract a "different range of buyers." Is this merely a ploy to give him another six-month listing?*

A. While it sounds like the agent does want to keep your listing, lowering the price could help to market the property. If a property is overpriced, it is discounted by serious buyers who may not want to tie up their time negotiating with an unrealistic seller. Your agent wants to breathe new life into the listing by alerting agents and prospective buyers that the property has an attractive new price and deserves a second look.

Lowering the listing price means that more buyers can potentially qualify for financing (requiring lower down payments and lesser closing costs), which also can increase the number of prospects for your house.

Before you agree to lower the price, make sure the agent shows you an updated CMA. Evaluating information about what other similar properties have sold for, how long it took them to sell, and current competition for similar houses, can help convince you that a price reduction will help.

Because your house is one of the nicest in the neighborhood, setting the right listing price is critical. No buyer wants to overpay for a property, especially if the house is already highly improved and on the high side of market value for the area. As the adage goes, "It's wise to buy on the low side of the market." This means that often the house with the greatest potential is the one least improved in an area of higher-quality houses. It's up to you (and your agent) to convince buyers that the price is fair because it includes amenities not found in other houses in your neighborhood.

Q. *We listed our house with an agent with explicit instructions not to bring FHA or VA offers (so we wouldn't have to bother with discount points). He brought us a full-priced VA offer. Why did he do this?*

A. Most state laws governing real estate licensees require that all offers be presented. This not only makes you aware of interest in the property, but gives you an opportunity to evaluate each offer on a case-by-case basis.

For example, just because the offer requires VA financing doesn't mean that you (1) have to pay the discount points involved (they are negotiable between the parties); and (2) won't net as much as you would with another offer. A majority of the buyer and seller costs can be negotiated between the parties, which could actually net you more than with a non-FHA or VA offer. Additionally, points and fees are typically negotiated on conventional loans as well.

Ask the agent to pencil out what you would net. While you might need to make a counteroffer back to the buyers requesting that they pick up more costs of sale, you might negotiate a stronger bottom line than you would with another buyer and other types of financing.

Q. *We were shocked when the selling agent (from another company, representing a buyer) brought us an offer accompanied by a CMA he prepared for the buyer. Wasn't that MLS information about our property confidential?*

A. The information isn't confidential; but once it's interpreted by an agent for his client, *that* information is confidential.

A comparative market analysis is a composite of information from the marketplace showing properties similar to yours that have sold, are currently listed, or have not sold. This information is generally compiled through the MLS and is readily available to real estate agents who are members of the MLS representing both sellers and buyers.

Once the information is used to interpret whether a listed price, terms, etc., are competitive, *that* interpretation becomes confidential. For a client, preparing a CMA is actually one of the duties owed by the agent.

The buyer's agent was justifying in hard figures why his buyer was making this type of offer. They felt that this information would help convince you that the property was listed too high. Hopefully the agent had his client's permission to show you their CMA.

If the roles were reversed, you would clamor for the same information the buyer's agent provided to the buyer in order to make an informed decision.

Q. *The first we knew that the agent showing our house was working for the buyer was when he brought us an offer. Shouldn't this have occurred earlier?*

A. The amount and type of disclosure regarding who represents whom is determined by each state's licensing laws in tandem with state laws that apply. But most states, and licensees in those states, take the "earlier is better than later" approach to agency disclosure. This has come about by consumers such as yourself who want to know not only who represents them, but who represents the other players in the transaction as well.

Many states require that the showing agent specify (usually at first contact with the listing agent, the listing agent's office, and/or the seller) if he or she is representing someone other than the seller. At that point, if the seller has not agreed to work with agents representing buyers, that agent can be so informed. (This very rarely happens today as buyer agents comprise a large part of many marketplaces and therefore contribute to a high percentage of successful sales.)

Buyer agents are certainly not to be feared. The only difference between them and the agent representing your interests is that their allegiance is to their buyer/client—the party that many sellers thought the showing agent was representing all along!

DANGEROUS DOLLARS AND PERILOUS PENNIES ISSUES

As a seller preparing your house for sale, Dangerous Dollars can slowly slip away undetected unless you adhere to The Frugal Home-Owner Law of Seller Preparedness. To become financially aware of what you could be losing:

- Use only the services you know you'll require to market your house. Before you commit to work with real estate professionals (including real estate agents and real estate attorneys), check personal references, review service contracts in depth, and make sure marketing plans (if applicable) are reduced to writing.
- Thoroughly research data to determine the fair market value for your property. Identify whether it's a seller's or buyer's market and determine what that could mean to your marketing efforts and the proportionate amount of time it could take to sell the house.

Perilous Pennies issues usually don't become apparent until you're well into the marketing process—when you've spent money and the house still hasn't sold! So as not to part with one extra cent of equity:

- Extend your marketing efforts by placing your house listing on the Internet, either with a real estate agent or with a reputable for-sale-by-owner property listing service. The exposure should more than warrant any meager service fee you'd be required to pay.

- Be open to working with agents who represent buyers. Fast becoming the preferred way for buyers to purchase a home, your property will attract a myriad of agents who represent some of the most savvy, not to mention highly motivated, buyers in the marketplace.

CHAPTER 11

The Frugal HomeOwner Law of Savvy Sellers

What Goes Around, Comes Around . . . and Hopefully It Looks Like Profit!

The end is in sight. Showing appointments are feverish. Buyers seem pleased with what they see, and you have no doubt that offers will be sailing in momentarily.

Now is not the time to go euphoric over all the attention the house (and your potential equity) is garnering. Just as when you were in the buyer's seat trying to maximize your meager down payment and closing cost money, so, too, do you now need to keep focused on maximizing your equity right down to the wire.

Anyone who has been in your shoes can tell you how tough it is to do. Things are so close to coming full circle (remember your apprehension as a naïve first-time buyer?), you're just days away from receiving an equity proceeds check for more money than you can make in a year's wages. While the idea of it makes you giddy, get a grip and keep focused on your last duty as a homeseller—contract negotiations with a buyer.

It's all coming back to you, right? Trying to nickel and dime the seller, asking for more concessions than you know any logical person would give . . . and of course, willing to give very little in return. Only now, *you're* the seller.

It's the last chance to show just how much you've learned in your evolution as a Bargain Buyer progressed to Economizing Owner elevated to Savvy Seller. Let the games begin!

ATTRACTING AND QUALIFYING BUYERS

Q. *Does it make sense to offer to pay a buyer's closing costs? I want to create interest to get this house sold quickly.*

A. It's a great and productive idea. However, you really need to set some parameters so that you won't end up being taken to the cleaners! You might use a clause something like the following:

> The seller agrees to pay up to $_________________ of the buyer's closing costs (payable at closing), excluding the items of ____________________ [e.g., extra points to buy down the interest rate, etc.]. Any overage will be credited back to the seller at closing.

This way you still can contribute the funds, but not be stuck for the cost of a purchaser who never completes a sale (like credit report and appraisal fees, etc.). In addition, you could choose to exclude items that are not customary costs, such as extra points or additional inspection fees.

You also may want to specify that you will contribute closing costs only to a buyer who brings you a full-price offer, or an offer netting you a certain amount. Without addressing these issues in your listing agreement, you may be giving up more of your sales price than you intend to.

Q. *My buyer raised his offer to my list price which included exterior paint and my labor to apply it. Unfortunately we failed to negotiate the quality of paint as well as the number of coats and he's threatening to back out. Any suggestions on what's fair?*

A. I bet you're kicking yourself now for not being more specific in the purchase agreement. It's amazing how little details left out of a purchase agreement can become a sale-breaker.

I sense from the tone of your question that you're feeling like you've been taken advantage of, when the contrary may be true. Sit down and pencil out in dollars and sense what price the buyer really paid for that paint. You said he "raised his offer to my list price." Was that a few thousand dollars or even a few hundred? Either way, it's doubtful that the paint will cost anywhere near that much.

And what is the true extra cost of using quality paint? Again, the difference is peanuts compared to selling your house worth thousands!

Consider what you stand to lose if the buyer backs out. Because neither of you addressed this issue in the purchase agreement, it will take far more money than it's worth to get attorney opinions about who's right and who's wrong (if you can get a consensus at all!). Decide if this paint issue is really worth losing a buyer over and the time and effort of putting your house back on the market. Then do the right thing. Happy painting!

Q. *I'm trying to sell my house by myself and wonder what kind of questions I should (or can) ask to screen buyers who are calling about the property?*

A. Obviously you can't ask anything that would discriminate based on the prospect's race, color, creed, sex, national origin, or marital status. But you need to find out who you're dealing with because some buyers may not be financially qualified to buy and/or a supposed prospect may desire access to your home only to case it out and return later through an unlatched window!

Couch your questions much like a real estate agent would when working with a prospect. Ask for the prospect's name and phone number. Because some buyers are concerned that the seller will badger them after seeing the house, state that you'll only contact them should you need to cancel the showing appointment.

Ask them over the phone if they've been preapproved for a mortgage loan. This gives you an indication of not only their preparedness, but their motivation to buy because preapproved buyers are the norm in an active market. If they've not been preapproved but would do so, give them the names and numbers of several lenders who would do so online or over the phone before you set the appointment.

For safety reasons, it's important for more than one person to be present when the home is shown. It doesn't take long for even a novice thief to clean out a jewelry box in the bedroom while the other prospective buyer chats with the sellers in the living room.

Buyers working with a real estate agent would face many more questions than you'll be asking. A serious, motivated buyer won't let a few necessary questions get in the way.

Q. *We accepted the offer that was $2,000 higher than the second one even though the couple hadn't been to the lender. But the second buyer did have a preapproval certificate from his bank. Did we do the right thing?*

A. Only time will tell. But to hedge your bet, you might have asked that the second buyer allow his offer to stay in a backup position, should the first offer fall.

Both offers equal, you're safer going with the buyers who have been preapproved. This is a more in-depth level of prequalifying because the lender has already verified the buyer's credit, income, and cash deposits for the down payment and closing costs. The buyers are virtually cash buyers. The only contingency by the lender might be receiving a satisfactory appraisal on the property.

Just because an offer comes in first, doesn't mean you have to accept it or give it special treatment. Most offers remain open for a determined period of time (as stated on the purchase agreement). That gives you the flexibility to evaluate an offer on its merits, not on whether it came to you first or second.

Hopefully, the buyers you chose won't have any trouble qualifying. A prudent thing to do before you accepted their offer might have been to insist that they be preapproved by a lender. It doesn't take much time and even can be started over the phone. This would have given you the peace of mind you were looking for as well as the best of both worlds—a qualified buyer and a sales price of $2,000 more!

SELLER DISCLOSURE

Q. *I believe our state has a seller disclosure form that real estate agents use when they list a house. I'm selling on my own; do I need to prepare one of those to show the buyer?*

A. In more than 30 states, sellers are required to disclose material facts about the property and its condition to prospect buyers. Unless your state law is out of the norm, the answer is yes. The disclosure law pertains to for sale by owners as well as properties listed with real estate agents. (You can refer to Chapter 4 where we cover disclosure forms.)

Q. *When we purchased this home five years ago, the seller told us about a room addition he had just completed but failed to obtain a building permit for. Now that we're selling, do we have to share that same information with the next buyer? It seems like old news.*

A. It doesn't matter when the addition occurred. Informing a prospective buyer about the lack of a building permit is a material fact about the property. While there may never be any repercussions to the new owner, it's important that you make it known and add a written disclosure to any purchase agreement you might sign. To know about the missing permit and not inform the buyer could be considered fraud and end up costing you more in damages than any sale would be worth.

Permits are obtained for various reasons, the most obvious to make sure that the new construction is in compliance with zoning regulations, lot setback requirements, and construction codes. A new buyer would be wise to make sure the room addition does not encroach over the lot line because most title insurance policies do not require surveys when property changes hands.

"Experience is a dear school,
but fools will learn in no other."
—*Ben Franklin*

EARNEST MONEY FROM BUYERS

Q. *A young couple made an offer on our house, gave us $200 in earnest money, and said they'd pay the balance in cash at closing (in two months). But we wonder if they're really good for it. Because they're not getting a loan from a lender, is there any way we can check this out?*

A. With only $200 in earnest money and no third party to run interference for you, I can see why you're leery. It would have been easier to investigate the buyers' financial ability before you accepted the offer. As a condition of the sale, you could have spelled out in the agreement the type of verification you required (a copy of a bank statement, verification from a personal banker, funds placed with a third party for safekeeping, etc.). But there may still be a way to get the information you need.

If you can contact the buyer (preferably in writing) to ask for financial verification, you might receive it. If you frame the request by saying that just as a lender would want to verify its down payment for a mortgage loan, you would like to receive the same information, especially because you're taking the property off the market. Of course, the buyer can tell you to take a hike.

If that happens, you could use a second approach—reopen negotiations. Yes, this is risky because it would give the buyers a way out of the purchase, if they desired, or they could try to hammer you on the price or other negotiation wins. And, of course, they have to mutually agree to renegotiate. But think about it. Equally risky is having your home off the market for two months for a mere $200! If the buyers are financially sound and sincere, it's likely that they'll follow through and purchase the house. They'll also realize you mean business.

In adding new financial verifications to the contract, you might also request that more earnest money be placed with a third party for safekeeping, like a title company or an attorney. While money verified in an account today can be gone tomorrow, it will be more difficult for the buyers to walk away from a substantial earnest money deposit.

Don't forget to change the purchase contract with changes you agree on, and have the buyers initial them. If the changes are detailed, drafting a new agreement may be best.

Q. *We are selling without an agent and the buyer wants to give us a promissory note and convert it to cash soon. What precautions do we need to take?*

A. A promissory note is a promise to pay. If the promissory note is not converted to cash in the time specified, you would have legal recourse against the buyer. But this is usually an exercise in futility; a buyer who can't convert a note to cash in time may have other financial difficulties in swinging the purchase.

Here are some ways to hedge your bet. First, make sure the buyer is financially qualified to buy. This could be verified by a lender who has preapproved the buyer for a certain loan amount. Often the buyer will have a certificate to prove this.

Second, set a short time frame for the note to be converted to cash. Based on the buyer's situation, this could be as little as a few hours to a few days. As with many phases of the real estate transaction, things will no doubt get worse if the buyer's performance takes too long. Know what the buyer must do to convert the note to cash and set the time frame accordingly.

Third, put a clause in the purchase agreement stating that until the note is converted to cash, you reserve the right to keep marketing the property and take backup offers. Besides being a motivator to the buyer, this protects you should the buyer not perform. It also won't take precious time from your marketing efforts, waiting for something that may not happen.

Before accepting an offer with a promissory note, you should understand what must happen before the buyer turns the note into cash, decide if it's realistic, and then decide if the risks are worth it.

Q. *A woman asked us to "hold the house for her" until her attorney could write us an offer and wire us a deposit. She called yesterday to say it was in transit. Did we do the right thing?*

A. The answer to your question lies in whether the buyer makes good on her promise and follows through with the purchase. But there are several cautions here.

First, she has virtually nothing to lose if she doesn't buy your house. You are the ones who are on the line with lost marketing time, inconvenience, and interrupting what might have been positive inquiries to see the house. Verbal agreements to purchase real estate are not enforceable. Besides legally binding a buyer, signing a contract and putting down earnest money is important to a buyer's commitment. Most buyers will think twice before leaving earnest money on the table.

Second, do you know what kind of an offer she will make? Taking the house off the market makes no sense if you haven't talked about specifics like price, terms, closing date, etc. Any or all of the terms and conditions might not be acceptable to you. Just as you wouldn't stop advertising your house until you found a ready, willing, and able buyer, why take it off the market now if you don't know the exact terms and conditions? Many of these are stated in the purchase agreement and not before.

Before any additional time goes by, contact the prospective buyer and get things nailed down. If you want to stand by your agreement with her, give her a short time (e.g., two working days) to get both a check and an offer to purchase to you. Let her know that you will review the offer she makes, but if it isn't acceptable you will be placing the house back on the active market.

You've been more than patient. To wait longer (promise or not) is to hurt only one party—you.

NEGOTIATING WITH THE BUYER

Q. *We were negotiating on our own with a buyer but she didn't respond when we countered for $3,000 more. Because we took another offer before she got back to us, she's threatening to sue. Can she do this?*

A. Your question is probably not can she sue, but will she win if she does? Only a court of law could say, but it doesn't appear that her position is strong for several reasons.

First, a counteroffer is a brand new offer that the other party doesn't have to accept. Once changes are made, it's a whole new ball game. If the tables were turned (with her countering back for $3,000 less price), she could withdraw her offer at any time prior to the time she gets communication from you that you accept the offer.

Second, a contract is not binding on the parties until it is bilaterally accepted (with word of that acceptance communicated back to the person making the offer). This means that in order for the contract to be binding, she would not only have to agree to the changes you made and sign the contract, but communicate back to you that she accepted those terms and conditions.

It's likely that this will all end as soon as she speaks to an attorney. Unless there are other circumstances surrounding these offers (like unreturned earnest money, etc.), it would probably be tough to prove that she was damaged in the way you handled the offers.

"Bad gains are truly losses."
—*Ben Franklin*

Q. *The buyer called us direct just as our agent was taking our offer to her. We settled the terms over the phone, but now she contends that we didn't decide things like points and costs. Can she get out of the purchase?*

A. Yes. She hadn't signed the counteroffer. While she agreed in theory to the broad picture, she hadn't yet agreed to the particulars of the offer and those are part of the contract as well.

If you turn the tables, it may help to see her point. You might have told her that you would take a certain price for the property, but until you saw an offer from her you might not be aware that she'd asked you to pay for all of her closing costs. You would have wanted the same opportunity to back out.

It seems that if a seller and buyer can agree to large, important sale points like price, they can work out the details. If you let the contract address the particulars, and the agent you've hired handle the balance of the negotiations, you'll hopefully be on your way to a quick closing.

Q. *Just as I received one offer, the agent informed me that another agent might have an offer. It never came. Why did the agent tell me this?*

A. The agent was working legally and ethically in your best interest. Because you are her client, she must disclose everything to you that she knows. This includes the fact that a second offer might be on the horizon. This would allow you to choose the better of the two offers and perhaps select the lesser offer as a backup, should the first one fall through.

You were under no obligation to wait for a second offer, but businesswise it makes sense. The agent was definitely doing her duty by informing you of what she heard.

Q. *Doesn't the buyer have to respond to my offer with a counteroffer? I excluded some personal property and haven't heard back from him. Also, how long does he have to withdraw an offer?*

A. By amending the purchase contract, you created an entirely new agreement that the buyer didn't have to accept. Any change, whether major or minor, voids the first offer, and the buyer is under no legal obligation to respond to the new offer. You should have been sure that you were willing to risk losing the buyer over a few minor changes to the contract.

When you fail to accept a buyer's offer, you are basically buying your house back for that price. It would be a business courtesy for the buyer to respond to your offer, but since he didn't, why not submit another offer to him?

If you feel you were hasty in excluding the personal property, include it in a new offer. If the buyer has another "hot button" you feel might entice him to accept the offer, include that, too. Just because you are the seller doesn't mean you can't propose new contract terms and conditions to the buyer.

The person making the offer can withdraw it prior to receiving word that it has been accepted. This means that a buyer could withdraw the offer (with earnest money being returned) anytime prior to receiving word that you accepted the offer.

Q. *The buyer we sold our house to is driving us crazy. He keeps coming back, asking for more. In fact, he's now asking that we leave $4,000 worth of appliances (and has refused to apply for financing if he can't have them). Do we have any leverage here?*

A. The buyer is using a negotiating technique described as nibbling or whittling. Even though he knows the purchase agreement has been negotiated, he's coming back to nibble at getting more. At this stage, he's testing you to see if you'll give in.

If you tell him no, he may do nothing. If he still threatens to back out, you could point out that he may lose his earnest money deposit (depending on how the purchase agreement is written). That could be the end of the discussion.

If he wants to reopen the contract for negotiations, remind him that it would invalidate the original agreement. In other words, a counteroffer creates a whole new offer, one that you don't have to agree to! This means opening up every term and condition for negotiation, including price, closing costs, and other items that could end up costing him more than $4,000 in the long run. In fact, you could decide not to sell the property to him at all if negotiations reopen.

If he still won't back down on the appliances, you can do several things to hold the sale together. You could rewrite the purchase agreement at a higher price to compensate for the appliances (if it's still within what you think would be the appraised value). He could give up something else he's won in the purchase (like you agreeing to pay some of the closing costs). If you don't want to move the appliances, you might be able to sell them to him at a reduced price. (But keep in mind that *you* would then have to replace them in your new house.)

If you try the steps in the order we've listed them, you may be able to end this appliance discussion in short order.

DELAYED CLOSINGS

Q. *What's the best way to orchestrate a delayed closing with the buyer 60 days in the future? We don't want to move until the kids are out of school.*

A. It's good that you're addressing this issue up front because the closing and occupancy dates are a critical part of the purchase agreement. But don't forget that requesting a closing in 60 days is not unusual.

First, depending on the type of financing the buyer is securing, loan processing will take time. Add extra time for any repairs or additional inspections, and you could easily stretch to 60 days.

Clearly state in the purchase agreement what you could do and the trade-offs you'd make. Options could include renting back on a daily basis from the purchaser after the sale closes. The rent could reflect fair market rental value or be a pro-rata share of their new payment. You might sell the fact that this would be extra money to them because they may not have a payment on their new loan for up to 30 days.

If you only need space for storing furniture, why not negotiate the rental of one or more of their rooms or a garage for a short time? This would allow them to move in, but would not cause you two moves.

Do you have a formal rental agreement, spelling out how the utilities will be prorated, transferred, and any renter's insurance coverage you'll carry? You also will need a final date to move. Most buyers, no matter how great the compensation, will ask that the seller move by a predetermined date. In fact, the buyer might ask that the daily rental fee be doubled should it extend beyond that date. It's in the best interests of all parties to design a time frame, and an alternative plan if necessary, to move from the property when you say you will.

Q. *The sale of our house is delayed and the buyers are moving in early so we can relocate as a family. How do I convince my husband that even though the buyers aren't reimbursing us as much as our monthly payment, it's worth it to be together?*

A. Besides the emotional issues of not being together as a family, there are many tangible financial issues you can show him. If you don't move together, you could be supporting two households and two moves (just pencil *that* out!). Also, if the buyers don't occupy the house before closing and you do move, you'll be leaving an unattended house. You could have maintenance costs, some utility costs, potential vandalism, plus two house payments! Even if the buyer's rent didn't cover all of the house payment, the property would be occupied and the other maintenance costs eliminated.

If the previous financial issues aren't enough, remind your husband that not every move in home ownership has to make financial sense to be the best alternative. Sometimes there are emotional trade-offs (like the family moving together) where value can't be solely measured by the difference in mortgage payments.

"At a great pennyworth, pause a while."
—*Ben Franklin*

USE BARTER FOR EVEN MORE LEVERAGE

Q. *As part of the purchase price, the buyer has agreed to pay $5,000 directly to my daughter's school to help with the tuition. How can we guarantee that it's paid as it will be after closing?*

A. Your creativity is great! But you are correct, you do need to make sure the balance of the terms are met after the sale is closed.

There are several steps to take to accomplish this. First, make sure the purchase and sale agreement reflects the terms. Second, find yourself a good real estate attorney to draft the proper legal language between you and the buyer to enforce payment after the closing.

It's best to get the funds from the buyer as soon as possible. In fact, if the buyer can pay something monthly, it helps establish a sound repayment pattern and reminds the buyer of the obligation. If you have to wait, make sure that a deadline is set for payment and that financial penalties arise if the deadline isn't met. This could be done with daily penalties or with interest charged after the due date.

An impartial third-party escrow holder (such as a bank, legal firm, or title company) can monitor the final payment, will collect the payment, and make the disbursement to the school on your behalf.

Your attorney may advise you to take a mortgage lien position in the buyer's property (your former house) until the debt is satisfied. This would allow you to foreclose to get the funds if the buyer didn't pay.

Q. *I have a lot of debt against my house, but I need to get it sold to get on with my life. Is there any way I can use this negative as a positive to get the house sold?*

A. A great question with a potentially workable answer—allow the buyer to assume some of your debt as a down payment. In other words, at closing you transfer the debt (on paper) as part of her down payment. She agrees to assume that debt and retire it over a period of time (probably based on what she can negotiate with your lender and other creditors you owe).

For example, assume that you owe $5,000 in debt (including delinquent water, sewer and garbage charges, property taxes, and two late payments on your mortgage). Find a buyer who is creditworthy, but who is perhaps short of cash for the down payment. Depending on what your loan requires, have the buyer approach the lender to either take over your loan or create a new loan by catching up your two delinquent payments as the down payment. Sometimes the lender will even waive the down payment (or tack the delinquent payments onto the end of the loan) when a creditworthy borrower is taking over the obligation of a delinquent loan.

Will your lender do it? Perhaps, especially if the buyer is financially stronger than you are and the lender can sidestep foreclosure and reselling the property.

Granted, this alternative probably won't give you a check at closing, but you'll have the property sold and be able to move on with your life.

CONTESTING THE APPRAISAL

Q. *Our agent brought us an offer for $140,000, but the appraisal came in at $135,000, which seems low. Can we contest it?*

A. Absolutely. An appraisal is one person's estimate of value. Even though statistical data is used to arrive at the value, you and the agent are more than justified in questioning the appraiser's findings.

Most agents would handle the problem by providing comparable sales (called comps), to the appraiser. These sales can come from Multiple Listing Service information, sales within the brokerage, or from for-sale-by-owner properties. Be sure to alert the agent to any sales of properties you're aware of in your neighborhood that could be checked out.

The agent would prepare the information in written form and submit it to the appraiser. An appraiser may not be aware of a particular recent sale, or may have overlooked a property feature on the report that could lend extra value to the property.

Most appraisers welcome inquiries and have been known to make adjustments to a report if the new information warrants.

SELLING A PROPERTY "AS IS"

Q. *I'm selling a house that's in bad shape and I wonder if using an "as is" clause will let me off disclosing how rotten the roof is, etc.?*

A. A majority of states require that sellers provide data to prospective buyers outlining the condition of the property as well as the material defects known by the seller (this would include the rotten roof!). That's why court cases where sellers try to use "as is" as a defense against disclosing to the buyer the true condition of the property very rarely swing in the seller's favor.

"As is" has broad interpretation. And it's possible that "as is" could even change between the time the buyer first views the property and the closing of the purchase.

Before you use "as is" for anything you sell, get counsel from your real estate attorney. If he or she says "as is" is worth using, have the attorney draft the documents and close the sale to help shift some of your liability!

"What shall it profit a man, if he gain the whole world,
and lose his own soul?"
—Ben Franklin, from Mark 8:36

LEGAL ISSUES WHEN DEALING WITH BUYERS

Q. *I want to assume a seller's mortgage, but his loan has a due on sale clause in it. What would happen if we just "forgot" to tell the lender about me buying the house?*

A. Most lenders (and investors who purchase mortgage loans) feel that their business decision to lend money to the original borrower does not subsequently extend to other buyers who purchase the property (and the loan) from the seller. Lenders want the ability not only to approve the new buyer, but to make him or her a new loan, complete with new discount points and fees!

If the lender uncovers that the seller has transferred the property, the loan can be called entirely due and payable. While this request would be made to the seller, you could stand to lose some or all of your down payment, payments made into the loan, and the ability to renegotiate this loan (or any other) with that lender. All things considered, it's a pretty stiff penalty just to get around a few requirements.

UNDERSTANDING BUYER MOTIVATIONS

Q. *I'm interested in what motivates buyers. Are there different levels of motivation?*

A. There are not only different levels of motivation, but distinct types of motivation as well. A seller's job may become easier when a buyer has a strong degree of motivation. Sales settle quicker, fewer sales collapse midstream, and motivated buyers tend to be less fanatical about minor issues and points they can't control. While there's no litmus test for buyer motivation, there are certain situations and housebuying emotions that tend to dominate motivation in housebuyers.

Time pressures are a very real motivator. For example, a buyer who has only 60 days to relocate would show a high level of motivation. Contrary to this, a buyer who has been a long-time renter and/or has been looking at houses for some time, may have less time pressure motivation.

Next comes situational or life pressure motivation. Couples pending divorce, empty nesters interested in selling their big house, or seniors desiring a house with less maintenance are all candidates.

Perhaps the toughest motivation to analyze comes from emotional pressure. This category could be comprised of widows or widowers who want to move from memories the house brings, or a family wanting out of a crime-ridden area. Emotional pressure motivation can be difficult to interpret and handle. For example, while it may seem like the best thing to do at the time, a widow could realize too late that buying a new house to replace the one she and her spouse shared was a mistake. Sometimes the best thing you can do with a buyer under emotional pressure is to wait it out.

And don't forget "fear of loss" as a motivator. After volleys of offers from various buyers back and forth to the seller, a buyer might not remember why he wanted a property; but he does know he doesn't want somebody else to get it!

While motivation is certainly not a science where buyers are concerned, asking questions based on the motivators we've mentioned helps sellers (and agents) have a bit more insight into what makes buyers tick.

FINANCING YOUR NEW HOME WITH A BRIDGE LOAN

Q. *Our house has sold, but not closed, and we'd like to consider getting a bridge loan to close on our new house. How do those work?*

A. A bridge loan is a type of second mortgage used for the purpose of financially "bridging" between sale and new purchase. The lender takes a second mortgage against your old house in order to advance you the down payment and closing costs for your new house.

You may be allowed between 75 and 80 percent total mortgage debt against your old house, so having strong equity in the property is important to get the maximum amount you need to purchase the new house.

A bridge loan can be used to fund a down payment and closing costs only if you have the ability to qualify for both the payment on the new house and the old house plus the bridge loan repayment. Often the lender helps out a bit by requiring interest-only payments on the new loan, or payments deferred entirely until your house sells.

DANGEROUS DOLLARS AND PERILOUS PENNIES ISSUES

Dangerous Dollars and their dastardly deeds have come full circle, impacting you as a Bargain Buyer, an Economizing Owner, and now with The Frugal HomeOwner Law of Savvy Sellers. Here's your last chance to control those dollars as you gravitate toward your very own proceeds check! To retain more of those Dangerous Dollars as a Savvy Seller:

- Show your house only to preapproved, creditworthy buyers. To do less will tempt the Gods of Speedy Closings, the Gods of Equity Fate, and engage the wrath of the truly qualified buyer who's also interested in seeing, and buying, your house!
- Negotiate strongly, yet fairly, with the buyer (especially on equity-sparing issues that will impact your bottom line).
- Address all purchase issues in the purchase agreement—right down to who gets the pink flamingo in the front yard!

Left to their own design, Perilous Pennies issues won't be kind to your net proceeds check either. So you must:

- Refrain from greed to win all the marbles at the negotiating table, only to lose on the ones you really wanted to win (reflect back on your negotiating experiences as a buyer—it's just the other side of the coin)!
- Structure any new purchase you're making conditioned on the closing of your old house, naming a minimum amount of proceeds you'll require from that sale. Otherwise, you'll be scrambling to find money for your new down payment, potentially be strapped with two mortgage payments, plus be off to a bad start as a Bargain Buyer.

Here's to a profitable sale and your next exciting frugal home purchase!

EPILOGUE

Here's hoping that *The Frugal HomeOwner* has provided you with answers to all your financial home ownership questions.

In the inimitable words of Benjamin Franklin:

> If you wou'd not be forgotten
> As soon as you are dead and rotten,
> Either write things worth reading,
> Or do things worth the writing.

Ben and I wish you a productive lifetime of both!

—Julie Garton-Good
"The Frugal HomeOwner™"
www.frugalhomeowner.com

RESOURCE GUIDE

PRINT RESOURCES

The following free booklets are available from:
The Mortgage Bankers' Association
1125 15th St., NW
Washington, DC 20005

"A Consumer's Glossary of Mortgage Terms"

- Great for the first-time buyer who needs to know the language, players, and the plays.

"Self Test"

- Ideal to use prior to qualifying with a lender. Will help you determine how much house you can afford and what documentation the lender may require.

"What Happens after You Apply for a Mortgage"

- Walks you through the process and explains the mysteries of underwriting the mortgage loan.

Choosing the Best Loan and Lender

The following booklet is available from:
Federal National Mortgage Association
Drawer MM
3900 Wisconsin Ave., NW
Washington, DC 20006

"Unraveling the Mortgage Loan Mystery"

- Great for information on who makes loans, types of loans available, and how to choose the best loan and lender.

"When Your Home Is on the Line"

- A comprehensive booklet describing how to evaluate equity lines of credit.

When writing, ask for a list of other publications available, or request information on a certain topic.

Evaluating Various Loans

Available from the:
Federal Trade Commission Bureau of Consumer Protection
Pennsylvania Ave. and 6th St., NW
Washington, DC 20580

"The Mortgage Money Guide"

- Gives detailed comparisons of costs borrowers can expect to pay for various types of loans. Good for loan comparison shopping.

General Real Estate and Homebuying Information

Write for a free catalog from the federal government's:
Consumer Information Center
P.O. Box 100
Pueblo, CO 81002

- A selection of booklets on homebuying, insurance, radon, and home hazards. While most of the government's booklets are free of charge, others may cost up to $1.50.

Other Booklets

Home Safety

"Home Modifications for the Elderly," available from the National Association of Home Builders (NAHB). A preplanning home safety audit. For a free copy, write to NAHB Research Center, 400 Prince George's Blvd., Upper Marlboro, MD 20772. Attn: L. Rickman.

Home safety booklet for the elderly, "The Doable, Renewable Home," is available free of charge from the AARP. Write for booklet D12470, AARP Fulfillment, EE094, 1909 K St., NW, Washington, DC 20049.

Environmental Safety

To obtain a copy of the free brochure, "A Home Buyer's Guide to Environmental Hazards," write to: The Federal National Mortgage Association, Department E., P.O. Box 23867, Baltimore, MD 21201-9998.

Accessability

Free of charge from the National Easter Seal Society, a booklet entitled "Easy Access Housing." Write to them at 70 East Lake St., Chicago, IL 60601.

Discriminatory Practices in Housing

Call the HUD hotline at 1-800-669-9777 to speak to a HUD representative or to order a free booklet, "Fair Housing: It's Your Right" (publication #HUD-1260-FHEO/July 1990).

ONLINE RESOURCES

Sorted alphabetically by topic. All are preceded by http://www.

City Comparisons

cityguide.com

Credit Agencies

experian.com
equifax.com
tuc.com

Crime Information

crimewatch.com

Environmental Information

epa.gov

FHA (Federal Housing Administration)

hud.gov

Flood Insurance

fema.gov

Foreclosure

fanniemae.com
freddiemac.com
ginniemae.com

For Sale by Owners

fizbo.com
fisbo.net
fsbo.com
ired.com
open-house-online.com
owners.com

Governmental Sites

hud.gov
epa.gov
ftc.gov

Homebuilding

nahb.com

Homebuyer/seller Information

frugalhomeowner.com
homeadvisor.com
inman.com
ired.com
ourbroker.com
realtimes.com
realtor.com

Home Inspections

ashi.com

Home Repair

askbuild.com
buildnet.com
misterfixit.com

Interest Rates

hsh.com
interest.com

Insurance

homefair.com
homeshark.com
insweb.com
prudential.com
safeco.com

Listings Online

cyberhomes.com
homeadvisor.com
homescout.com
homeseeker.com
listinglink.com
matchpoint.com
realtor.com

Manufactured Housing

mfdhousing.com

Mortgages

bankofamerica.com
countrywide.com
e-loan.com
homefair.com
homeshark.com
loanshop.com
loanworks.com
mortgage-mart.com
quickenmortgage.com
wellsfargo.com

Payment Calculators

homefair.com
loanguide.com

Pricing Property

cswonline.com
experian.com

Private Mortgage Insurance

mgic.com
pmirescue.com

Real Estate Education

reea.org

Refinancing

countrywide.com
homeshark.com
loanshop.com

Relocation

homefair.com

Rentals

rentnet.com

Rent versus Buy

homefair.com

School Information

schoolreport.com

Tax Rates

irs.gov

Unbundled Services

realestatecafe.com
helpusell.net

VA (Department of Veterans Affairs)

va.gov

GLOSSARY

acquisition cost The cost of acquiring a property, in addition to purchase price, such as title insurance and lender's fees (e.g., with FHA, acquisition is a set amount based on the appraised value of the property).

adjustable-rate mortgage (ARM) A mortgage tied to an index that adjusts based on changes in the economy.

adjustment period The period during which an ARM adjusts (e.g., six months, one year, or three years).

a la carte real estate services Paying for and receiving professional real estate services one by one rather than via a full-service "bundled" approach (e.g., paying a real estate agent to write an ad versus receiving advertising as merely one of the services under a full-service, commission-based brokerage relationship).

alienation clause (due-on-sale clause) A type of acceleration clause in a loan, calling for payment of the entire principal balance in full, triggered by the transfer or sale of a property.

American Society of Home Inspectors (ASHI) An organization of professional inspectors who attain membership only after submitting proof that they have completed over 250 fee-paid property inspections.

amortization Retiring a debt through predetermined periodic payments, including principal and interest.

appraisal An estimate of value.

ARM See *adjustable-rate mortgage.*

assignment The transfer of rights to pay an obligation from one party to another, with the original party remaining secondarily liable for the debt, should the second party default.

assumption To take over one's obligation under an existing agreement. (Note: This can be done with varying degrees of release; see *assignment, novation,* and *subject-to.*)

balloon payment A principal sum coming due at a predetermined period of time (may also contain payment of accrued interest).

biweekly mortgage A mortgage under which one-half of the regular amortized monthly payment is payable every two weeks, giving the benefit of 13 full payments per year; this allows a 30-year loan to retire in approximately 18 years.

blended rate The melding together of two rates to create a lower overall rate of interest. For example, blending the rate of a 7 percent first mortgage, and a 9 percent second mortgage, allows the buyer to more readily qualify.

buydown Permanent: Prepaid interest that brings the note rate on the loan down to a lower, permanent rate. Temporary: Prepaid interest that lowers the note rate temporarily on the loan, allowing the buyer to more readily qualify and to increase payments as income grows. (A common example of a temporary buydown is the 3-2-1 plan—3 percent lower interest the first year, 2 percent the second, and 1 percent the third.)

buyer's market Real estate market condition when there are more properties available than there are qualified buyers; thereby giving buyers potentially more negotiating power over sellers.

cash reserves The amount of a buyer's liquid cash remaining after making the down payment and paying all closing costs.

Certificate of Eligibility VA certification, showing the amount of entitlement used and the remaining guaranty available.

Certificate of Reasonable Value (CRV) The formal name for a VA appraisal.

chattel Personal property.

collateral/collateral agreement Means "additional," but is generally termed to mean security for a debt.

comparative market analysis (CMA) An approach to help determine the market value of a property by analyzing what similar properties with similar locations and similar amenities have recently sold for, as compared to the subject property.

compensating factors Additional positive factors a lender looks for in order to strengthen a buyer's loan qualifying position (e.g., good pattern of savings).

Consumer Credit Counseling Service A nonprofit organization with locations throughout the United States, designed to help consumers analyze income and debt and orchestrate repayment programs in an effort to reestablish good credit.

contract for deed (installment sales and land sales contract) A document used to secure real property when it is seller-financed; contains the full agreement between the parties, including purchase price, terms of payment, and any additional agreements.

convertible ARM An adjustable-rate mortgage containing a clause allowing for the rate to become fixed during a certain period (e.g., between months 13 and 60 of the loan term).

convertibility option The clause that allows the ARM loan to convert to a fixed rate during a certain period.

counteroffer A follow-up offer made after the offeror has made an initial offer; a counteroffer is a brand new offer that the offeree is under no obligation to accept and that the offeror can withdraw at any time prior to notification of the offeree's acceptance.

credit scoring Electronically giving a numerical weight to various financial factors in the borrower's credit in order to determine the risk of lending to that borrower.

CRV See *Certificate of Reasonable Value.*

debt assumption letter/assignment of debt The formal transfer of debt from one person to another, backed by a formal contract of assumption signed by the parties. This is done to reduce the amount of a person's long-term debt.

debt ratios The comparison of a buyer's housing costs to his or her gross or net effective income (based on the loan program); and the comparison of a buyer's total long-term debt to his or her gross or net effective income (based on the loan program used). The first ratio is termed housing ratio; the second ratio is total debt ratio. (See particular programs for applicable ratios.)

deed of trust (trust deed) A document used to secure the collateral in financing the property; title is transferred to the trustee, with payments made to the beneficiary by the trustor (grantor in some states).

desktop underwriting Using software programs to automatically underwrite and otherwise evaluate the repayment capacity of the borrower.

discount points (points) A point is equal to 1 percent of the amount financed. Points are used to increase the lender's yield on the loan, so as to bridge the gap between what the lender could get with conventional monies, and the lower rates of VA and FHA.

discounting, seller Reducing the sales price in lieu of paying points or other fees from the seller's gross price.

distributive share MIP The FHA mortgage insurance plan in effect prior to 1983.

due diligence The series of activities performed by real estate professionals (agents, lenders, appraisers) that constitute proper representation of the consumer.

due-on-sale clause (alienation clause) See *alienation clause.*

entitlement Also known as VA guaranty; the amount of the veteran's eligibility in qualifying for a VA loan.

equity The difference between what is owed and what the property could be sold for.

equity lines of credit Lien positions against a property that allow the consumer to access a line of cash (credit) with a predetermined cap and scheduled repayment requirements.

equity loans Tapping into an owner's equity, with the property used as the collateral.

escrow An impartial holding of documents pertinent to the sale and transfer of real estate; also the term used to describe the long-term holding of documents, such as with seller financing. Called a long-term escrow or escrow collection.

escrow holder An impartial third party who holds the documents pertinent to the transfer and sale of real estate.

facilitator Also known as transaction broker or intermediary; a real estate licensee who has no client relationship with the party he or she is assisting in the real estate transaction and whose position is to provide generic, informational material to the customer.

Federal Home Loan Mortgage Corporation (FHLMC) Also called Freddie Mac; a part of the secondary market, particularly used to purchase loans from savings and loan lenders within the Federal Home Loan Bank Board.

Federal Housing Administration (FHA) Part of the federal government's Department of Housing and Urban Development, it exists to underwrite insured loans made by lenders to provide economical housing for moderate-income persons.

Federal National Mortgage Association (FNMA) Also called Fannie Mae; a privately owned part of the secondary mortgage market used to recycle mortgages made in the primary market; purchases conventional, FHA, and VA loans.

FHLMC See *Federal Home Loan Mortgage Corporation.*

FICO The Fair, Isaac and Company credit scoring system used by many lenders to determine the borrower's ability to repay a mortgage; uses a scoring range of 450 to 850—the lower the score, the higher the risk.

fixed-rate mortgage (FRM) A conventional loan with a single interest rate for the life of the loan.

float downs Provisions in the mortgage rate lock-in agreement that allow the consumer to access a lower rate of interest (and lock it in) should interest rates drop during the prescribed lock-in period.

FNMA See *Federal National Mortgage Association.*

foreclosure A proceeding, in or out of court, to extinguish one's rights in a property, and pay off all outstanding debts via a sale of the property.

FRM See *fixed-rate mortgage.*

fully indexed rate The maximum interest rate on an ARM that can be reached at the first adjustment.

full-service broker A real estate broker who performs all transaction services for consumers including (but not limited to) listing and selling.

funding fee An origination fee on VA loans, usually equal to 1 percent of the amount financed.

gift letter A letter from a relative (or party with whom a strong relationship has been established for some loans) stating that an amount will be gifted to the buyer, and that said amount is not to be repaid.

GNMA See *Government National Mortgage Association.*

Government National Mortgage Association (GNMA) Also called Ginnie Mae, a governmental part of the secondary market that deals primarily in recycling VA and FHA mortgages, particularly those that are highly leveraged (e.g., no or low down payment).

guaranteed sales program A real estate brokerage program designed to buy out the consumer's equity should the property not sell during a predetermined period of time (e.g., four months).

guaranty, VA The amount that the Department of Veterans Affairs will indemnify the lender against loss on a VA loan.

Homeownership Bridal Registry The FHA marketing program that allows potential buyers to accumulate monies from relatives and friends for down payment and closing costs.

housing expense ratio The amount of either gross income or net effective income (depending on the loan program) that can be allocated for a borrower's housing expense. This percent also varies based on the loan-to-value ratio of the loan.

income qualifications The amount of either gross income or net effective income (depending on the loan program) required by the lender for loan qualifying.

index An indicator used to measure inflation, which is a basis for the ARM. There are various sources of indexes, including Treasury securities, Treasury bills, 11th district cost of funds, and the index of the Federal Home Loan Bank Board. The index, plus the margin, becomes the interest rate in the ARM.

inflation An increase in value; most often used as an indicator of the economy. When inflation is high, real estate performs well, because it appreciates in times of inflation.

initial interest rate The introductory interest rate on a loan; signals that there may be rate adjustments later in the loan.

in-service eligibility Qualifying a veteran buyer for a VA loan while still in active duty.

installment sales contract (contract for deed) See *contract for deed.*

interest only Payments received are only applied to accrued interest on the loan; therefore, there is no principal reduction.

interest rate The note rate charged on the loan.

interest rate cap The maximum amount of interest that can be charged on an ARM. Can be expressed in terms of annual or lifetime figures.

jumbo loans Mortgages that exceed the loan amounts acceptable for sale in the secondary market; these jumbos must be packaged and sold differently to investors and therefore have separate underwriting guidelines.

lease option A lease with an option to buy; either can be exercised to culminate in a purchase or forfeited by the optionee.

lease purchase A type of delayed closing. A lease purchase is drafted on a purchase and sales contract, stating the terms of the purchase, as well as a date for closing the sale. Should the buyer default, the seller has all of the remedies available under the sales contract.

leverage Using a small asset to purchase a larger asset; using "OPM" other people's money! Leverage allows a buyer's down payment to go further (e.g.; instead of using $50,000 down on a $100,000 property, the buyer could use $10,000 down on five properties of $100,000).

liability, release of The type of liability release for the original borrower; found under a novation.

lifetime cap The maximum amount of interest an ARM can reach during the life of the loan.

loan qualifying Meeting the criteria for a loan as required by a lender; varies greatly from program to program.

loan servicer The entity servicing (collecting payments and managing) the closed mortgage.

loan-to-value ratio The amount of the loan as compared to the appraised value of the property.

local improvement district (LID) A legal entity (district) established under state law to benefit a certain geographic area. Districts issue bonds to finance real property improvements such as water distribution systems, sidewalks, and sewer systems. To repay funds, districts then levy assessments on real estate located in the geographic area affected.

lock-in The fixing of an interest rate or points at a certain level, usually during the loan application process. It is usually done for a certain period, such as 60 days, and may require a fee or premium in the form of a higher interest rate.

long-term debt For qualifying purposes, debts that cannot be paid off within a certain amount of time, which varies depending on the loan type. (e.g., Conventional long-term debts are considered to be those in excess of 10 months, 6 months for FHA, and 12 months for VA. Note, however, that individual lenders could choose to be more restrictive than these national guidelines.)

margin An amount added by the lender to an ARM index in order to compute the interest rate. The margin is set by the lender at the time of loan inception and remains constant for the life of the loan. The margin is considered to be the lender's cost of doing business plus profit.

maximum entitlement The maximum amount of VA guaranty available to a veteran.

mortgage insurance premium (MIP) The mortgage insurance required on FHA loans for the life of said loans. MIP can either be paid in cash at closing or financed in its entirety in the loan.

Multiple Listing Service (MLS) Listing information repositories, often managed in tandem with National Association of REALTORS® local members.

National Association of Exclusive Buyers Agents (NAEBA) A professional organization for agents who solely represent buyer/clients in the purchase of real estate.

negative amortization An interest payment shortfall that is added back onto the principal balance.

note rate The rate of interest shown on the face of the promissory note or in the contract of sale language; the rate of interest charged on an obligation.

notice of separation The VA form received when the veteran is discharged from the service.

novation From the root word nova, meaning new. A novation is a total release of liability to the first borrower under a loan, and the substitution of a subsequent borrower;

usually not automatic, requiring a lender's approval (see assignment, assumption, and subject-to).

online lending Accessing mortgage programs and lenders via the World Wide Web.

overimproved property Real estate that could not be sold high enough in the marketplace to recoup the cost of its improvements.

owner occupancy Occupied by the buyer of the property; a requirement in VA loans; many times a requirement in conventional and FHA programs as well.

PAM See *pledged account mortgage.*

paid outside of closing (POC) Funds disbursed on behalf of the borrower outside the formal closing with that borrower.

payment cap The maximum amount the payment can adjust in any one time frame (e.g., 7.5 percent per period).

PITI Principal, interest, taxes (property), and insurance.

pledged account mortgage (PAM) Instead of using all of the down payment at closing, part of the funds are placed in an interest-bearing account and drawn from over time to help pay the mortgage payment. These impounded funds are said to be "pledged" to the lender. Also known as pledged asset mortgage.

PMI See *private mortgage insurance.*

portfolio lending Instead of selling the mortgage into the secondary market, the lender keeps it "in portfolio" (in its in-house file) for the life of the loan.

preapproval A lender's term meaning that the borrower has been preapproved to receive a mortgage loan at a determined maximum amount given a certain cap on the rate of interest.

premium pricing When the lender agrees to pay (or waive) a portion of the cash required by the borrower to close the mortgage (e.g., down payment or closing costs) and in return charges a premium rate over and above the market interest rate.

premium yield adjustment Denotes that a lender is receiving compensation from the party funding the real estate mortgage.

prepaids Property expenses that are paid in advance and are usually prorated at the time of closing (e.g., insurance).

prepayment privilege The right of the borrower to prepay the entire principal sum remaining on the loan without penalty.

private mortgage insurance (PMI) Insurance that indemnifies the lender from the borrower's default, usually on the top 20 percent of the loan. Premiums are paid as an initial fee at time of closing, and as a recurring annual fee based on the principal balance, but paid monthly with the PITI payment. The buyer customarily pays both the initial and recurring fees.

qualifying ratio Percentages used by lenders to compare the amount of housing expense and total debt to that of the buyer's gross income or net effective income (depending on the loan program).

rate cap The maximum amount of interest that can be charged on an ARM, expressed as per period, per lifetime, or both.

rate ceiling The maximum to which the rate can go in an ARM, specified in an interest amount (e.g., 14 percent).

ratio A percentage that is used as a qualifying guideline in mortgage lending.

Real Estate Settlement Procedures Act (RESPA) The up-front view of the costs of borrowing in a mortgage loan, including the APR (annual percentage rate), which is the note rate plus the up-front costs of borrowing.

Regulation Z A federal regulation requiring disclosure of the overall cost of borrowing (truth in lending); states that if you disclose one piece of financial information, you must disclose in its entirety (including the total of all payments and the number of payments). The only exception to this rule is the use of the annual percentage rate. If this is used, no other piece of financial information is necessary.

reservist A person who has served in a reserve branch of the armed forces.

R-factor R stands for resistance and is used to measure the amount of insulation in the walls, ceilings, and floors of homes.

right of first refusal The privilege extended to a potential buyer to remove contingencies on a contract should the seller receive another acceptable offer (e.g., a buyer with a contingency of selling his home before purchasing the seller's home would be given a right of first refusal to either remove the contingency and purchase the property or forfeit the purchase should the seller receive another acceptable offer).

sales concession A cost paid by the seller or a third party, even though the cost is customarily paid by the buyer. Some loan programs have limits as to the amount of sales concessions that can occur before overage would decrease the amount of loan available.

secondary market Comprised of FNMA, GNMA and FHLMC, which recycle lent funds from the primary market.

self-insure When providers of materials and services use personal or corporate savings to stand behind warranties, rather than providing formal protection written through insurance companies.

seller financing The seller allows the borrower to finance the property using a portion of the seller's equity in the property.

seller's market Real estate market condition when there are more buyers than there are properties available, giving an upper hand to sellers.

setback Space required between structures and side lots, front lots, and the street and/or sidewalk, as well as from structures and the rear of the property line. Size of setbacks is usually determined through local zoning requirements.

simple assumption A type of loan assumption that is actually a no-qualifying assignment with the lender. The original obligor remains secondarily liable should the assumptor default.

subject-to The transfer of rights to pay an obligation from one party to another, with the first party remaining secondarily liable should the second party default. In addition, the first obligor could be responsible for any deficiency judgment caused by the second borrower. (See *assignment, assumption,* and *novation.*)

subprime loans Mortgage loans of A–, B, C, and D grades (less than the standard A grade mortgage) that are available to credit-damaged borrowers. Subprime loans are made at rates in excess of standard market rates and typically require more points and fees to be paid.

surviving spouse The widow or widower of a deceased veteran.

sweat equity Materials or labor used by a buyer in addition to, or in lieu of, cash.

teaser rate An unusually low introductory rate for an ARM, used to entice borrowers into a loan and allow them to more readily qualify.

trailing spouse An employable spouse, accompanying the other spouse in relocating for job reasons, who expects to return to work. Lenders often use trailing spouses as compensating factors when making mortgages to relocating buyers.

unbundled real estate services Services not bound together (e.g., in traditional listing packages from brokerages) that can be purchased by consumers a la carte (one by one).

Uniform Resource Locator (URL) A Web site's location or address on the Internet, preceded by *http://*.

WDAGO A veteran's notice of separation.

wraparound An original loan obligation remains stationary, while a new amortizing obligation wraps around the other loan. One payment is made (often to an escrow holder), out of which the underlying payment is made, with the remainder going to the seller.

yield Return on investment.

zero-net When the seller is receiving little or no net proceeds from selling the property.

INDEX

D

E

F

G

H

I

J–K

L

M

N

O

P

Q–R

S

T

U

V

W